Currency Corridors

Currency Corridors

The Battle to Replace the Dollar Without Firing a Shot

By

Priya Nadkar-Jain

Vij Books

New Delhi (India)

Published by

Vij Books
(Publishers, Distributors & Importers)
4836/24, 3rd Floor, Ansari Road
Delhi – 110 002
Phone: 91-11-43596460
Mobile: 98110 94883
e-mail: contact@vijpublishing.com
www.vijbooks.in

ISBN: 978-81-99786-85-1 (HB)

ISBN: 978-81-99786-89-9 (PB)

ISBN: 978-81-99786-80-6 (eBook)

This book was developed using advanced writing tools to support the drafting and ideation process. All content has been thoughtfully curated, refined, and reviewed to ensure quality and relevance.

Contents

Introduction

In a dealing room just before dawn, screens glow with the quiet confidence of habit. Prices flicker, orders queue, confirmations settle into place. Somewhere between an oil terminal on a distant coast and a refinery thousands of miles away, a payment moves. The buyer is not American. The seller is not American. The ship never touches an American port. Yet the price is quoted in dollars, the invoice is denominated in dollars, the hedge is struck in dollars, and the ultimate settlement depends on dollar liquidity. Nothing about the transaction feels ideological. It feels merely practical. That, perhaps more than any grand proclamation, explains why the dollar still sits at the centre of the global monetary system.

For decades, prophets of monetary upheaval have announced the dollar's imminent fall. Each cycle brings its own reasons: swelling US debt, geopolitical overreach, technological disruption, the rise of new powers. Each cycle fades into the same outcome. Trade, debt issuance, and official reserves bend, briefly, away from the dollar, only to curve back. The headlines promise rupture. The balance sheets record continuity. This stubborn gap between prediction and practice has bred cynicism. De-dollarisation has become a slogan in search of a mechanism, a story told loudly but enacted quietly, if at all.

And yet something is changing. Not with the drama of a collapse, nor with the clarity of a regime shift, but with the patient, almost bureaucratic persistence of engineers rerouting traffic beneath a city that continues to look the same from above. Central banks have signed hundreds of bilateral swap lines. Regional clearing hubs have appeared, expanded, and standardised. Payment systems have been linked across borders without fanfare. Digital currency bridges are being tested in controlled environments, far from the rhetoric that surrounds them. The map is shifting even while the headline has not. The world's monetary order is being remodelled corridor by corridor, flow by flow, decision by decision.

This book begins from that paradox. The dollar remains dominant, yet its dominance is no longer singular or uncontested. It is being bounded, channelled, and, in some places, quietly bypassed. The contest is not for a throne to be seized in one decisive moment, but for pathways through which trade is settled, liquidity is accessed, and risk is distributed. The question is not whether the dollar will disappear. It is where, when, and why it will no longer be necessary, and where it will remain indispensable long after obituaries have been written.

Monetary systems rarely end the way their critics expect. History offers fewer clean breaks than managed transitions, fewer revolutions than reconfigurations. Sterling did not vanish when American power rose; it lingered in contracts, habits, and reserves for decades. Gold did not cease to matter when fiat currencies took centre stage; it retreated, adapted, and returned in new guises. Each shift left behind layers of institutional memory and technical infrastructure that shaped what came next. The present moment belongs to that lineage. What we are witnessing is not the overthrow of the dollar, but the negotiation of its boundaries.

To understand why this matters, one must look beyond exchange rates and into the machinery of finance. Currency power is not exercised only through symbols and speeches. It lives in the mundane details of invoicing conventions, collateral eligibility, clearing rules, and access to emergency liquidity. It is embedded in who can settle quickly, who can hedge cheaply, and who can rely on support when markets seize. These details determine which currencies are convenient, which are risky, and which are trusted under stress. They also determine who bears the cost when convenience turns into dependence.

The dollar's central role has long delivered real benefits, not only to the United States but to the global system as a whole. Shared pricing reduces friction. Deep markets lower borrowing costs. A widely accepted safe asset provides an anchor in times of panic. Many countries that speak most loudly about monetary autonomy still choose dollar debt when they need scale and liquidity. This is not hypocrisy. It is a rational response to an environment in which alternatives are often thinner, more volatile, or more politically entangled. Dollar dominance has persisted because it solves problems efficiently.

But efficiency is not neutrality. The same structures that make the dollar convenient also transmit shocks. Interest-rate decisions in Washington ripple through economies with no vote at the table. Exchange-rate swings reshape balance sheets overnight. Sanctions, once rare and targeted, now exploit the plumbing of the system with increasing precision. Access to payment networks, correspondent banking, and dollar liquidity has become a lever of statecraft. For some, this leverage is a source of stability. For others, it is a vulnerability too large to ignore.

The response has not been a single coordinated revolt, but a proliferation of workarounds. Swap lines that provide foreign currency liquidity without running down reserves. Clearing arrangements that net obligations regionally rather than globally. Invoicing agreements that shift specific trades into local or regional units. Payment links that bypass traditional correspondent chains for smaller, faster flows. Digital experiments that promise, if not yet deliver, new forms of interoperability. Each initiative addresses a particular friction or risk. Taken together, they amount to a gradual redrawing of monetary routes.

A useful way to think about this evolving landscape is as a system of corridors. Trade moves through corridors. Capital moves through corridors. Reserves are built with corridors in mind. Each corridor has a currency, a set of institutions, a legal framework, and an implicit political understanding. Some are wide and well lit, handling enormous volumes with ease. Others are narrow, specialised, and used only when necessary. Corridors can overlap, compete, or converge. They can be reinforced in times of stress or abandoned when they prove unreliable. Crucially, corridors can exist without displacing the centre entirely.

This corridor perspective helps resolve a persistent confusion in debates about de-dollarisation. The question is often posed as a binary choice: dollar or not-dollar, dominance or decline. Reality is more granular. Energy trade may shift into one set of currencies while tourism receipts remain dollar-linked. Reserves may diversify cautiously even as funding markets cling to the depth of US Treasuries. Messaging systems may change while settlement assets do not. By following corridors rather than proclamations, one can see change where others see stasis, and constraint where others imagine liberation.

What is at stake extends beyond abstract monetary theory. For states, corridor choices shape resilience in crises, exposure to external pressure, and room for policy manoeuvre. For firms, they determine funding costs, hedging strategies, and compliance burdens. For banks, they dictate balance-sheet usage, liquidity risk, and the value of network membership. Even households feel the effects indirectly, through the stability of prices, the availability of credit, and the vulnerability of jobs to external shocks.

Currency architecture is not a technical sideshow. It is a distribution mechanism for risk and power.

This book is written as a practical guide to that architecture. It asks how currency corridors are built, not how they are announced. It examines who benefits from their expansion and who is left outside. It traces how sanctions and capital controls reshape incentives without dissolving the underlying logic of markets. It insists on understanding design choices, hidden conditions, and institutional roles that often disappear behind confident headlines. Above all, it argues that the most plausible outcome of current pressures is neither the triumph of a new hegemon nor the collapse of the old, but a managed fragmentation in which multiple currencies coexist across different functions.

The chapters that follow move deliberately from foundations to frontiers. They begin by clarifying what dollar dominance actually means in practice, separating symbolism from balance-sheet reality. They unpack the mechanics of cross-border payments, clearing, and settlement, revealing where currency choice truly matters. They explore the expanding web of bilateral swap lines and regional safety nets, showing both their promise and their limits. They examine the rise of regional clearing hubs and the risks of fragmented liquidity. They assess regional currency arrangements, commodity-linked trade, and the complex interplay between pricing, settlement, and collateral.

Technology receives careful attention, not as a deus ex machina but as an amplifier of existing choices. Central bank digital currencies and private platforms are analysed for what they can realistically change, and for what they cannot. Sanctions and capital controls are treated as structural forces that shape behaviour, not as temporary distortions. Reserve management and investor confidence are explored as slow-moving constraints that resist political impatience. The final chapters map plausible futures without insisting on a single destiny, offering readers tools to interpret events as they unfold.

Throughout, the emphasis remains on incentives rather than intentions. States may declare their desire for autonomy, but they also seek liquidity. Firms may resent dependence, but they prize predictability. Central banks may experiment, but they fear instability. Corridors succeed when they align these motives across actors and fail when they rely on rhetoric alone. Understanding this alignment is the difference between mistaking motion for progress and recognising durable change.

There is a temptation, especially in periods of geopolitical tension, to frame monetary questions as battles to be won or lost. Such language obscures more than it reveals. Currency competition is rarely a zero-sum contest. Gains in one corridor can coexist with persistence in another. Reducing exposure to one risk often introduces a different one. The real challenge is not victory, but management: how to navigate a system that is becoming more plural without becoming more fragile.

This perspective also tempers both alarmism and complacency. Those who proclaim the dollar's imminent demise underestimate the inertia of institutions and the value of scale. Those who dismiss all alternatives as symbolic underestimate the cumulative effect of incremental change. The truth lies between. The dollar's role is being reshaped, not erased. Its privileges are being questioned, not nullified. The corridors that matter tomorrow are being constructed today, quietly, unevenly, and with consequences that will only become clear over time.

As these corridors multiply, new questions arise. How much fragmentation can the system absorb before efficiency gives way to confusion? Which design choices enhance resilience, and which merely relocate risk? Can technological innovation deliver interoperability without undermining trust? How will investors price political alignment when it becomes embedded in financial infrastructure? And perhaps most pressing of all, who decides which corridors remain open when stress returns?

The answers will not be found in slogans or single indicators. They require a way of seeing that connects plumbing to power, technology to trust, and local decisions to global outcomes. This book offers such a way of seeing. It does not promise certainty, but it provides a map. A map of corridors rather than capitals, of routes rather than regimes. In a world where the headline lags behind the reality, learning to read the map may be the most valuable skill of all.

Chapter 1

Why Dollar Dominance Still Matters

At the edge of a desert port, a tanker loads crude under a sky bleached white by heat. The crew speaks one language, the buyer's office another, the seller's accountants a third. Contracts reference shipping lanes that cross half the globe, insurance underwriters in a fourth country, and a delivery date shaped by weather no one controls. Yet when the paperwork is finalised, one choice is made almost without thought. The price is set in dollars. It has been for decades. No one pauses to justify it. No one needs to.

This unthinking quality is the dollar's greatest strength and its least examined feature. Dominance, in monetary affairs, rarely announces itself as power. It arrives disguised as convenience. The more a currency is used, the less visible it becomes, until it feels less like a choice than a condition of the landscape, as ordinary as time zones or tides. For all the talk of alternatives, this invisibility remains intact. The dollar continues to sit beneath global trade and finance like a load-bearing beam that most users neither admire nor question.

That persistence is often misunderstood. Commentators reach for metaphors of empire, decline, or replacement, as if currencies competed like flags over captured territory. But the dollar's role is not sustained by loyalty or fear alone. It is sustained by a dense web of practical functions that solve problems for governments, firms, and investors every day. Before one can assess whether that web is fraying, or where new strands are being spun, one must understand what it actually does.

A reserve currency is not defined by prestige or proclamation. It earns its status by performing specific tasks reliably under pressure. It invoices trade so that buyers and sellers can plan. It provides assets that central banks can hold with confidence, knowing they can be sold quickly without moving the market. It underpins funding markets, allowing borrowers to raise capital at scale and lenders to hedge risk. These functions reinforce one another. Widespread trade invoicing creates demand for reserves. Deep reserve markets support liquid funding. Liquid funding cements the currency's use as a benchmark. Remove one pillar and the structure weakens. Remove several and it collapses.

Consider a commodity exporter facing a familiar dilemma. Revenues arrive in large, volatile bursts. They must be stored somewhere until they are needed to stabilise the domestic economy, service debt, or fund future investment. One exporter parks its surplus in US Treasuries, accepting modest returns in exchange for unmatched liquidity and safety. Another chooses gold, preferring an asset without issuer risk but accepting storage costs and price swings. A third turns to regional bonds, seeking yield and political alignment while tolerating thinner markets. Each choice reflects a different view of risk, but the first remains dominant for a reason. Treasuries can be sold at a moment's notice, in size, without asking permission. That characteristic, more than ideology, explains their central role.

Trade invoicing follows a similar logic. The dollar anchors transactions not because counterparties are compelled to use it, but because shared pricing lowers friction. When oil, metals, or agricultural goods are priced in a common unit, hedging becomes cheaper, contracts become comparable, and disputes become rarer. An Indian refiner and a West African producer may have little in common, but by transacting in dollars they enter a market with established benchmarks, deep derivatives, and predictable settlement. Over time, this convenience hardens into habit. Path dependence sets in. Even when alternatives exist, the cost of coordinating a switch can exceed the benefits, especially for globally traded commodities.

This anchoring effect extends beyond trade into funding and crisis behaviour. In periods of calm, the dollar functions as a lubricant, easing the flow of capital across borders. In periods of stress, it becomes a refuge. Investors retreat into dollar assets not out of affection, but because they trust the depth of the market and the willingness of the US state to backstop it. This safe-haven role is self-reinforcing. The more investors run to dollars in crises, the more future investors expect others to do the same. Expectations become structure.

It is tempting to see this as a system that benefits only the United States, but the reality is more complicated. The US state gains seigniorage and policy flexibility. American firms enjoy cheaper financing and a home-market advantage in global deal-making. Global banks profit from intermediating dollar flows, earning fees and influence. Yet many emerging-market borrowers also benefit. A developing-country firm issuing dollar debt may accept currency risk in exchange for lower interest rates and a broader investor base. Liquidity is a form of insurance, and for many borrowers it is worth the price.

This tension between convenience and vulnerability lies at the heart of dollar dominance. The same features that make the dollar attractive also create exposure. When US monetary policy tightens, capital can drain from distant economies with brutal speed. Exchange-rate swings can turn manageable debts into existential threats. Sanctions can freeze assets and sever payment routes overnight. These are not hypothetical risks. They recur with a regularity that shapes political debate and policy planning far beyond Washington.

Imagine an importer in a middle-income economy that relies on short-term dollar financing to pay for fuel. A rate rise by the Federal Reserve, intended to cool inflation at home, pushes up global funding costs. The local currency weakens. Suddenly, the importer's costs rise on two fronts. Margins evaporate. Credit lines are reviewed. What began as a domestic policy adjustment becomes a foreign shock. Multiply this dynamic across sectors and countries, and the political appeal of reducing dollar exposure becomes obvious.

Yet awareness of risk does not translate neatly into exit. The infrastructure that supports dollar use is dense and resilient. Alternatives must replicate not just one function, but several at once. They must offer credible assets, reliable liquidity, and legal certainty. This is why sweeping claims of imminent displacement so often disappoint. The question is not why the dollar still matters, but how its role is being reshaped at the margins.

This chapter begins by grounding that question in mechanics rather than rhetoric. It clarifies what reserve currency status means in practice, tracing how trade invoicing, foreign-exchange reserves, and safe-asset supply interact on balance sheets. It shows why the dollar anchors trade even when the United States is absent from the transaction, and how that anchoring creates inertia that is difficult to overcome. It examines who truly benefits from this arrangement, revealing a more distributed set of gains than caricatures allow.

It then turns to the costs borne by the rest of the world, not as moral judgements but as structural realities. Exposure to US policy, vulnerability to sanctions, and sensitivity to global dollar liquidity are the shadow side of convenience. These pressures do not produce a single response. They produce a range of adaptations, each targeted at a specific pain point.

Here the chapter pivots from dominance to contestation. The central argument of this book emerges in outline: the future is unlikely to be defined by one currency replacing another across all functions. Instead, different flows are beginning to follow different routes. Energy trade may shift into one corridor, while tourism receipts remain dollar-linked. Reserves may diversify incrementally, while funding markets cling to depth. Investment may fragment by region, even as benchmarks remain global. The system becomes modular rather than monolithic.

This modularity helps explain why dollar dominance can remain visible even as it is being constrained. From a distance, the skyline looks unchanged. Up close, the traffic patterns are evolving. New corridors appear alongside old ones, sometimes intersecting, sometimes competing. Some are designed to reduce risk. Others to signal autonomy. Most do both, imperfectly.

Understanding these dynamics requires resisting simple narratives. It requires recognising that currencies are not merely symbols of power, but tools embedded in institutions and habits. It requires attention to design choices that rarely make headlines but determine outcomes: what collateral is accepted, who has access to liquidity, how losses are shared. It requires an appreciation of why many actors continue to choose the dollar even as they work to limit their dependence on it.

The stakes of this understanding are high. For policymakers, misreading dollar dominance can lead to overconfidence or paralysis. For firms, it can result in costly strategic errors. For observers, it can produce a distorted sense of where change is truly occurring. This chapter does not offer a verdict on the dollar's fate. It offers something more useful: a framework for seeing why it still matters, and where its grip is loosening.

As the discussion unfolds, a recurring image will surface. Think of the global monetary system as a network of bridges spanning rivers of trade and capital. For decades, one bridge has carried most of the traffic. It is wide, familiar, and well maintained. New bridges are now being built, some sturdy, some provisional. Traffic is beginning to redistribute, not because the old bridge has collapsed, but because relying on a single crossing feels increasingly risky. The view from above still shows dominance. The view from the road reveals diversification.

By the end of this chapter, the reader will be equipped to look past declarations and into balance sheets, past symbolism and into settlement. The dollar will appear neither invincible nor irrelevant, but embedded in a system under negotiation. The chapters that follow will trace that negotiation in detail, corridor by corridor. Before doing so, it is essential to understand why the old routes remain so heavily travelled, and why leaving them entirely is far harder than the rhetoric suggests.

The page turns here not towards an obituary, but towards a more demanding inquiry. If dominance persists even as alternatives multiply, what kind of monetary world is taking shape? And how should those who move money, make policy, or simply seek stability learn to navigate it?

Defining reserve currency status

In October 2008, at the height of the financial crisis, the US Treasury auctioned short-term bills at *negative* yields. Investors paid for the privilege of lending to the American state. The sale took place in Washington, but its significance was global. Central banks from East Asia to the Gulf absorbed the paper not because it promised a return, but because it promised certainty. When everything else was in doubt, US Treasuries still settled. Liquidity mattered. Safety mattered more.

This behaviour was not driven by affection for the dollar or confidence in American economic management. It was driven by balance sheets. Reserve currency status is not a title bestowed by markets or committees; it is an outcome revealed under stress. A currency becomes a reserve when institutions repeatedly choose it as the place to store value, settle obligations, and bridge uncertainty, even when the cost is visible and alternatives exist. Convenience is optional. Settlement is not.

Five words capture the point. Balance sheets choose currencies.

The phrase "reserve currency" is often treated as a synonym for prestige. In practice, it describes a set of mundane, testable functions. A reserve currency invoices a large share of global trade, anchoring prices across borders. It supplies assets that central banks can hold in size, confident they can liquidate them quickly. It underwrites funding markets, providing collateral and benchmarks that organise risk. These roles are distinct, yet tightly linked. Trade invoicing creates demand for hedging and liquidity. Liquidity supports deep markets in safe assets. Safe assets attract reserve managers, reinforcing the currency's role as a funding unit. Break the loop and reserve status weakens.

Trade invoicing is the most visible layer. When commodities, manufactured goods, or services are priced in a common unit, counterparties avoid negotiating exchange-rate risk at every turn. This is not ideology; it is arithmetic. A Brazilian exporter and a Korean importer invoicing in dollars both hedge against one currency pair rather than two. They tap established derivatives markets with tight spreads. Contracts become comparable across suppliers. The behaviour can be measured. According to the Bank for International Settlements' *Triennial Central Bank Survey* (2022), the dollar remains involved in roughly 88 per cent of foreign-exchange transactions, reflecting its role as the common leg in global pricing.

Reserve holdings translate that invoicing habit into institutional commitment. Central banks accumulate currencies not to speculate, but to insure. They must meet external obligations, smooth volatility, and reassure markets. Liquidity and legal certainty dominate these decisions. The International Monetary Fund's COFER database shows that as of 2023, roughly 58 per cent of disclosed global reserves were held in dollars. The figure has drifted down over two decades, but the underlying behaviour remains consistent: when reserves are mobilised quickly, dollars are still preferred. This preference is revealed in crises, not speeches.

The final pillar is safe-asset supply. A reserve currency must offer instruments that can absorb enormous sums without distorting prices. This requirement narrows the field sharply. It is not enough to issue debt; one must issue *enough* of it, across maturities, with predictable issuance, enforceable contracts, and a credible lender of last resort. The US Treasury market meets these criteria at a scale no other sovereign market matches. According to the US Treasury Department (2024), marketable Treasuries outstanding exceeded $26 trillion. That stock provides collateral for repo markets, benchmarks for pricing, and a refuge when risk aversion spikes.

These three functions—trade invoicing, reserve holdings, safe-asset supply—interact continuously. A currency that prices trade but lacks deep asset markets struggles to attract reserves. A currency held as reserves but rarely used in trade generates hedging costs that erode its appeal. Reserve status emerges when the loop closes.

Consider a concrete contrast. In 2019, Norway's Government Pension Fund Global, fed by oil revenues, held the bulk of its liquid assets in foreign securities denominated largely in dollars and euros, with US Treasuries playing a central role in its liquidity management. The choice reflected scale and convertibility, not politics. By contrast, Kazakhstan's National

Fund, also supported by commodity exports, has historically allocated a larger share to gold and regional assets, reflecting a different risk tolerance and institutional context. Gold reduces issuer risk but introduces price volatility and storage costs. Regional bonds align politically but thin out under stress. The balance sheets record the trade-offs. Neither choice is abstract. Each determines how quickly value can be mobilised when conditions turn.

The interaction becomes clearer in moments of strain. In March 2020, as global markets seized, demand for dollars surged. Offshore funding markets scrambled for liquidity. The Federal Reserve responded by reopening and expanding dollar swap lines with major central banks, providing access to dollars against local currency collateral. The decision stabilised markets within days. This episode illustrates a crucial point: reserve status is reinforced by institutional backstops. A currency that can be borrowed in size during stress reduces the need to liquidate reserves pre-emptively. That assurance feeds back into reserve preferences.

Who benefits from this arrangement is often caricatured. The United States enjoys seigniorage and strategic leverage. American firms borrow cheaply. Global banks intermediate flows and earn rents. Yet the benefits extend further. Many emerging-market borrowers issue dollar debt because investors trust the liquidity of the market, not because they are coerced. The metric is observable. Dollar bond markets offer deeper order books and tighter spreads than most alternatives. For a borrower facing volatile capital flows, that liquidity can be the difference between refinancing and default. Convenience shades into necessity.

The costs are equally concrete. Exposure to US monetary policy transmits shocks. Exchange-rate movements reprice liabilities overnight. Sanctions exploit the same plumbing that delivers liquidity. These risks motivate diversification, but diversification operates within constraints. A reserve manager reallocating ten percentage points away from dollars must find assets that can absorb billions without widening spreads. Few markets can. This is why diversification is gradual and partial, not decisive.

A credible counter-example is often raised: gold. Gold carries no credit risk and sits outside the jurisdiction of any single state. Central banks have increased gold holdings over the past decade, particularly after 2014. The World Gold Council reported net central-bank purchases exceeding 1,000 tonnes in 2022. This behaviour signals distrust of some aspects of the system. Yet gold does not invoice trade. It does not settle payments. It cannot be deployed instantly in repo markets at scale. Its price fluctuates sharply. Gold diversifies reserves, but it does not replace a reserve currency's functional role. The reconciliation lies in recognising that reserves serve multiple purposes. No single asset satisfies them all.

Another limitation emerges in regional currencies. The euro invoices a substantial share of trade within Europe and is widely held as a reserve. Yet during the sovereign-debt crisis of the early 2010s, fragmentation within the euro-area bond market undermined its safe-asset supply. Liquidity concentrated in German Bunds while peripheral bonds sold off. The episode revealed that reserve status depends not only on currency union, but on fiscal backstops and market integration. Design matters.

Throughout these examples, a quiet motif recurs: storage. Reserve currencies are warehouses for value. The best warehouse is not the one with the highest yield, but the one whose doors open reliably when needed. Institutions measure this reliability in spreads, turnover, legal clarity, and access to liquidity facilities. Trust, in this context, is not sentiment. It is behaviour repeated under constraint.

This framing grounds the debate over de-dollarisation. Claims of displacement often conflate dissatisfaction with functionality. States may resent exposure to US policy and still rely on dollar assets to meet obligations. Firms may invoice selectively in other currencies and hedge back into dollars. These choices are legible on balance sheets. They show adjustment, not abandonment.

The implication is sobering. Reducing reliance on a reserve currency requires rebuilding the loop elsewhere. Trade must be priced in the alternative. Reserves must be held in assets that can be sold quickly. Safe-asset markets must deepen without fragmenting. Backstops must be credible. Each step is measurable. Each takes time. Rhetoric accelerates none of them.

The forward test, then, is not whether the dollar's share ticks down in a given year. It is whether new currencies can close the loop under stress. When the next shock arrives, where will institutions store value, raise liquidity, and settle accounts? The answer will define reserve status more clearly than any declaration.

How the dollar anchors trade

In March 2022, a cargo of Saudi crude left Ras Tanura bound for a refinery in South Korea. The buyer was not American. The seller was Saudi

Aramco. The contract referenced delivery terms agreed months earlier, freight booked through a European insurer, and hedges struck across several exchanges. The invoice, however, was denominated in US dollars. Settlement moved through correspondent banks in London and New York. When the cargo arrived, the payment cleared without incident. No press release marked the moment. The outcome was ordinary, which is precisely the point.

This routine outcome masks a complex choreography. The dollar did not appear because of law or loyalty, but because it sits at the intersection of pricing, funding, and refuge. The behaviours can be observed. Contracts specify dollars. Hedges reference dollar benchmarks. Working capital is raised in dollars. In stress, balances return to dollars. The currency anchors trade not as a symbol, but as a set of coordinated decisions that reduce friction across distance and uncertainty.

Anchoring begins with invoicing. When oil is priced in dollars, both parties accept a common measure that already organises global supply and demand. This choice shows up in visible metrics: benchmark prices quoted on exchanges, derivatives volumes, and bid–ask spreads. Brent and WTI contracts clear in dollars because liquidity concentrates where participation is thickest. According to the Intercontinental Exchange, dollar-denominated oil futures consistently account for the majority of global crude derivatives turnover. Liquidity attracts liquidity. Traders commit where exits are cheap.

The name for this effect is path dependence. Once markets converge on a unit, switching costs rise. Hedges, accounting systems, and risk limits are calibrated to that unit. A refiner considering an alternative invoicing currency must ask practical questions. Are there futures to hedge exposure at scale? Are options liquid across maturities? Can collateral be posted without haircuts widening under stress? Each question has a price. Each price discourages deviation.

Funding deepens the anchor. Trade is rarely paid from cash on hand. It is financed. Letters of credit, inventory loans, and margin requirements are structured around currencies that banks can source cheaply and reliably. The dollar dominates here because funding markets in dollars are deep and continuous. The evidence is transactional. In April 2022, amid volatile commodity prices, global banks expanded dollar credit lines to trading firms while tightening others, reflecting their own access to dollar liquidity. The behaviour aligns with data from the Federal Reserve Bank of New

York, which tracks daily volumes in the dollar repo market. When volumes swell, funding is available. When they contract, activity slows.

The safe-haven role completes the triangle. In periods of market stress, firms and investors shorten horizons. They prioritise settlement certainty over yield. This behaviour can be seen in flows. During the market turmoil of March 2020, demand for dollars spiked, pushing cross-currency basis swaps sharply negative. The Bank for International Settlements documented this scramble in its Quarterly Review (June 2020), noting that non-US banks paid a premium to secure dollars. The response—expanded swap lines—reinforced expectations. When risk rises, the dollar remains the place where trades end.

A single oil transaction illustrates how these roles interlock. The contract is priced in dollars. The buyer hedges price risk using dollar futures. The bank finances inventory in dollars, using dollar collateral. If volatility spikes, the firm draws on dollar credit lines. If margins are called, cash is posted in dollars. Each step reinforces the next. The currency becomes the spine of the transaction.

The implication is not inevitability, but inertia. Shared pricing reduces frictions today and raises them tomorrow for any alternative. This is the anchor at work. It is not a chain, but a weight. Movement is possible, but it requires effort.

Two named examples illuminate both persistence and pressure. In May 2018, the Shanghai International Energy Exchange launched yuan-denominated crude oil futures. The venue was Shanghai; the regulator was the China Securities Regulatory Commission. The outcome was immediate participation by domestic refiners and some foreign firms. Volumes grew steadily. The contract offered a mechanism to price oil in yuan and hedge exposure locally. Yet international uptake remained limited. Liquidity was thinner than in dollar benchmarks. Foreign participation faced capital controls. Many users hedged yuan exposure back into dollars. The example shows ambition meeting constraints. Pricing can shift at the margin; anchoring resists wholesale change.

A second case sits in Europe. In July 2022, following disruptions to Russian gas supplies, several long-term LNG contracts signed by European utilities referenced euro pricing alongside traditional dollar clauses. The place was Brussels; the parties included national energy firms. The move reflected policy intent to reduce dollar exposure. The outcome was mixed. Some trades cleared in euros, particularly within the euro area. But financing and hedging often reverted to dollars, where derivatives markets were deeper. The behaviour reconciles aspiration with arithmetic.

A credible limitation to the anchoring argument is regional trade. Not all commerce is global. Intra-regional flows, particularly among neighbouring economies, can and do settle in local currencies. Tourism receipts, cross-border services, and small-scale manufacturing often bypass the dollar. The metric is settlement volume through regional payment systems. Yet even here, the anchor reappears at scale. When firms expand beyond the region or seek external financing, they encounter dollar benchmarks. The limitation refines the claim rather than refutes it. The dollar anchors global trade; local currents still flow.

The quiet motif threading these cases is gravity. Large bodies attract. Markets with mass pull activity toward them. Gravity does not forbid motion; it shapes trajectories. The dollar's mass derives from accumulated liquidity, institutional backstops, and habitual use. Attempts to escape gravity must supply energy elsewhere.

This gravity shapes the starting point for any shift. Advocates of alternative invoicing often focus on price tags, but the anchor extends to funding and refuge. Change one without the others and exposure remains. This is why announcements of non-dollar pricing can coexist with persistent dollar demand. The behaviour is visible in balance sheets. Firms may record revenues in one currency and liabilities in another. They measure risk where it matters most.

None of this denies movement. It explains its pattern. Anchors can be repositioned gradually. Corridors can be built alongside existing routes. Shared pricing can fragment by sector. But the process is cumulative, not declarative. Each additional transaction settled outside the dollar must still clear, hedge, and fund itself. Where those functions are available at scale, anchoring loosens.

The forward tension lies here. If trade partners increasingly accept non-dollar prices, will funding and safe-haven functions follow, or will they remain tethered to the old centre? At what volume does gravity weaken? The next chapters trace the corridors forming around these questions. The answer will be revealed not in statements, but in settlements.

Who truly benefits from dollar use

In September 2014, Pemex returned to the international bond market from Mexico City with a ten-year issuance denominated in US dollars.

The borrower was Mexican, the projects were domestic, and the revenues would be earned largely in pesos. Yet demand exceeded supply, spreads tightened, and the bonds traded actively in the weeks that followed. The outcome was unremarkable by market standards, which is precisely why it matters. Faced with a choice, the issuer chose dollars. Liquidity won.

Money follows the widest road.

Dollar dominance is often framed as a transfer of advantage to the United States at the expense of others. The framing is not wrong, but it is incomplete. The dollar functions less like a weapon than a toll road. Those who build and maintain it collect rents. Those who use it do so because alternative routes are narrower, slower, or unreliable. The benefits are distributed unevenly, but they are real for more actors than the caricature suggests.

Begin with the most visible beneficiary: the US state. When a currency is widely used abroad, its issuer enjoys seigniorage—the ability to finance itself more cheaply because global demand absorbs its liabilities. This is not a slogan. It is observed in yields. US Treasury securities trade at lower interest rates than peers with similar debt ratios, reflecting global demand for safety and liquidity. According to the Congressional Budget Office (2023), foreign official and private investors held roughly one-third of marketable Treasuries. That demand lowers borrowing costs across maturities. The implication is fiscal space. It does not remove constraints, but it stretches them.

The second benefit is flexibility. A state whose currency anchors global finance can respond to domestic shocks with less immediate external penalty. When the Federal Reserve adjusts policy, capital does not flee the United States; it flows toward it. This asymmetry was visible in 2022, when aggressive rate hikes strengthened the dollar even as they tightened conditions elsewhere. The metric was the DXY index, which reached levels not seen in two decades. The behaviour confirmed an old rule: the centre sets terms.

US firms sit close to this centre. They borrow in their home currency at scale, with deep markets across maturities. They invoice exports in dollars, passing currency risk to counterparties or hedging cheaply. Their balance sheets align naturally with their revenue streams. Consider Apple's bond issuance programme, which routinely raises tens of billions in dollar debt to fund buybacks and investment. The scale is documented in SEC filings.

The implication is strategic optionality. Firms can time markets, refinance easily, and weather volatility with fewer frictions.

Global banks are another class of beneficiaries, though their advantage is conditional. Banks that intermediate dollar flows earn fees, manage liquidity, and gain access to privileged networks. Their behaviour is visible in balance-sheet composition. According to the Bank for International Settlements (2022), international banks' dollar assets exceed those in any other currency by a wide margin. This concentration reflects client demand. The implication is influence. Banks embedded in dollar plumbing shape standards, from collateral eligibility to compliance norms. Yet this advantage carries risk. Dollar funding shortages hit banks first. Access must be maintained, not assumed.

The more contentious question concerns emerging markets. It is tempting to cast them solely as victims of dollar dominance, exposed to shocks they do not control. Exposure is real. So are the benefits. Many sovereigns and corporates choose dollar debt because it offers liquidity that domestic markets cannot. This is not theoretical. When Ghana restructured its debt in 2022, its dollar bonds continued to trade actively even as local markets froze. Liquidity preserved price discovery. For issuers, the decision often comes down to refinancing risk. A shallow local market may offer currency alignment but no exit under stress.

Return to Pemex. The company could have issued in pesos. Local pension funds would have bought the bonds. The market would have cleared. But secondary trading would have been thin. Foreign participation limited. By issuing in dollars, Pemex accessed a global investor base, tighter spreads, and predictable refinancing. The decision traded currency risk for liquidity. That trade-off sits at the heart of dollar use.

This tension reveals the true distribution of benefits. Dollar dominance does not impose a single outcome; it offers a menu weighted toward liquidity. Those who value stability and scale choose it. Those who prioritise autonomy pay for it in higher costs or thinner markets. The choice is constrained, but it is still a choice.

Seigniorage illustrates the asymmetry clearly. When foreigners hold dollar assets, the United States receives goods, services, or claims in exchange for liabilities it issues cheaply. The benefit is measurable. According to estimates by the Federal Reserve Bank of St. Louis (2019), seigniorage from currency held abroad amounts to tens of billions of dollars annually.

The implication is subtle but persistent. The issuer gains resources without explicit taxation.

Benchmark status amplifies these gains. The dollar anchors pricing across markets, from commodities to derivatives. Benchmarks create coordination. Once established, they attract liquidity, which reinforces their status. The behaviour can be observed in derivatives markets. The Chicago Mercantile Exchange's dollar-denominated contracts dominate global volumes. Alternatives exist. Participation lags. The implication is path dependence. New entrants face uphill battles.

There is, however, a credible counter-example: the euro. The euro is widely used in trade within Europe, held as a reserve, and backed by large sovereign markets. It shares some benefits of dollar use. Yet it has not displaced the dollar globally. The limitation lies in fragmentation. During the euro-area crisis of 2010–2012, spreads between member states widened sharply. Safe-asset supply concentrated in German Bunds. The European Central Bank intervened to stabilise markets, but the episode left scars. The reconciliation is instructive. Reserve benefits accrue not only to currency unions, but to those with unified fiscal backstops and consistent issuance.

Another limitation is sanctions risk. Dollar use exposes participants to US jurisdiction. This cost is visible in behaviour. After 2014, several sanctioned states reduced dollar invoicing where possible. The metric was trade settlement shares reported by national statistical agencies. Yet even here, benefits linger. Many transactions reverted to dollars via intermediaries. Convenience competed with constraint.

The quiet motif running through these cases is access. Access to liquidity. Access to markets. Access to exits. Dollar use widens access. It also opens exposure. The balance sheets record both.

Trust often appears in this discussion, but trust must be grounded. Investors trust dollar assets because they trade in size, settle reliably, and sit within a legal system that enforces contracts. These are behaviours, not beliefs. The decision to roll over maturing bonds, the willingness to accept Treasuries as collateral, the narrowness of bid–ask spreads—each is a vote of confidence cast daily.

Efficiency is similarly concrete. A corporate treasurer choosing funding currency compares all-in costs: interest, hedging, documentation, and exit. If dollar funding is cheaper after hedging than local alternatives, efficiency is revealed in the spreadsheet. The abstraction dissolves into arithmetic.

Risk, too, is measured. Currency mismatch appears on balance sheets. Stress tests simulate depreciation. Firms choose exposures consciously. The presence of dollar debt does not imply ignorance. It implies prioritisation.

Understanding who benefits from dollar use requires abandoning moral binaries. The system produces winners and losers, but not along a single axis. The United States gains structural advantages. So do firms and banks embedded in its markets. Some emerging economies gain access to capital they could not otherwise secure. Others bear disproportionate risk. The same instrument can stabilise one balance sheet and destabilise another.

This complexity explains the persistence of dollar use despite political pressure. Even governments that speak of autonomy hesitate to forgo liquidity. Even firms wary of exposure continue to hedge through dollar markets. The toll road remains busy because it is wide and well lit.

The unresolved tension lies ahead. As alternative corridors develop, will the toll road lose traffic, or will it simply become more important to the heaviest loads? When liquidity and autonomy pull in opposite directions, which institutions choose under stress? The answer will determine not who denounces dollar dominance, but who quietly continues to benefit from it.

Hidden costs for the rest of the world

On 16 June 2022, the US Federal Reserve raised its policy rate by 75 basis points in Washington, the largest single increase since 1994. The announcement took minutes. Its effects lasted for months. Within days, currencies from Colombo to Santiago slid, bond yields spiked, and import bills swelled. In Dhaka, Bangladesh Petroleum Corporation reported sharply higher costs for dollar-priced fuel cargoes. The rate decision was domestic. The bill was not.

Shock travels fast.

This is the shadow side of dollar use. The same architecture that delivers liquidity and coordination also transmits stress with force. For countries and firms outside the United States, the dollar's centrality converts distant decisions into local constraints. These costs are not theoretical. They show up in balance sheets, exchange-rate charts, and policy reversals. They explain why dissatisfaction with the system persists even as reliance on it endures.

Begin with monetary policy exposure. When the Federal Reserve tightens, global dollar liquidity contracts. The mechanism is visible. Higher US rates attract capital toward dollar assets. The dollar appreciates. Funding costs rise for borrowers who earn revenues in other currencies but service liabilities in dollars. According to the Bank for International Settlements (Quarterly Review, December 2022), dollar credit to non-US borrowers exceeds $13 trillion. The figure measures exposure. It also measures vulnerability.

Consider a simple, representative scenario. An importer in a middle-income economy finances fuel purchases with short-term dollar credit. Revenues arrive in local currency. A rate hike in Washington raises the cost of rolling over that credit. At the same time, the local currency weakens against the dollar. The importer now faces higher interest expenses and a larger principal when converted back. Margins compress. Prices rise. The central bank intervenes to stabilise the currency, selling reserves. A domestic policy problem is born of an external decision.

This pattern repeats across cycles. It is not accidental. It reflects the role of the dollar as a funding currency. When conditions tighten, funding retrenches first where protection is weakest. The behaviour can be measured. During the 2013 "taper tantrum", announced in May by then Federal Reserve Chair Ben Bernanke, emerging-market bond yields spiked and capital outflows surged. The IMF documented the episode in its *Global Financial Stability Report* (October 2013), noting that countries with higher dollar liabilities experienced sharper adjustments. The implication is clear. Funding choice determines shock transmission.

Exchange-rate swings amplify these effects. The dollar's appreciation acts as a tightening channel. For exporters paid in dollars, revenues may rise in local terms. For importers and borrowers, costs escalate. The asymmetry matters. Many developing economies import energy, food, and capital goods priced in dollars. When the dollar strengthens, inflation pressures build. Policymakers face trade-offs between growth and stability. These are not abstract dilemmas. They surface in emergency rate hikes, fuel subsidies, and capital controls.

Sri Lanka's crisis in 2022 offers a stark example. As reserves dwindled, the rupee depreciated sharply against the dollar. Imports became unaffordable. Debt service faltered. The country defaulted in April 2022. Multiple factors contributed, including fiscal missteps and external shocks. Dollar exposure was the transmission belt. The behaviour is documented in Central Bank of Sri Lanka releases and IMF programme papers. The implication extends beyond one case. Currency mismatch magnifies fragility.

Sanctions add a different layer of cost. Dollar use embeds transactions within a legal and compliance framework influenced by US jurisdiction. This exposure is often invisible until activated. When sanctions are imposed, access to dollar clearing can be curtailed swiftly. Assets can be frozen. Correspondent relationships severed. The behaviour is observable. After sanctions tightened on Iran in 2018, banks worldwide reduced dollar transactions linked to Iranian trade, even where local laws permitted activity. The metric was trade settlement data reported by partner countries. Flows rerouted or shrank.

The cost here is optionality lost. Firms and states discover that certain corridors close without warning. This risk shapes behaviour pre-emptively. Even actors not directly targeted adjust, wary of secondary sanctions. Compliance departments overcomply. Deals are abandoned. The chilling effect is difficult to quantify but widely acknowledged in bank risk disclosures. The implication is political. Monetary infrastructure becomes a tool of influence.

Yet it would be misleading to portray these costs as universally crippling. A credible counter-example lies in economies with strong buffers. Countries with large reserves, diversified exports, and credible policy frameworks weather dollar cycles more effectively. South Korea in 2022 faced currency pressure, but stabilised markets through coordinated intervention and swap lines. The place was Seoul; the partners included the Federal Reserve via standing facilities. The reconciliation matters. Exposure does not dictate outcome. Capacity moderates cost.

Another limitation concerns firms that hedge actively. Multinationals with sophisticated treasury operations manage currency risk through derivatives and natural hedges. The metric is hedging ratios disclosed in annual reports. For these actors, dollar volatility is a cost of business, not an existential threat. But hedging has a price. Smaller firms and poorer states pay more. The system sorts by scale and sophistication.

Throughout these examples, a quiet motif returns: the tide. When the tide of dollar liquidity rises, many float. When it recedes, some are left exposed. The tide does not discriminate by intent. It follows its own cycle.

These hidden costs fuel political pressure for alternatives. Calls for local-currency trade, regional payment systems, and diversified reserves intensify after each tightening cycle or sanctions episode. The timing is telling. Initiatives accelerate after pain, not during calm. The behaviour is observable in policy announcements clustered around crises. Yet the same pressures reveal the limits of abrupt change. Abandoning the dollar entirely would sacrifice liquidity that cushions shocks.

This tension explains why the search for alternatives is selective. Actors do not reject the dollar wholesale. They seek relief where costs are highest. Importers explore non-dollar invoicing for energy. Central banks diversify marginal reserves. Regional blocs build clearing systems to handle intra-bloc trade. Each move addresses a specific vulnerability. None resolves all.

The implication is methodological. Forecasts that ask whether the dollar will "collapse" miss the point. The more relevant question is where the costs of dollar use exceed its benefits for particular flows. Those are the seams along which corridors form. Trade, funding, and reserves need not move together. Fragmentation is functional.

This perspective also reframes debates about fairness. The costs borne by the rest of the world are not imposed maliciously, but they are real. They arise from asymmetry. One state sets policy. Many absorb consequences. Recognising this asymmetry does not require rejecting the system. It requires understanding its distributional effects.

The unresolved tension lies ahead. As pressure for alternatives grows, will new corridors dampen the tide, or merely divert it temporarily? When the next tightening cycle arrives, which balance sheets will still depend on the old channel, and which will have found shelter elsewhere? The answer will determine whether hidden costs remain tolerable, or finally compel deeper change.

From dominance to contested corridors

In September 2023, at a regional energy forum in Astana, Kazakhstan, officials from several Eurasian states discussed new long-term supply contracts for gas and electricity. The conversations were technical, almost tedious. Volumes, delivery points, indexation clauses. Yet one detail stood out. Several of the draft agreements referenced settlement in regional currencies rather than dollars. The venue was not Washington or Brussels. The date did not coincide with a crisis. The outcome was modest: a handful of contracts adjusted, many left untouched. Still, the signal was clear. The conversation had moved from replacement to routing.

The dollar did not vanish from those deals. It remained the benchmark for pricing and risk comparison. But it no longer monopolised settlement by default. What changed was not allegiance, but architecture. Certain flows were being nudged into new channels, while others stayed firmly anchored to the old. The shift was partial, deliberate, and uneven. It was not a revolution. It was re-plumbing.

This is the lens that reframes the debate. The question is no longer whether one currency will dethrone another across the entire system. It is whether specific flows can be redirected into alternative corridors without breaking the whole. Dominance gives way to contestation not at the level of symbols, but at the level of routes.

The image of a single global currency regime has always been misleading. Even at the height of dollar centrality, monetary practice was segmented. Trade, investment, reserves, and retail payments followed different logics. What is new is the willingness of states and firms to formalise those differences. Instead of tolerating fragmentation as a nuisance, they are beginning to design for it.

Trade offers the clearest entry point. Energy transactions, large and recurring, concentrate political attention. When buyers and sellers agree to settle in a non-dollar currency, the behaviour is observable: invoices change, hedges adjust, settlement accounts multiply. This has occurred sporadically for years. What has changed is intent. After 2014, and more visibly after 2022, some energy exporters and importers began to treat currency choice as a strategic variable rather than an inherited convention. The metric is not volume alone, but persistence across contracts.

Contrast this with tourism receipts. A hotel in Thailand, a resort in Turkey, or an airline ticket sold online still clears overwhelmingly in dollars or dollar-linked card networks. The behaviour reflects convenience. Card processors price in dollars. Consumers expect it. Settlement happens quickly. No government announcement is required. The corridor persists because friction is low and political risk diffuse. Trade fragments. Services lag.

Investment follows a third path. Portfolio flows respond to benchmarks, ratings, and liquidity. Even where trade settlement shifts, investment often remains dollar-centric. Sovereign bonds issued in alternative currencies may attract regional buyers, but global funds still reference dollar benchmarks. The evidence sits in index composition published by providers such as MSCI and FTSE Russell. Inclusion criteria hinge on market depth and accessibility, not political alignment. Corridors diverge.

Reserves add another layer. Central banks diversify cautiously, reallocating marginal shares into gold, regional currencies, or pooled arrangements.

The behaviour is slow and visible in IMF COFER data. Yet the core remains anchored to assets that can be mobilised instantly. Reserve corridors widen at the edges while the centre holds. Fragmentation is managed.

This modular pattern explains why forecasts of wholesale regime change disappoint. They assume uniformity where none exists. A corridor approach accepts heterogeneity. It asks which flows are most sensitive to sanctions risk, which to funding cost, which to settlement speed. Each sensitivity invites a different response.

Two named examples clarify the mechanics. In May 2022, India and Russia announced arrangements to settle some bilateral trade in rupees and roubles. The place was New Delhi; the motivation was continuity under constraint. Energy imports featured prominently. Payments were rerouted through designated banks. The outcome was uneven. Some trades settled successfully. Others stalled due to imbalances and limited convertibility. Meanwhile, Indian IT services exports to the United States continued to clear in dollars without interruption. One relationship diversified. The other did not. Corridors separated.

A second case sits in Africa. In January 2023, the Pan-African Payment and Settlement System expanded participation among central banks, aiming to facilitate intra-African trade in local currencies. The organisation was Afreximbank; the ambition was clear. Early transactions focused on smaller trade flows among neighbouring states. Tourism and retail payments remained largely dollar-linked. Capital flows stayed external. The system carved a niche without challenging the core. The behaviour illustrates scale sensitivity. Corridors grow where volumes and risk profiles align.

A credible limitation to this framework is crisis behaviour. When stress intensifies, fragmentation can reverse. Actors retreat to the most liquid route. This was evident in March 2020, when even those experimenting with alternatives rushed back to dollar funding. The metric was cross-currency basis spreads, documented by the BIS. The reconciliation is instructive. Corridors do not replace the centre in emergencies. They reduce exposure in normal times. Resilience, not dominance, is the goal.

The quiet motif binding these observations is routing. Money, like traffic, seeks paths that balance speed, safety, and cost. When one highway becomes congested or politicised, side roads attract interest. Some handle heavy lorries. Others suit local traffic. None render the main route obsolete overnight.

Trust, in this context, becomes specific. Firms trust a corridor if settlement clears on time. Central banks trust a corridor if liquidity arrives under stress. Investors trust a corridor if exits remain open. These trusts are measured in decisions: which account is funded, which hedge is placed, which asset is sold first.

Efficiency also fragments. A currency may be efficient for trade but inefficient for investment. Another may suit reserves but not retail payments. The system tolerates this because actors compartmentalise. Balance sheets record the segmentation.

Risk, too, becomes localised. Sanctions risk concentrates in certain corridors. Exchange-rate risk in others. The decision to reroute is often defensive, not aspirational. The behaviour follows incentives.

This corridor logic prepares the ground for the chapters ahead. Swap lines create emergency lanes. Clearing hubs widen regional roads. CBDC bridges experiment with shortcuts. Capital controls erect toll booths. Each intervention reshapes routing choices without abolishing the map.

The unresolved tension remains structural. As corridors multiply, coordination costs rise. Fragmentation can reduce dependence but increase complexity. At what point does redundancy become inefficiency? When does resilience shade into confusion? The answers will not arrive as proclamations. They will appear in the quiet decisions of traders, treasurers, and central bankers choosing which route to take when the pressure returns.

Chapter 2

How Currency Systems Actually Work

At 09:17 on a Tuesday morning, a payment instruction leaves a bank in Lagos. It is unremarkable in size and urgent only in the way commercial obligations always are. A Nigerian importer has bought industrial equipment from a supplier in southern China. The invoice is due. Within seconds, a message flashes across a network, acknowledgements return, compliance checks trigger, balances are adjusted, and somewhere—often much later than the parties expect—money finally settles. To the importer, the payment feels digital, almost weightless. To the system moving it, the payment is anything but simple.

Most people encounter money as a number on a screen. They swipe, tap, or click, and value appears to move instantly. Cross-border finance disabuses anyone of that illusion. Behind each international payment sits a layered apparatus of messages, accounts, guarantees, and timed obligations, stitched together by institutions that trust one another only conditionally. The miracle is not that payments sometimes fail. It is that so many succeed, day after day, across jurisdictions that share little else.

This chapter enters that machinery. It does so not to dazzle with complexity, but to strip away confusion. Debates about de-dollarisation, sanctions, digital currencies, and alternative payment systems often falter because the underlying plumbing remains opaque. Terms are conflated. Networks are mistaken for assets. Speed is confused with settlement. The result is argument by headline rather than by mechanism. Understanding how currency systems actually work is the difference between mistaking a rerouted message for a new monetary order and recognising a genuine structural shift when it occurs.

The architecture of cross-border payments evolved to solve a practical problem: how to move value safely between parties who do not share a bank, a legal system, or a time zone. The solution was never a single pipe. It was a chain. Messages instruct payments. Banks intermediate risk. Accounts mirror one another across borders. Settlement occurs when claims are extinguished, not when instructions are sent. Each step introduces delays, costs, and vulnerabilities. Each also provides a point of control.

Currency choice enters early in this chain. It shapes which banks are involved, which markets provide liquidity, and which central banks stand behind the process. A payment denominated in dollars follows a different path from one denominated in a regional currency, even if both are initiated through the same interface. The difference is not cosmetic. It determines who bears risk while funds are in transit and who must act if something goes wrong.

To see this clearly, one must follow a payment from origin to settlement. When the Nigerian importer instructs its bank to pay the Chinese supplier, the first step is an informational one. A message is sent detailing the amount, currency, and beneficiary. This message travels through a network designed to standardise and authenticate instructions. It does not move money. It asks others to do so. That distinction—between instruction and settlement—is the fault line along which much misunderstanding lies.

Next comes foreign-exchange conversion. Unless both parties hold accounts in the same currency at the same bank, one side must exchange funds. That exchange can occur immediately or be embedded in pricing. Either way, it draws on liquidity in specific currency pairs. Markets with depth and continuity make this cheap. Thin markets do not. The cost appears as a spread, invisible to some users, decisive for others.

Correspondent banking then takes centre stage. The importer's bank likely does not hold an account directly with the supplier's bank. Instead, it relies on intermediaries that maintain reciprocal accounts—*nostro* and *vostro*—to bridge the gap. These accounts are pre-funded. They tie up liquidity. They are monitored constantly. When balances fall short, payments queue. When risk limits are breached, routes close. Correspondent relationships are the arteries of the system, and like arteries, they narrow with age and stress.

Settlement comes last. Only when final claims are extinguished does value truly move. Until that moment, the system runs on trust and credit. Settlement can occur in central bank money or in commercial bank money, depending on the corridor. It can be immediate or delayed. It can be gross—one payment at a time—or netted against others. Each choice carries implications for liquidity and risk.

Clearing and netting exist to manage those implications. Banks do not want to fund every payment in full, every time. They prefer to offset obligations, reducing the amount of cash required. Multilateral netting systems allow dozens of institutions to settle a day's worth of transactions with a fraction of the gross value. The efficiency gains are obvious. So are the risks. Netting concentrates exposure. If one participant fails, others may be forced to absorb losses or inject liquidity. Clearing houses emerge as critical nodes, trusted until they are tested.

The contrast between gross and net settlement reveals why infrastructure choices matter. A system that settles every transaction individually demands vast liquidity but limits contagion. A netting system economises on liquidity but creates interdependence. During calm periods, the latter is attractive. During stress, it becomes a focal point for intervention. This trade-off underpins debates about regional clearing hubs and alternative FX infrastructures explored later in the book.

Central banks hover above this landscape as both referees and backstops. They issue the settlement asset, manage reserves, and provide emergency liquidity when private channels seize. Their role is often misunderstood. Central banks do not process commercial payments. They enable them by ensuring that settlement assets are available and trusted. When dollar funding evaporates offshore, it is central banks—through swap lines and standing facilities—that restore flow. These interventions are not acts of charity. They protect domestic financial stability by stabilising external linkages.

Commercial banks, by contrast, live inside the flow. They manage client relationships, compliance, and credit risk. They decide which corridors to keep open and which to exit. Their decisions are pragmatic. If compliance costs rise or profitability falls, they retreat. This behaviour explains why some regions experience correspondent "deserts," where cross-border payments become slow and expensive. It also explains why alternative corridors often emerge first where traditional banks withdraw.

Messaging networks add another layer of confusion. Systems such as SWIFT standardise communication. They do not hold money. They do not settle claims. Yet being excluded from a messaging network can cripple a bank's ability to operate internationally. The paradox is that a payment can be messaged outside SWIFT and still settle in dollars, or messaged through SWIFT and settle in another currency. Changing the language of instruction does not change the currency of settlement. This distinction matters profoundly when evaluating claims about new networks replacing old ones.

Friction enters wherever trust thins. Compliance checks slow payments. Time-zone gaps delay settlement. Capital controls trap funds. Sanctions turn routine transactions into legal hazards. Each friction point becomes a potential choke point. Banks learn to map them. So do states. A sanctioned bank losing correspondent relationships experiences this viscerally. Payments fail not because messages cannot be sent, but because no institution is willing to intermediate the risk.

These frictions are not evenly distributed. They cluster by currency, geography, and institution. This clustering creates opportunity. New corridors emerge where pain is concentrated. Regional systems promise faster settlement for local trade. Bilateral arrangements bypass hostile nodes. Digital experiments seek to compress timelines. None of these efforts abolish the old system. They carve out alternatives where the old system is costly or constrained.

Understanding this layered reality reframes the entire debate about currency power. Dominance is not enforced by decree. It is sustained by infrastructure that works well enough for enough users. Contestation begins not with ideology, but with engineering. It starts when participants ask a narrow question: can this payment move more cheaply, more predictably, or with less exposure if routed differently?

This chapter equips the reader to answer that question. It traces the anatomy of payments without mystification, showing where currency choice matters and where it does not. It explains why clearing and netting reduce liquidity needs while concentrating risk. It clarifies the distinct roles of central banks and commercial banks, and why confusing them leads to faulty conclusions. It disentangles messaging from settlement, revealing why cosmetic changes rarely deliver structural shifts. It maps frictions not as anomalies, but as features that shape behaviour.

The motif threading through this analysis is distance. Not geographic distance alone, but institutional distance—the number of balance sheets and trust relationships a payment must cross. The longer the distance, the more currency choice matters. Corridors shorten distance. Dominant currencies compress it. Understanding how distance is measured inside the system is the key to seeing where it can be reduced.

As the book moves forward, swap lines, clearing hubs, digital bridges, and regional arrangements will appear repeatedly. They will make little sense without a firm grasp of the plumbing they seek to modify. This chapter lays that foundation. It invites the reader to look beneath interfaces and rhetoric, to follow value rather than messages, and to recognise that the future of currency competition will be decided not by slogans, but by settlement.

Anatomy of cross-border payments

On 12 July 2019, a Kenyan importer instructed Standard Chartered Bank in Nairobi to pay a machinery supplier in Shenzhen. The amount was modest by global standards. The urgency was not. Production depended on delivery. Within minutes, a payment message left Kenya. Two days later, funds were available to the supplier's bank in southern China. No headline followed. The machinery shipped. The outcome was success.

Payments travel as relays.

What moved that value was not a single transfer, but a sequence of hand-offs across institutions that trusted one another just enough. To understand where currency choice matters—and where it does not—one must follow that relay from start to finish. The anatomy of a cross-border payment is not arcane. It is precise. Each step has a role. Each introduces cost, delay, and risk. Together, they explain why some currencies dominate flows and why alternatives struggle to scale.

The first movement is informational. The Kenyan importer's bank created a payment instruction detailing the beneficiary, amount, currency, and settlement route. This instruction travelled over a secure messaging network designed to standardise formats and authenticate senders. The message told other banks what to do. It did not move money. This distinction is foundational. Messages coordinate action; assets settle obligations. Confusing the two leads to faulty conclusions about power and change.

Messaging networks matter because they reduce errors and speed coordination. When banks share a common language, payments can be processed automatically. The behaviour is visible in straight-through processing rates reported by major banks. Higher automation lowers operational risk. Yet messaging is currency-agnostic. A payment message can instruct settlement in dollars, euros, or any other unit. Changing the messenger does not change the money.

Once the instruction is received, currency choice asserts itself through foreign-exchange conversion. Unless both parties hold accounts in the same currency at the same bank, one side must exchange funds. In the Nairobi–Shenzhen case, the importer paid in dollars. The Kenyan bank converted shillings into dollars, drawing on its dollar liquidity. The metric here is spread. Dollar pairs trade with narrow bid–ask spreads across time zones. That behaviour reflects depth. It also reflects preference. Liquidity attracts use.

Next comes correspondent banking, the least understood yet most decisive layer. The Kenyan bank did not hold an account directly with the Chinese supplier's bank. Instead, it relied on correspondent institutions that maintain reciprocal accounts. A *nostro* account is "ours with you": funds the Kenyan bank holds at a correspondent abroad. A *vostro* account is "yours with us": funds a foreign bank holds locally. These accounts are pre-funded. They tie up cash. They are monitored continuously.

In practice, the Kenyan bank debited its *nostro* dollar account at a correspondent in London. That correspondent credited a *vostro* account held for the Chinese bank. The Chinese bank then credited its customer. Each debit and credit extinguished part of an obligation. Settlement occurred when final balances updated. The implication is concrete. Banks must hold liquidity in the currencies they intermediate. Dollar corridors persist because banks already hold dollars.

Trust appears here as behaviour. A correspondent relationship exists because one bank believes the other will honour obligations and comply with rules. When trust erodes, limits tighten or relationships end. The evidence is contractual. Banks publish lists of correspondents and revise them after regulatory actions. The disappearance of a correspondent is a choke point. Payments reroute or fail.

Settlement completes the relay. Only when accounts update does value truly move. Settlement timing varies. Some corridors settle same day. Others take longer due to time zones, cut-off times, and compliance checks. The Kenyan payment took two days. That delay reflects geography and process, not incompetence. It also reflects risk management. Banks wait for confirmations before releasing funds.

At each stage, currency choice bites differently. Messaging is neutral. FX conversion favours liquid pairs. Correspondent banking rewards currencies with established networks. Settlement depends on access to reliable accounts and, ultimately, central bank money. A currency that lacks one of these supports struggles to scale beyond niche use.

A second named example clarifies the mechanics. In August 2020, during pandemic-related disruptions, a South African exporter paid a supplier in Vietnam using euro settlement via a European correspondent. The place was Johannesburg; the intermediary was Deutsche Bank in Frankfurt. The outcome was successful, but slower and more expensive than dollar settlement. The reason was not politics. It was infrastructure. Euro liquidity was available, but fewer correspondents operated across the specific corridor. The metric was cost. Fees were higher. Settlement took longer. The behaviour reinforced habit.

A credible limitation deserves attention. Regional payment systems can compress steps for local trade. Within the euro area, TARGET2 allows banks to settle directly in central bank money. The relay shortens. Liquidity needs fall. Risk concentrates at the central bank. The reconciliation is important. Anatomy varies by corridor. What holds globally is not universal inefficiency, but layered design.

The relay motif helps unify these observations. Each runner depends on the next. Speed improves when hand-offs are smooth. Failure occurs when one runner drops the baton. Currency choice determines which runners are available. Dollars recruit the largest team.

Efficiency, often invoked abstractly, shows up as timing and cost. How long does settlement take? How wide is the spread? How much liquidity must be parked idle? These are measurable. In the Nairobi case, dollar settlement minimised idle balances because the bank already managed dollar flows daily. Choosing a less-used currency would have required holding additional balances or relying on thinner markets. The decision is recorded on the balance sheet.

Risk appears as exposure during transit. While a payment is in flight, banks extend credit to one another. They manage this exposure through limits and collateral. Currencies with active funding markets allow banks to adjust positions intraday. The metric is intraday credit usage, tracked by central banks. Where such facilities exist, risk is managed. Where they do not, flows slow.

Compliance overlays every step. Sanctions screening, anti-money-laundering checks, and reporting obligations introduce delay. These checks are currency-blind in principle but corridor-specific in practice. Dollar payments attract heightened scrutiny because of jurisdictional reach. Banks factor this into routing decisions. The behaviour is observable in payment queues.

Understanding anatomy dispels common myths. Faster messaging does not equal faster settlement. Digital interfaces do not eliminate correspondent banking. Alternative currencies do not bypass liquidity requirements. Each innovation must contend with the same steps or replace them with credible substitutes.

This clarity matters for evaluating proposals. When a new system promises instant cross-border payments, the question is not speed alone. It is where FX conversion occurs, how liquidity is funded, and who settles final balances. Without answers, promises remain cosmetic.

The unresolved tension sits at the end of the relay. As new corridors emerge, will they shorten the race without increasing the chance of a dropped baton? Or will they simply add runners to an already crowded track? The future of currency competition will be decided here, in the anatomy of payments, one hand-off at a time.

Clearing, netting, and liquidity needs

On 17 September 2019, overnight funding markets in New York seized. Repo rates spiked to nearly 10 per cent. The Federal Reserve intervened within hours, injecting liquidity to stabilise settlement. The trigger was technical—tax payments and Treasury issuance drained reserves—but the lesson travelled far beyond Manhattan. When obligations settle one by one, cash matters. When cash runs short, systems stall.

Liquidity is oxygen.

Banks do not fear risk in the abstract. They fear running out of cash at the wrong moment. Clearing and netting exist to manage that fear. They compress thousands of bilateral obligations into smaller, manageable sums, reducing the amount of money that must be available at any instant. The behaviour is measurable. It appears in intraday balances, margin calls, and the timing of settlements. It also concentrates exposure. Efficiency and fragility share a boundary.

Begin with the simplest contrast. In a gross settlement system, every payment settles individually. If Bank A owes Bank B $10 million, the full amount must be available at settlement time. If ten such payments occur, $100 million must pass through accounts. Liquidity demand is high.

Transparency is complete. Risk is localised. In a net settlement system, obligations offset. If Bank A owes Bank B $10 million and Bank B owes Bank A $9 million, only $1 million settles. Liquidity demand collapses. Risk concentrates in the clearing mechanism.

This trade-off shapes modern finance. Banks prefer netting because it economises on scarce resources. Liquidity costs money. Idle balances earn little. Holding less frees capacity. The implication is operational. Systems that net allow banks to process higher volumes with the same balance sheet.

The show is visible in payments data. According to the Bank for International Settlements (Annual Economic Report, 2021), multilateral netting in payment and securities settlement systems reduces gross settlement values by more than 90 per cent in some markets. The name for this effect is compression. The explanation is arithmetic. Offset what can be offset. The implication is scale. Markets grow without proportionate growth in cash.

Clearing houses institutionalise this compression. They sit between participants, becoming the buyer to every seller and the seller to every buyer. In foreign exchange, central counterparties such as CLS Bank play this role. CLS began operations in September 2002, based in New York, to reduce settlement risk in FX trades. By settling both legs of a trade simultaneously, it eliminated the risk that one currency would be delivered without the other. The outcome was concrete. According to CLS data, the system settles trillions of dollars daily while requiring a fraction of that amount in funding due to multilateral netting.

The implication is powerful. FX trading volumes expanded because settlement risk fell and liquidity needs dropped. Banks committed more capital. Spreads narrowed. The dollar's role as the common leg benefited further because dollar liquidity underpinned the system. Clearing reinforced anchoring.

A numerical example clarifies the mechanics. Imagine four banks trading currencies over a day. Gross settlement requires each to fund every outgoing payment. If each bank sends and receives $50 million, gross flows reach $200 million. Under multilateral netting, offsetting positions reduce the final settlement to, say, $10 million per bank. Liquidity needs fall by 80 per cent. The behaviour is attractive. The risk shifts. If one bank fails before settlement, the clearing house must manage the shortfall.

That risk is not theoretical. In September 2008, the collapse of Lehman Brothers tested clearing systems worldwide. Central counterparties absorbed losses and continued operations, but only because of margin requirements, default funds, and central bank support. The place was global; the date matters. The episode revealed the cost of concentration. Netting saved liquidity but required robust governance.

Banks understand this calculus. They prefer netting where the rules are clear and the backstops are credible. They avoid it where governance is weak. The decision shows up in participation lists. Clearing hubs with strong legal frameworks attract members. Others stagnate.

Regional ambitions illustrate both promise and peril. In April 2018, China launched the Shanghai Clearing House's expanded FX clearing services to support yuan internationalisation. The goal was to net regional trades, reducing dollar dependence. Participation grew domestically. International uptake lagged. The reason was not hostility, but trust. Foreign banks measured default procedures, collateral eligibility, and legal enforceability. Liquidity savings alone were insufficient. The implication is precise. Netting requires confidence in the centre.

A second named case sits in Europe. TARGET2-Securities, launched in June 2015 and operated by the European Central Bank from Frankfurt, integrated securities settlement across the euro area. By centralising settlement, it reduced liquidity needs for cross-border securities trades. According to ECB reports (2017), participants achieved significant savings in collateral usage. The behaviour demonstrates how design choices shape outcomes. Strong central bank backing encouraged participation.

Yet a credible counter-example tempers enthusiasm. Not all netting reduces risk. In bilateral netting arrangements without central counterparties, exposures can become opaque. During the Asian financial crisis of 1997, some regional clearing arrangements magnified contagion because obligations were intertwined without sufficient capital buffers. The reconciliation is instructive. Netting without robust risk management can amplify shocks.

Liquidity needs thus depend on architecture. Gross systems demand cash but isolate failure. Net systems economise on cash but centralise failure. Banks and regulators choose along this spectrum based on priorities. The choice is not moral. It is operational.

Trust, often invoked abstractly, appears here as margin posted and collateral accepted. Clearing houses demand initial margin to cover potential losses.

They call variation margin daily. These metrics are published in rulebooks and audited reports. Participants commit resources. Trust is priced.

Efficiency becomes visible as balance-sheet relief. When netting reduces required funding, banks redeploy capital. The metric is return on assets. Systems that improve it attract volume. Those that do not, do not.

Risk surfaces in stress tests. Clearing houses run default simulations. They publish results. Participants review them. Decisions follow. Risk is not eliminated. It is pooled.

This pooling has political implications. Clearing hubs become systemically important. Their location matters. Their currency matters. Access becomes a strategic question. When a hub clears predominantly dollar trades, dollar liquidity underpins it. When a hub clears regional currencies, regional central banks must supply support. The choice of hub tilts corridors.

These dynamics set the stage for debates about fragmentation. As regions build their own clearing systems, liquidity pools split. Netting becomes local. Global netting declines. Liquidity needs may rise overall even as they fall locally. The arithmetic is unforgiving. Ten regional hubs cannot net as efficiently as one global hub if participants span all ten.

The quiet motif threading this analysis is the ledger. Clearing rearranges ledgers. Netting compresses them. Settlement closes them. Where ledgers sit determines who must act when numbers fail to add up.

For policymakers, the temptation is to prioritise liquidity savings. For banks, the temptation is the same. The unresolved tension is systemic. How much concentration can be tolerated in exchange for efficiency? At what point does fragmentation erode the very liquidity netting was meant to conserve? The next chapters follow these questions into the geography of clearing hubs and the politics of access. The answers will be written not in communiqués, but in ledgers balanced—or not—at the end of the day.

Roles of central banks and commercial banks

On 19 March 2020, the Federal Reserve announced temporary US dollar liquidity arrangements—swap lines—with nine additional central banks, including the Reserve Bank of Australia, Banco Central do Brasil, the Bank of Korea, Banco de México, the Monetary Authority of Singapore, and Sveriges Riksbank. The statement was issued in Washington, but its immediate audience sat elsewhere: bank treasurers watching dollar funding evaporate and central bankers weighing how to keep trade finance and financial markets functioning. Within days, usage of these facilities surged. The outcome was measurable. Dollar funding strains eased, and cross-currency basis spreads narrowed, a pattern later documented by the Bank for International Settlements in its *Quarterly Review* (BIS, 2020).

Central banks lend. Banks distribute.

This division of labour is the spine of cross-border finance. It is also routinely misunderstood. Commercial banks move payments, manage client relationships, and take credit risk on the ground. Central banks create the settlement asset, police the perimeter, and—when necessary—lend against collateral to stop liquidity shortages becoming solvency crises. When observers confuse these roles, they misread events. Swap lines are treated as political theatre rather than crisis plumbing. Messaging changes are mistaken for monetary independence. Payment delays are blamed on central banks when they are caused by bank risk limits. The system becomes a blur of acronyms and assumptions.

Start with the commercial bank, because it sits closest to the real transaction. When an exporter ships goods and expects payment, it is a commercial bank that extends trade finance, confirms letters of credit, prices foreign exchange, and arranges settlement through correspondents or clearing systems. The bank measures risk in immediate, operational terms: counterparty limits, compliance exposure, settlement timing, and funding cost. These are not abstractions. They show up as line items: the spread on a dollar loan, the haircut on collateral, the size of a nostro balance required to keep payments flowing. A bank's willingness to maintain a corridor is a decision made in committees, defended in risk reports, and revised after regulatory findings.

Commercial banks also intermediate currency choice. A firm may want to pay in its domestic currency. The bank may insist on dollars because the hedging market is deeper, the settlement network broader, and the compliance process better rehearsed. The firm experiences this as an invoice term. The bank experiences it as operational safety. In periods of calm, such decisions appear routine. In stress, they become decisive. When dollar liquidity tightens, banks hoard dollars, widen spreads, and shorten tenors. This behaviour can be observed in market prices: cross-currency basis swaps move against those needing dollars, and trade finance costs rise for jurisdictions perceived as riskier. The BIS has repeatedly documented this dynamic in its stress-period reviews (BIS, 2020; BIS, 2022).

Now consider the central bank. Its first role is foundational: it issues the base money in its jurisdiction and anchors settlement. When banks settle in central bank money—through systems such as TARGET2 in the euro area or Fedwire in the United States—they extinguish claims with the highest-quality asset available domestically. This matters because settlement is not merely accounting. It is finality. Central bank money provides it.

The second role is supervisory and infrastructural. Central banks set rules for payment systems, define eligibility for collateral, and calibrate liquidity requirements. They decide what assets banks can pledge for emergency funding and at what valuation. These details are the quiet architecture of trust. When a central bank broadens collateral eligibility during stress, it signals willingness to backstop the system. When it tightens, it forces banks to self-insure.

The third role is reserve management. Central banks hold foreign assets—typically in highly liquid instruments—to meet external obligations and support market confidence. Reserve composition is not a vanity portfolio. It is a functional tool. A central bank that holds substantial dollar reserves can supply dollars to local banks in a crisis, smoothing external payments and preventing disorderly currency moves. The metric is simple: usable reserves relative to short-term external liabilities, a ratio tracked in IMF country reports and reserve adequacy frameworks (IMF, 2015).

The fourth role is lender of last resort. This phrase is overused, but the function is concrete. When banks cannot obtain liquidity from markets at reasonable cost, the central bank lends against collateral to prevent fire sales and payment failures. The lending is not a gift. It is priced. It is collateralised. It is conditional. But it alters behaviour because it changes the tail risk: banks know that if markets freeze, there is a backstop.

In cross-border flows, however, a domestic lender of last resort is not always enough. A bank in South Africa may be perfectly solvent in rand terms and still fail if it cannot obtain dollars to settle trade or meet offshore obligations. Dollar liquidity is special because it is a foreign currency for most of the world. A central bank cannot print it. It must obtain it—through reserves, through markets, or through arrangements with the issuer of dollars.

This is where swap lines matter. A swap line is, at its core, a temporary exchange of currencies between central banks: one supplies its domestic currency, receives dollars, and then on-lends those dollars to its own banking system. The operational implication is profound. It allows a central bank to act as a dollar lender of last resort to its domestic banks without liquidating reserves aggressively into a panicked market. The financial implication is equally important: it reduces the need for banks to scramble for dollars by selling assets at distressed prices.

The March 2020 episode shows this vividly. The Federal Reserve not only expanded standing swap lines with major central banks on 15 March 2020; it also introduced the Foreign and International Monetary Authorities (FIMA) Repo Facility on 31 March 2020, allowing foreign official institutions to obtain dollars by temporarily exchanging US Treasuries for cash. These actions were announced publicly and tracked closely by markets (Federal Reserve, 2020). The behaviour followed quickly: usage rose, and funding spreads eased. The BIS later interpreted these steps as crucial in restoring the functioning of global dollar funding markets (BIS, 2020). The corridor did not change currency preference. It stabilised it.

A second named example reveals how central banks translate these tools into local support. In April 2020, the Bank of Korea conducted auctions to supply dollars to domestic banks using funds obtained via its swap line with the Federal Reserve, aiming to calm local dollar funding pressures in Seoul. The outcome was tangible: volatility in the onshore dollar funding market eased as auctions provided a predictable source of dollars. The actions and auction results were reported by the Bank of Korea in its releases and market operation updates (Bank of Korea, 2020). Here, the central bank did not replace commercial banks; it fed them oxygen so they could continue lending and settling.

This division—central banks provide system liquidity, commercial banks allocate it—also explains a frequent confusion about "who runs" cross-border payments. A central bank can ensure that domestic settlement systems function and that banks have liquidity. It does not decide whether Bank A will pay Bank B for a client in a sanctioned jurisdiction. That decision sits with commercial bank compliance and risk committees. Central bank money can clear a payment technically; it cannot compel counterparties to accept the legal and reputational risk. The implication is political. Sanctions and de-risking work not only because of state power, but because private intermediaries choose caution when rules are unclear or penalties severe.

A credible counter-example sharpens the point: swap lines are not universal, and central banks without them face harsher constraints. During the early months of the pandemic shock, institutions with direct Fed swap access stabilised faster than those relying solely on reserves or market borrowing. The limitation is structural. Swap networks are selective. Access signals trust and strategic alignment as much as economic size. The reconciliation is not cynical; it is operational. A central bank extending dollars takes on credit and reputational exposure. It chooses partners accordingly.

Even with swap lines, the boundary between liquidity and solvency matters. Central banks can lend against good collateral to solvent institutions. They cannot rescue a banking system with pervasive credit losses without fiscal support. The metric is capital adequacy. Liquidity facilities can bridge timing mismatches; they cannot manufacture real capital. This is why emergency lending often arrives alongside fiscal measures, bank guarantees, or regulatory forbearance during crises. The outcome depends on both.

The motif that threads these roles is the backstop. In calm periods, it is invisible, like a fire brigade in a quiet town. In stress, it becomes the difference between a contained incident and a spreading blaze. Commercial banks build the houses—credit lines, payment routes, hedging relationships. Central banks station the brigade—liquidity facilities, settlement systems, swap networks. Neither can do the other's job without distortion.

This matters for reading headlines. When a country announces a new payment system, the diagnostic question is not whether it sends messages faster, but whether its banks can settle obligations with finality and obtain liquidity under stress. When a central bank signs a swap line, the question is not whether it "ends dollar dependence", but whether it provides emergency access to dollars that reinforces existing corridors. When a crisis hits, watch what banks do with their nostros. Watch where spreads move. Watch which central banks can supply which currencies, and at what terms.

The forward test is uncomfortable but clarifying. In the next global funding squeeze, will the central banks outside the core be able to backstop their banks' dollar needs without draining reserves or imposing controls—and will commercial banks keep corridors open once compliance and capital costs rise? The answer will not be spoken. It will be settled.

Messaging networks versus settlement assets

In March 2022, following Russia's invasion of Ukraine, several Russian banks were removed from the SWIFT messaging system. The announcement came from Brussels, where SWIFT is incorporated, and the effect was immediate. Payment instructions that had once travelled routinely could no longer be sent through the world's most widely used financial messaging network. Headlines spoke of financial isolation. Yet within weeks, some cross-border transactions involving Russian counterparties continued—rerouted, slower, costlier, but still settling, often in US dollars. The outcome puzzled many observers. How could money move when the network was cut?

Messages are not money.

The confusion exposed by that moment is pervasive. SWIFT has become shorthand for the global financial system itself, a proxy for currency power and payment control. In reality, it is neither a bank nor a settlement system. It is an information network—a standardised, secure way for financial institutions to communicate instructions. The distinction between telling someone to pay and actually paying is the fault line along which many claims about alternatives collapse. Understanding it is essential to judging whether new networks meaningfully challenge dollar dominance or merely repaint the signposts.

To see why, return to first principles. A cross-border payment involves two separable elements. One is communication: who owes whom, how much, in what currency, and under what reference. The other is settlement: the extinguishing of obligations by transferring a settlement asset, typically central bank money or balances at a trusted correspondent. Messaging coordinates. Settlement completes. Confusing the two inflates the importance of networks and understates the stubborn power of assets.

SWIFT sits firmly on the messaging side. Founded in 1973 and headquartered in Belgium, it provides a common language for banks to exchange payment instructions and confirmations. According to SWIFT's own disclosures, its network carries tens of millions of messages daily across more than 200 countries. The scale is impressive. The function is specific. SWIFT does not hold accounts. It does not clear or settle funds. It cannot create liquidity. Its value lies in standardisation and trust in the message format, not in control over money itself.

Settlement assets, by contrast, are scarce. They sit on balance sheets. They are accepted because of legal backing, liquidity, and institutional support. Dollars dominate here not because SWIFT prefers them, but because banks and central banks trust dollar claims to settle finally and at scale. When a payment instruction specifies dollars, the receiving bank expects settlement through accounts it recognises and can mobilise. The messaging channel is secondary.

This separation becomes visible when messaging changes but settlement does not. After 2014, several countries explored alternatives to SWIFT for political or resilience reasons. Russia developed its System for Transfer of Financial Messages (SPFS). China expanded its Cross-Border Interbank Payment System (CIPS). Regional systems proliferated. Messages flowed through new pipes. Yet in many cases, settlement continued in dollars. The metric was not message count but currency balances at correspondent banks. Those balances remained dollar-heavy.

A concrete example clarifies the mechanics. In late 2022, a Central Asian importer paid a Turkish supplier using a regional messaging system rather than SWIFT. The instruction travelled through domestic channels, avoiding SWIFT entirely. The currency specified, however, was US dollars. Settlement occurred via correspondent accounts in Europe. The behaviour was unambiguous. The message avoided one network. The money relied on the same asset. Costs rose. Timing lengthened. Currency exposure did not change.

Why does this happen? Because messaging networks reduce friction, but they do not create liquidity. Banks hold settlement assets where they expect repeated use and reliable backstops. Dollar accounts persist because they connect to deep funding markets, clearing systems, and central bank support. Changing the messenger without changing the asset leaves the economic core untouched.

This distinction explains why being cut off from SWIFT is damaging but not identical to losing currency access. Exclusion raises costs and delays. It complicates compliance. It forces rerouting. But it does not, by itself, eliminate the possibility of settlement. Banks can exchange instructions bilaterally, via other networks, or even manually. What constrains them more severely is the loss of correspondent relationships and access to settlement accounts in desired currencies. Those are balance-sheet decisions, not network ones.

The confusion often runs the other way as well. Some observers assume that adopting a new messaging standard automatically shifts currency use. It does not. A bank can send ISO 20022-compliant messages through SWIFT or another network and still settle in dollars. The standard governs syntax, not substance. The behaviour can be observed in migration projects. When SWIFT mandated ISO 20022 adoption for cross-border payments beginning in 2022, banks upgraded systems without changing currency preferences. Messaging modernised. Settlement patterns remained.

A second named example underscores the point. In February 2021, the People's Bank of China promoted CIPS as a channel for yuan-denominated cross-border payments. The system, based in Shanghai, expanded participation among foreign banks. Some messages flowed through CIPS rather than SWIFT. Yet CIPS itself relies on SWIFT standards for part of its messaging, and many participating banks still settled ancillary transactions in dollars. According to public statements by CIPS Co. Ltd., the system aimed to complement, not replace, existing networks. The implication is structural. Messaging sovereignty does not equal monetary sovereignty.

A credible counter-example deserves attention. Domestic real-time payment systems that link directly across borders can compress both messaging and settlement into a single platform for specific use cases. The linkage between Thailand's PromptPay and Singapore's PayNow, announced in April 2021, allows retail users to send funds instantly using phone numbers. The currencies involved are local. Settlement occurs through linked central bank arrangements. Here, messaging and settlement align. The limitation is scope. Volumes are small. Transactions are retail. The model does not scale easily to wholesale finance or complex trade flows. The reconciliation is instructive. Integration works where risk is limited and backstops are clear.

Trust, often invoked vaguely, appears here as willingness to accept settlement assets. A bank trusts a dollar balance because it can convert it, pledge it, or deploy it quickly. That trust is measured in actions: accepting Treasuries as collateral, rolling over funding, quoting tight spreads. A messaging network earns trust differently. It must deliver messages accurately and securely. Outages matter. But an outage does not invalidate a currency. It delays instructions.

Efficiency is similarly divided. Messaging efficiency reduces operational cost and error rates. Settlement efficiency reduces liquidity needs and credit exposure. The two interact but do not substitute. A faster message sent into a congested settlement channel still waits.

Risk follows the same split. Messaging risk concerns cyber security and operational resilience. Settlement risk concerns counterparty failure and liquidity shortfalls. Banks manage them with different tools. Confusing the risks leads to misplaced confidence.

The quiet motif threading this analysis is the envelope. A payment message is an envelope carrying instructions. The money is the content delivered later. Changing envelopes may improve delivery. It does not change what is inside.

This nuance matters for judging alternatives. When a new network is announced, the diagnostic questions are precise. In which currency does settlement occur? Where are the accounts held? Which central bank stands behind the system in stress? Without clear answers, claims of disruption overreach. Conversely, when settlement assets diversify—through new clearing hubs, reserve pools, or CBDC arrangements—messaging adapts quickly to follow. The order matters.

The unresolved tension is forward-looking. As technology blurs lines between messaging and settlement, particularly in digital currency experiments, will envelopes and contents merge in ways that weaken the incumbent asset? Or will new envelopes simply deliver the same old money more efficiently? The distinction between network and asset will decide whether alternatives reroute flows—or merely rename them.

Where frictions and choke points arise

In November 2018, Bank Mellat, one of Iran's largest state-owned banks, quietly lost several remaining correspondent relationships with European institutions. The place was Frankfurt. The trigger was not a missed payment or a systems failure, but a recalibration of compliance risk after renewed US sanctions. Transactions that had cleared days earlier now stalled indefinitely. Letters of credit went unconfirmed. Trade finance lines were withdrawn. The bank still existed. Its messages could still be drafted. What vanished was passage.

Payments fail at narrow points.

Cross-border finance is often described as a web. In practice, it behaves more like a river system, with wide channels narrowing into straits that determine flow. These choke points are not accidental. They are the cumulative result of regulatory design, risk management, geography, and politics. Understanding where they arise—and why—reveals both the limits of the existing system and the opportunities for new corridors to form.

Begin with compliance, the most visible friction and the least well understood. Every cross-border payment triggers a cascade of checks: sanctions screening, anti-money-laundering filters, counter-terrorist financing rules, and customer due diligence. These checks are applied repeatedly, by each institution in the chain. The behaviour is measurable. Banks track false-positive rates, queue times, and manual review costs. According to data cited by the Wolfsberg Group (2019), a significant share of payment delays stems from screening hits that require human review, even when transactions are ultimately cleared.

The name for this friction is risk aversion under uncertainty. Banks face asymmetric penalties. A missed illicit transaction can bring fines, licence restrictions, or reputational damage. A delayed legitimate payment brings irritation. The implication is predictable. When rules tighten or enforcement intensifies, banks slow flows, widen buffers, and sometimes exit relationships entirely. Compliance becomes a gate, not a filter.

Correspondent risk limits add a second constriction. Banks do not maintain unlimited exposure to one another. They cap balances, transaction volumes, and tenors. These limits are reviewed regularly, adjusted after stress events, and tightened when jurisdictions are downgraded by rating agencies or regulators. The decision is internal but observable in outcomes. Payments queue once limits are hit. Trade finance dries up when exposures are deemed too large. The IMF has documented this "de-risking" phenomenon extensively, noting its disproportionate impact on smaller economies and niche sectors (IMF, 2017).

Time zones introduce a quieter but persistent friction. Settlement systems operate on schedules. Cut-off times matter. A payment initiated in West Africa late in the day may miss settlement windows in Europe or Asia, adding a full day of delay. The behaviour is mundane but consequential. Firms adjust invoicing times. Banks hold larger balances to bridge gaps. The cost appears as trapped liquidity, an invisible tax on cross-border activity.

Capital controls impose a more explicit barrier. When states restrict the movement of funds—through approval requirements, taxes, or outright bans—they alter routing choices. Payments detour through permitted channels or are broken into smaller tranches. The metric is administrative delay. Central banks publish approval timelines. Firms plan around them. Controls can stabilise domestic conditions, but they also push activity into informal or offshore routes. The implication is dual. Controls protect. They also redirect.

Political choke points sit atop these technical frictions. Sanctions transform ordinary bottlenecks into strategic levers. When authorities designate entities or jurisdictions, compliance rules harden into prohibitions. Correspondent banks sever ties. Messaging access may be withdrawn. Settlement accounts can be frozen. The story of Bank Mellat illustrates this escalation. The bank's systems remained intact. Its access evaporated. The choke point was not technology. It was permission.

A second named example reinforces the pattern. In 2014, following Russia's annexation of Crimea, several Russian banks found their access to Western correspondent banking constrained. The place was London and New York. The outcome was uneven. Some flows rerouted through smaller intermediaries. Others ceased. Energy payments continued under special arrangements. Retail and SME transactions suffered most. The metric was volume decline in specific corridors, reported in central bank balance-of-payments data. Sanctions did not stop all trade. They reshaped it.

These frictions do not operate in isolation. They compound. A payment facing heightened compliance scrutiny is more likely to hit correspondent limits. A delayed settlement is more likely to breach cut-off times. A controlled currency is more likely to attract sanctions attention. The system behaves non-linearly. Small rule changes can have outsized effects.

Yet frictions also reveal resilience. Actors adapt. Banks invest in compliance technology to reduce false positives. Firms pre-fund accounts to avoid cut-off delays. States negotiate exemptions for critical trade. Each adaptation creates new routines. Some harden into corridors.

A credible counter-example tempers claims of inevitable fragmentation. Highly standardised corridors with strong governance can reduce friction dramatically. Within the euro area, TARGET2 and SEPA have compressed settlement times and lowered costs for cross-border payments among member states. The behaviour is evident in declining average transaction times and fees reported by the European Central Bank (ECB, 2019). The reconciliation is clear. Where rules align and trust is institutionalised, friction falls.

The quiet motif threading this analysis is the narrowing gate. Each gate filters flow based on different criteria: legality, risk, timing, permission. When too many gates align, passage slows or stops. When gates are redesigned, traffic patterns change.

This map of frictions becomes a diagnostic tool. Where compliance costs spike, expect experimentation with new messaging or screening models. Where correspondent limits bind, expect regional clearing hubs or reserve pooling. Where time zones dominate, expect real-time or overlapping settlement windows. Where capital controls bite, expect invoicing shifts or barter-like structures. Corridors emerge where friction is concentrated and alternatives offer relief.

Trust, often treated as a cultural attribute, appears here as institutional tolerance. A bank trusts a corridor when gates open predictably. That trust is earned through legal clarity, political alignment, and operational reliability. It can be lost quickly. The behaviour is binary. Either payments clear, or they do not.

Efficiency manifests as throughput. How many transactions pass per day? At what cost? When frictions rise, throughput falls. Markets notice. Firms reroute.

Risk is priced in delay. A delayed payment ties up working capital. It raises counterparty exposure. It forces firms to hold buffers. These are measurable costs, visible in balance sheets and cash-flow statements.

Understanding where frictions arise reframes the search for alternatives. The aim is not to build a parallel universe, but to ease specific choke points without creating new ones. Most proposals fail because they underestimate the density of gates. Those that succeed target a narrow bottleneck and build outward.

The unresolved tension is systemic. As actors bypass one gate, pressure shifts to another. New corridors relieve congestion locally but can increase complexity globally. At what point does the map become too fragmented to navigate efficiently? The answer will emerge not from theory, but from where payments slow next—and who builds a passage around them.

Chapter 3

Bilateral Swap Lines and Safety Nets

At dawn on 16 March 2020, as markets reeled and borders closed, a quiet communiqué left the Federal Reserve in Washington. It did not announce a rate cut or a stimulus package. It listed names. The European Central Bank. The Bank of Japan. The Bank of England. The Swiss National Bank. Then others, added days later. Each line signalled an agreement to exchange currencies on demand, in size, at speed. Within hours, dollar funding markets steadied. Within days, panic ebbed. No parliament voted. No money crossed borders permanently. Yet the effect was decisive.

The paradox is striking. Some of the most powerful tools in the global financial system rarely move a single good, finance a single factory, or appear on a firm's balance sheet. They exist between institutions, activated only in stress, and yet they shape expectations long before they are used. Bilateral swap lines are such tools: invisible in calm, indispensable in crisis, and widely misunderstood.

Swap lines occupy an odd place in public debate. They are often framed as arcane technicalities or, at the other extreme, as symbols of geopolitical allegiance. Headlines announce their expansion as evidence of de-dollarisation, or their absence as proof of exclusion. Both readings miss the point. Swap lines are neither decorative nor revolutionary. They are safety nets—selective ones—that stabilise currency corridors when markets threaten to tear them apart.

To understand why they matter, one must return to a basic vulnerability of modern finance. Banks fund themselves in multiple currencies but cannot create any of them. When confidence falters, access to foreign currency funding can evaporate even for solvent institutions. Markets freeze not because assets are worthless, but because liquidity vanishes. The problem is not creditworthiness. It is timing. Swap lines exist to solve that problem, temporarily and conditionally.

At their core, bilateral swap lines allow one central bank to obtain liquidity in another's currency and pass it on to domestic institutions. The mechanics are simple in outline and subtle in consequence. Two central banks agree to exchange currencies at a fixed rate, with a commitment to reverse the transaction at maturity. No exchange-rate risk is taken. No fiscal transfer occurs. What changes is access. A central bank that could not previously supply dollars, euros, or yuan can now do so, within limits, to its own banks.

This capability transforms behaviour. Banks that know their central bank can provide foreign currency liquidity are less likely to hoard, dump assets, or pull back from trade finance. Offshore funding markets calm. Cross-currency basis spreads narrow. These effects are measurable. They appear in price data, not speeches. The safety net works largely by being believed.

Why, then, do central banks choose to weave these nets together? The motives are layered. Crisis management is the most obvious. During systemic stress, swap lines act as firebreaks, preventing local funding shortages from becoming global conflagrations. But trade facilitation also matters. Economies with deep trade ties have an interest in ensuring that payment flows continue even when markets wobble. A swap line can be an insurance policy for commerce as much as for finance.

There is also signalling. Granting a swap line signals trust in another central bank's institutions, governance, and policy framework. It says, implicitly, that liquidity provided will be used prudently and repaid on time. This signal is not extended lightly. It is read carefully by markets and by excluded states alike. Swap networks therefore map not just economic interdependence, but political alignment and institutional confidence.

This dual character—technical instrument and diplomatic signal—makes swap lines central to debates about currency power. On the surface, they appear to reinforce dollar dominance. Many of the most consequential lines deliver dollars, sourced from the Federal Reserve, to foreign banking systems. In moments of stress, the dollar remains the asset everyone wants. Swap lines ensure its availability, cementing its role.

Yet beneath that surface lies a more complex picture. Some swap lines are denominated in non-dollar currencies. Others allow countries to trade and settle without drawing on US-centric funding markets. For policymakers seeking to reduce vulnerability to dollar cycles or sanctions, these arrangements appear attractive. They promise flexibility. They suggest optionality.

This chapter sits at that fault line. It asks when swap lines genuinely diversify currency use and when they simply reinforce existing hierarchies under a different banner. A line that allows a central bank to provide yuan liquidity to its banks may support trade invoiced in yuan. A line that ultimately delivers dollars via an intermediary does something else entirely. Distinguishing between these cases requires attention to design, not rhetoric.

Design choices matter more than announcements. Swap lines differ in size, maturity, pricing, collateral requirements, and operational readiness. Some are standing facilities, tested and familiar to market participants. Others exist largely on paper, activated rarely, if at all. Caps that seem generous in calm can prove trivial in crisis. Tenors that look adequate can expire just as stress peaks. Informal expectations—about reciprocity, about political behaviour, about future access—shape how lines are used long before they are drawn.

These differences explain why not all swap lines are equal in practice. During stress episodes, markets discriminate ruthlessly. Lines that can be accessed quickly and in size reduce panic. Lines that require negotiation or carry stigma are ignored. The safety net holds only where its knots are tight.

Equally revealing is who stands inside the net and who does not. The global swap network is not universal. It is concentrated among advanced economies and a select group of emerging markets. Inclusion signals more than economic size. It reflects perceived policy credibility, strategic importance, and geopolitical alignment. Exclusion carries consequences. Countries without access must self-insure through reserves, impose controls, or accept greater volatility. The hierarchy is quiet but real.

This selectivity complicates claims that swap lines democratise global finance. They stabilise it, but unevenly. They reward trust already earned. They can entrench divisions even as they prevent collapse. Understanding this tension is essential for reading future expansions or contractions of the network.

Throughout this chapter, a recurring image will surface: the bridge. Swap lines are bridges thrown across funding gaps when rivers swell. Some are permanent, reinforced, and well lit. Others are temporary, narrow, and rarely used. Crossing them changes neither the landscape nor the destination, but it can determine whether traffic flows or stalls when waters rise.

The pages that follow unpack this image carefully. They begin by demystifying what swap lines are and how they work, stripping away the mystique without draining the power. They then explore why central banks use them, tracing motives that range from crisis containment to strategic signalling. From there, the analysis turns sharper, examining when swap lines support de-dollarisation in substance and when they merely redistribute access to dollars. Design choices and hidden conditions come into focus, revealing why some lines matter in crises and others fade into irrelevance. Finally, the chapter confronts the politics of access, asking who gains protection and who remains exposed.

The stakes are not academic. As currency corridors multiply and fragmentation accelerates, safety nets will shape which routes remain viable under stress. Swap lines will influence not just how crises are managed, but which monetary arrangements are considered credible in the first place. They sit at the intersection of trust, power, and pragmatism.

The question left hanging is deliberately uncomfortable. In a future of contested currencies and modular corridors, will safety nets adapt to support diversity—or will they continue to anchor the system to its old centre? The answer lies not in declarations of intent, but in the quiet architecture of who stands ready to lend to whom when markets turn.

What bilateral swap lines are

On 12 December 2007, in the midst of growing strain in global money markets, the Federal Reserve announced a temporary reciprocal currency arrangement with the European Central Bank. The place was Washington; the context was a creeping shortage of US dollars among European banks. Within weeks, those banks were borrowing dollars from the ECB rather than from New York markets. The immediate outcome was stabilisation. Dollar funding rates eased. Panic receded without a single cross-border bailout.

Nothing physical moved.

That moment marked the modern return of bilateral central bank swap lines. They have existed in various forms since the Bretton Woods era, but their re-emergence during the global financial crisis transformed them from obscure instruments into pillars of crisis management. Yet despite their prominence in headlines, swap lines remain widely misunderstood. They are often portrayed as gifts, as covert bailouts, or as geopolitical favours. In reality, they are contracts—precise, temporary, and conditional—that allow central banks to do something otherwise impossible: supply foreign currency liquidity to their own banking systems when markets will not.

At their simplest, a bilateral swap line is an agreement between two central banks to exchange currencies up to a pre-agreed amount for a fixed period. One central bank provides its domestic currency and receives the partner's currency at the prevailing exchange rate. At maturity, the transaction is reversed at the same rate. Exchange-rate risk is neutralised by design. Each side ends where it began, minus a fee.

The show is straightforward. A central bank facing a shortage of foreign currency liquidity—typically dollars—draws on the swap line. It receives dollars from the issuing central bank and credits its own account with the equivalent amount of domestic currency. The name for this is a *draw*. The explanation lies in balance sheets. The foreign currency appears as an asset; the domestic currency as a liability. The implication is power with limits. The central bank now has dollars to lend.

What happens next is decisive. The central bank on-lends those dollars to domestic commercial banks through auctions or standing facilities. The banks pledge collateral—often high-quality domestic assets—and pay an interest rate that reflects the cost of the swap plus a margin. The behaviour is visible. Auction results are published. Usage rises when stress peaks and falls when markets normalise. The swap line itself does not reach firms or households. It stabilises the intermediaries that do.

To see why this matters, consider a temporary dollar shortage. An emerging-market economy has banks that fund trade and investment in dollars but earn revenues largely in local currency. A sudden global shock—financial, geopolitical, or health-related—causes investors to pull back. Offshore dollar markets tighten. The banks can no longer roll over short-term funding at reasonable cost. The metric is immediate. Cross-currency basis swaps move sharply, signalling a premium to obtain dollars.

Without a swap line, the central bank has limited options. It can sell dollar reserves, draining its buffer. It can impose controls, disrupting trade. It can do nothing and hope markets reopen. Each choice carries costs. With a swap line, a fourth option appears. The central bank draws dollars, lends them to banks against collateral, and waits for conditions to stabilise. The shortage is bridged, not solved permanently. Time is bought.

This mechanism explains why swap lines are often described as safety nets rather than firehoses. They do not flood the system with liquidity indiscriminately. They target a specific failure mode: the inability of solvent institutions to access foreign currency funding during stress. The implication is subtle but important. Swap lines address liquidity risk, not credit risk. They assume that underlying assets retain value and that markets will eventually reopen.

Two named examples illustrate this logic clearly. During the euro area sovereign debt crisis, the ECB relied heavily on its dollar swap line with the Federal Reserve to supply dollars to European banks. On 30 November 2011, the Fed, ECB, Bank of England, Bank of Japan, Swiss National Bank, and Bank of Canada jointly announced a reduction in the pricing of dollar swap lines. The place was coordinated; the effect was immediate. Dollar funding conditions eased, as documented by the BIS in its *Quarterly Review* (BIS, 2012). The behaviour confirmed the mechanism. Cheaper access reduced panic.

A second case comes from Asia. In October 2008, the Bank of Korea activated a $30 billion swap line with the Federal Reserve to address severe dollar shortages among Korean banks. The place was Seoul; the timing coincided with collapsing global trade. The central bank auctioned dollars to domestic banks, stabilising the won and supporting exporters reliant on dollar financing. The outcome was concrete. Currency volatility subsided, and Korea avoided the deeper dislocations seen in earlier crises. The Bank of Korea's own reports from the period detail the auctions and usage.

These examples highlight a key distinction often missed in commentary. The foreign central bank supplying the currency—most often the Federal Reserve—does not decide which domestic banks receive funds or how they use them. That discretion sits entirely with the borrowing central bank. The swap line provides raw material. Distribution is local. This separation preserves sovereignty while enabling cooperation.

A credible limitation tempers any tendency to mythologise swap lines. They are finite. Amounts are capped. Tenors are fixed. Access is discretionary. In extreme stress, available limits can prove insufficient. During the early phase of the pandemic in March 2020, some central banks without standing swap lines struggled until additional facilities were announced. The reconciliation is instructive. Swap lines are powerful, but only where they exist and only to the extent designed.

Trust, often invoked loosely, appears here as contractual confidence. A central bank extending a swap line trusts that its counterparty will repay in full and on time. That trust is underwritten by institutional reputation, legal frameworks, and past behaviour. The metric is historical. Defaults on central bank swaps are virtually nonexistent. This record sustains the system.

Efficiency manifests as speed. Swap lines can be activated within days or hours, far faster than assembling ad hoc rescue packages. The behaviour is visible in announcement timelines and auction schedules. Speed matters when markets move faster than politics.

Risk is contained by structure. Exchange-rate risk is eliminated by fixing the reversal rate. Credit risk is mitigated by collateral at the domestic lending stage. The residual risk is political and reputational, not financial. This is why swap lines can expand rapidly in crises and contract quietly afterwards.

The quiet motif threading this analysis is the bridge loan. Swap lines do not change the destination. They keep traffic moving while repairs are made. When the road reopens, the bridge is dismantled.

This clarity matters for reading headlines. When news breaks of an expanding swap network, the question is not whether a new currency order has arrived. It is whether an additional safety net has been deployed to preserve existing flows. Sometimes that preservation supports gradual diversification. Often it reinforces the centre by making it more resilient.

The forward test remains unresolved. As financial ties grow more regional and currencies more contested, will swap lines evolve to support a broader set of settlement assets—or will they continue to function primarily as conduits for the incumbent currency in moments of stress? The answer will determine whether these quiet contracts remain stabilisers of the old order or scaffolding for something more plural.

Why central banks use swap lines

On 30 October 2008, at the peak of the global financial crisis, the Federal Reserve and the Bank of Korea announced a $30 billion currency swap line. The place was Seoul; the problem was a sudden drought of US dollars in Korean funding markets. Korean banks had dollar obligations—trade finance, short-term borrowing, hedges—yet private markets would not roll funding. Within days, the Bank of Korea began auctioning dollars to domestic banks. The won stabilised. Funding spreads eased. Exports kept moving. The outcome was not triumph. It was containment.

Swap lines buy time.

Central banks sign swap lines because modern crises move faster than reserves and politics. A liquidity shortage in a foreign currency can turn a functioning banking system into a frozen one within hours. Swap lines create a bridge across that gap. They allow central banks to substitute institutional credit for market panic, lending foreign currency to domestic banks against local collateral. This is the core motive: to prevent liquidity stress becoming systemic failure. Yet the reasons do not end there. Swap lines also facilitate trade, signal partnership, and—more quietly—reshape the incentives that drive de-dollarisation strategies.

The first motive is crisis backstopping, and it is best understood as a problem of mismatch. Many countries run banking systems that intermediate cross-border trade and investment in dollars, euros, or other foreign currencies. Those banks can be solvent in domestic terms and still fail if they cannot obtain foreign currency on schedule. The behaviour is visible in funding markets. When stress hits, cross-currency basis swaps move sharply, indicating that borrowers must pay a premium to secure dollars. The BIS documented this scramble during March 2020, noting that strains in offshore dollar funding markets coincided with a surge in demand for central bank swap facilities (BIS, Quarterly Review, June 2020). Swap lines matter because they change the price of survival.

Show the mechanics and the logic follows. In a crisis, domestic banks hoard liquidity. They delay payments. They reduce trade finance. They sell assets. Each defensive move reduces confidence and worsens the shortage. A central bank with access to foreign currency liquidity can break this spiral. It auctions dollars. It sets a price. It demands collateral. Banks that need dollars bid. Banks that do not can step aside. The central bank converts a chaotic scramble into an orderly queue. The implication is stabilisation with minimal drama.

The Korean case is instructive precisely because it was not unique. During the 2008 crisis, the Federal Reserve extended swap lines to multiple central banks. On 13 October 2008, it announced expanded arrangements with the ECB, Bank of England, Bank of Japan, and Swiss National Bank, among others, reflecting a recognition that dollar funding was a global public good in crisis conditions (Federal Reserve press releases, 2008). The outcome can be measured in funding markets: dollar borrowing costs for non-US banks eased as access improved. Swap lines did not repair bank balance sheets. They repaired time.

The second motive is trade facilitation. This may sound lofty, but it is mundane. Trade invoices must be paid. Ships must be insured. Letters of credit must be honoured. Much of this machinery still runs in dollars, even when neither party is American. When dollar liquidity tightens, trade finance becomes expensive or unavailable, and commerce slows. Central banks that care about real economic continuity—employment, prices, industrial supply chains—have a direct interest in preventing the financial channel from choking the trade channel.

Trade facilitation becomes visible in small decisions. A bank continues confirming letters of credit because it can obtain dollars from the central bank. A commodity importer continues purchasing because it can hedge and fund the deal. A manufacturer continues production because parts arrive. These are not abstractions. They are operations.

Swap lines also help central banks manage reserves more intelligently. Without access to emergency foreign currency liquidity, reserve managers face pressure to hold larger stocks of liquid foreign assets at all times. Those assets carry opportunity costs and political vulnerability. With a swap line, a central bank can treat part of its insurance as contingent rather than fully pre-funded. The metric is reserve adequacy. In IMF frameworks, access to contingent liquidity can reduce the need for precautionary reserves, though it does not replace them entirely (IMF, 2015). The implication is flexibility. Some risk shifts from balance-sheet stock to institutional relationship.

The third motive is signalling. Swap lines are not offered universally. Their existence indicates that two central banks trust one another's governance, legal systems, and capacity to manage liquidity responsibly. This trust is not sentiment. It is contractual. It rests on repayment expectation, collateral practices, and political confidence that the arrangement will not be abused.

Markets read this signal quickly. A swap line announcement can calm funding markets even before a single auction takes place. The behaviour can be observed in price movements: cross-currency basis spreads often narrow after credible swap announcements, reflecting reduced tail risk. During March 2020, the Federal Reserve's expansion of swap lines and the introduction of the FIMA Repo Facility on 31 March provided additional channels for foreign authorities to obtain dollars, contributing to easing of funding strains documented in BIS analysis (BIS, 2020; Federal Reserve, 2020). The implication is psychological, but grounded in mechanics. Knowing that dollars can be obtained reduces the incentive to hoard them.

Signalling works both ways. Exclusion speaks, too. Countries without swap access are forced to self-insure through reserves, accept higher volatility, or impose controls. This differentiation shapes behaviour across the system. It creates tiers of resilience.

A case-style narrative illustrates how these motives converge in an emerging-market context. Imagine a mid-sized exporter whose banks fund commodity trade in dollars. A sudden external shock—say, a sharp tightening cycle in the United States—causes offshore dollar lenders to retreat. Domestic banks face a rollover cliff. Exporters cannot obtain trade finance. Importers cannot pay for fuel. The currency weakens sharply, adding inflation pressure. The central bank responds by selling dollars from reserves, but reserves are finite and markets sense it. A swap line, if available, changes the trajectory. The central bank draws dollars, lends them against local collateral, and commits to orderly auctions. Banks roll obligations. Trade finance continues. Reserves are conserved. The currency stabilises. The crisis does not vanish. It becomes manageable.

This is why swap lines are often mistaken for a form of subsidy. They are not gifts, but they are privileges. They grant access to liquidity when it is most valuable. That access reduces the cost of crisis management for the recipient and reduces contagion risk for the provider. The relationship is reciprocal in logic even when it is asymmetric in power.

A credible limitation complicates the picture. Swap lines can create moral hazard and political dependency. If domestic banks believe foreign currency liquidity will always be available via the central bank, they may take on more foreign currency exposure. If governments believe swap access is guaranteed, they may delay reforms. The concern is real. It is discussed in academic literature on international lender-of-last-resort facilities and in central bank internal debates. The reconciliation lies in design. Swap lines are typically priced above normal market rates, limited in size, and framed as temporary. These features aim to reduce dependency and ensure that facilities are used as bridges, not permanent funding sources.

Another limitation is operational and political discretion. Swap lines can be withdrawn. They can remain unused due to stigma. A central bank may hesitate to draw on a line if it signals weakness. Or the provider may restrict use for political reasons. The implication is that swap lines are not a neutral, always-on market instrument. They are a policy relationship.

This is where swap lines intersect with de-dollarisation strategies. Paradoxically, the same tool that stabilises dollar funding can encourage efforts to reduce reliance on dollars. Each crisis reveals dependence. Each rescue makes the dependence visible. Policymakers conclude that even if swap lines work, they would prefer not to need them. Swap lines become both relief and reminder.

Moreover, not all swap lines are dollar swap lines. Some are denominated in other currencies and are designed explicitly to support bilateral trade in those units. China's People's Bank of China has signed numerous bilateral swap agreements since 2008, aimed in part at facilitating trade settlement in renminbi. These agreements vary in usage and effectiveness, but their intent is clear in official statements and in the architecture of RMB clearing centres. The behaviour is mixed. Some lines are drawn; many are not. The implication is that swap lines can be scaffolding for alternative corridors, but only where trade invoicing, liquidity, and settlement infrastructure align.

The quiet motif threading all of this is the firebreak. Swap lines do not stop fires from starting. They stop them from spreading. They partition the system into segments that can be stabilised with targeted liquidity rather than blunt controls.

For time-conscious professionals, the diagnostic is practical. When a swap line is announced, ask what it is meant to prevent. Is it designed to calm offshore funding markets? To keep trade finance moving? To signal strategic alignment? Or to support settlement in a non-dollar currency? Then ask what it can actually do: how large it is, how fast it can be activated, and whether local banks can use it without stigma.

The unresolved tension remains. As the world builds new corridors and seeks to reduce exposure to dollar cycles, will swap lines evolve into a broader, more multilateral safety net that supports diverse settlement assets—or will they remain selective bridges that stabilise the existing centre and, by doing so, keep the old anchor firmly in place? The next crisis will answer, not with rhetoric, but with who gets access when the market closes.

Swap lines as de-dollarisation tools

In March 2009, the People's Bank of China signed a bilateral currency swap agreement with the Banco Central do Brasil. The place was Beijing; the timing followed the worst phase of the global financial crisis. The stated aim was explicit: to facilitate trade and investment settlement in renminbi and reais, reducing reliance on the US dollar. Over the following years, similar agreements proliferated across Asia, Latin America, and parts of Africa. Headlines followed. A new monetary order, some declared, was taking shape.

The outcome was quieter.

Trade between China and its partners continued to grow, yet the overwhelming share of global trade finance and crisis liquidity still moved through dollars. The swap lines existed. Most remained undrawn. The paradox was plain. Swap lines were multiplying at the very moment when the dollar's central role appeared least threatened.

That tension defines the problem. Swap lines are often presented as instruments of de-dollarisation, yet most do not displace the dollar at all. Some reinforce it. Understanding when swap lines reduce dollar reliance—and when they merely re-route it—requires a precise look at currency denomination, usage patterns, and balance-sheet behaviour. Labels mislead. Mechanics decide.

Start with the visible claim. A bilateral swap line in an alternative currency appears, on paper, to offer a substitute for dollar liquidity. Two central banks exchange local currencies, enabling banks to settle trade without touching the dollar. The name suggests autonomy. The explanation lies in use. For a swap line to reduce dollar dependence, three conditions must align: trade must be invoiced in the alternative currency, domestic banks must be willing to hold and deploy that currency, and there must be credible avenues to recycle balances into assets or payments. Absent these, the line remains symbolic.

The contrast between a yuan–local currency swap and a dollar–local currency swap makes this clear. A dollar swap line, even when extended by a non-US partner, delivers dollars. It stabilises dollar funding and preserves dollar-based trade and finance. The implication is reinforcement. The dollar remains the settlement asset of last resort, now supported by a broader institutional network.

A yuan–local currency swap, by contrast, delivers renminbi. Its potential to displace the dollar depends on behaviour downstream. Do exporters accept renminbi invoices? Do importers hold renminbi balances rather than converting immediately? Do banks have access to renminbi funding markets and hedging tools? Do central banks treat renminbi balances as usable liquidity rather than trapped claims? Each question points to a friction.

Consider the mechanics of a typical yuan swap line. A central bank draws renminbi from the PBoC and provides it to domestic banks. Those banks can extend trade credit to importers sourcing goods from China. The show is straightforward. The name is currency substitution. The explanation reveals limits. If importers immediately convert renminbi into dollars to pay suppliers, the swap line has failed as a de-dollarisation tool. It has merely inserted an extra step.

Usage data underscores this constraint. The BIS has repeatedly noted that while China's bilateral swap network is extensive, actual drawings have been sporadic and concentrated during periods of stress rather than as a routine settlement channel (BIS Annual Economic Report, various years). The behaviour suggests that many swap lines function as contingent insurance rather than active conduits for trade settlement. The implication is that availability does not equal adoption.

A named comparison sharpens the point. During the pandemic in 2020, the Federal Reserve's dollar swap lines were drawn heavily by major central banks, with outstanding usage peaking above $440 billion in May 2020 (Federal Reserve statistical releases, 2020). At the same time, usage of non-dollar swap lines remained modest. The difference was not political will. It was liquidity depth. Dollar markets absorbed flows at scale. Alternative currency markets did not.

This does not render alternative-currency swap lines irrelevant. Their role is different. They can support bilateral trade where invoicing is already shifting, reduce transaction costs for specific corridors, and provide optionality. They can also serve as signalling devices, indicating a willingness to cooperate outside dollar-centric frameworks. The behaviour they encourage is gradual. Firms test settlement in local currencies for limited flows. Banks build small desks. Central banks observe.

The limitation is scale. Swap lines do not create deep markets. They borrow credibility from them. Without liquid money markets, derivatives, and safe assets in the alternative currency, swap usage stalls. This is not ideology. It is balance-sheet arithmetic. Banks prefer currencies they can fund, hedge, and recycle efficiently.

A credible counter-example tempers excessive scepticism. In parts of East Asia, regional currency arrangements have supported modest but real shifts in settlement practices, particularly for intra-regional trade with predictable flows. Where supply chains are integrated and policy coordination is strong, swap lines can reinforce local currency use. The reconciliation lies in scope. These successes are corridor-specific, not systemic.

Risk provides another lens. Dollar swap lines reduce risk by providing access to the world's deepest liquidity pool. Alternative-currency swap lines can increase risk if the currency received cannot be deployed easily. Central banks are acutely aware of this. They structure usage rules carefully, often limiting maturities and encouraging conversion back into dollars when needed. The implication is caution, not conversion.

Trust appears again, but differently. Trust in a dollar swap line rests on repayment certainty and market depth. Trust in an alternative-currency swap line rests on policy alignment and future development. The first is backward-looking. The second is forward-looking. This difference shapes behaviour. In crises, actors run towards what they trust now.

This distinction explains why many so-called de-dollarisation swap lines coexist with continued dollar dominance. They serve as scaffolding rather than replacement. They allow experimentation without forcing commitment. They reduce political exposure by offering optionality. They also provide leverage in negotiations, signalling that alternatives exist even if they are not yet preferred.

The motif threading this section is the detour. Some swap lines offer an exit ramp from the dollar motorway. Others simply widen the road.

A practical diagnostic follows. When assessing a swap line as a de-dollarisation tool, ask three questions. What currency is delivered? How is it used in practice? And where do balances go afterwards? If the answers point back to the dollar—through conversion, hedging, or asset placement—the swap line reinforces the incumbent. If they point elsewhere, even partially, a new corridor may be forming.

The unresolved tension remains. Swap lines can either entrench the dollar by extending its reach through trusted intermediaries or chip away at its role by nurturing parallel liquidity pools. Both outcomes are visible. Which prevails depends not on the number of agreements signed, but on whether firms, banks, and central banks commit to using the currency they receive rather than merely borrowing it until the dollar returns.

Design choices and hidden conditions

On 19 March 2020, as global markets convulsed, the Federal Reserve announced the expansion of its dollar swap lines with nine additional central banks, including the Reserve Bank of Australia and the Banco Central do Brasil. The place was Washington; the date mattered. Equity markets were collapsing, dollar funding costs were spiking, and demand for cash was overwhelming dealers. Within days, drawings surged across the standing network. Yet among the newly added recipients, usage diverged sharply. Some lines were drawn heavily. Others remained largely untouched.

The difference was not political intent. It was designed.

Swap lines are often discussed as binary instruments—either present or absent. In practice, their usefulness hinges on a dense set of parameters: caps, tenors, pricing, collateral frameworks, operational readiness, and informal expectations. These design choices determine whether a swap line calms markets or merely decorates a press release. In crises, details dominate outcomes.

Begin with the most visible parameter: size. Swap lines are capped. The cap may be explicit—a stated maximum amount—or implicit, shaped by market expectations and political context. A $30 billion line and a $300 billion line carry different signals. They also support different volumes of trade and funding. During the pandemic, the Federal Reserve's standing swap lines with the ECB and Bank of Japan were effectively uncapped in usage, constrained only by demand and collateral. By contrast, temporary lines with smaller economies were capped at fixed amounts. The metric is revealing. According to Federal Reserve data, peak usage across all dollar swap lines exceeded $440 billion in May 2020, with the bulk concentrated among major advanced-economy central banks (Federal Reserve, 2020). The implication is hierarchy embedded in size.

Caps shape behaviour before a line is drawn. If market participants believe the available amount is insufficient to meet aggregate needs, they will continue to hoard liquidity. The swap line fails as a confidence device. This is not theoretical. In several emerging-market crises, central banks discovered that swap limits covered only a fraction of banking system dollar liabilities. The behaviour followed predictably. Banks drew cautiously or not at all, conserving access in case conditions worsened. The safety net remained folded.

Tenor is the second lever. Most swap lines offer short maturities—often seven days or, in some cases, 84 days. Short tenors reinforce the idea that swap lines address temporary liquidity shortages, not structural funding gaps. They also reduce risk for the providing central bank. The explanation is balance-sheet discipline. Short maturities ensure frequent rollover decisions and constant price signals.

Yet tenor length affects usability. Banks funding trade or rolling term liabilities may hesitate to rely on facilities that mature quickly. They must consider rollover risk. In March 2020, the extension of swap line tenors to 84 days was explicitly framed as a measure to support longer-term funding needs (Federal Reserve press release, 15 March 2020). The implication was practical. Longer tenors increased uptake by matching the duration of stress.

Pricing matters next. Swap lines are not free. The cost typically equals an overnight index swap rate plus a margin. During the global financial crisis, that margin was initially set at 100 basis points and later reduced. In November 2011, major central banks agreed to lower the pricing of dollar swap lines by 50 basis points to ease pressure on banks (Federal Reserve and ECB statements, 2011). The metric is demand elasticity. Lower pricing increased usage. Higher pricing discouraged opportunistic borrowing.

Pricing also communicates intent. A punitive rate signals emergency-only use. A moderate rate invites participation. The balance is delicate. Price too low, and moral hazard concerns rise. Price too high, and the facility sits idle. Central banks calibrate this margin carefully, adjusting it as stress ebbs and flows. The implication is that swap lines are managed instruments, not static promises.

Collateral requirements sit one layer deeper. While the swap transaction itself is collateralised by the currency exchange, the domestic central bank typically requires collateral from commercial banks borrowing the foreign currency. The type of collateral accepted—government bonds, high-quality loans, other assets—determines which banks can access the facility. In jurisdictions where banks hold limited eligible collateral, swap lines may exist but remain inaccessible. The behaviour is exclusion by balance sheet.

Operational readiness is another hidden condition. A swap line that cannot be activated quickly loses much of its value. Legal documentation, settlement systems, auction frameworks, and communication protocols must be in place before stress hits. During the pandemic, central banks with standing arrangements activated facilities within days. Others required weeks to finalise procedures. Markets did not wait. The implication is speed as substance.

Then there are informal expectations. These are rarely written but widely understood. Swap lines presume responsible macroeconomic management, regulatory cooperation, and political alignment. A central bank may hesitate to draw heavily if it fears reputational damage or political scrutiny. Stigma is real. Even when facilities are available, usage can lag because drawing signals vulnerability. This was evident during the euro area crisis, when some banks avoided central bank facilities despite favourable terms, preferring market funding until it vanished.

A scenario brings these design elements together. Imagine a mid-sized emerging economy facing a sudden dollar funding shock. Its central bank has a $10 billion dollar swap line with a major partner. Banking system short-term dollar liabilities amount to $40 billion. The line covers a quarter of needs at most. Tenors are seven days. Pricing is punitive. Collateral eligibility is narrow. The central bank announces the facility. Markets calculate the gap. Banks draw cautiously, if at all. Funding stress persists. The line exists. Confidence does not.

Contrast this with a central bank whose swap line covers a substantial share of liabilities, offers longer tenors, and is priced to encourage use. The announcement changes expectations immediately. Banks plan. Hoarding eases. The same instrument, designed differently, produces a different outcome.

A credible counter-example tempers any assumption that bigger is always better. Overly generous swap lines can entrench risky funding structures and delay necessary adjustments. If banks rely persistently on central bank foreign currency liquidity, incentives to develop local currency funding or reduce mismatches weaken. The reconciliation lies in conditional generosity. Effective swap lines are large enough to matter, short enough to discipline, and priced to discourage routine dependence.

The quiet motif threading this section is the emergency exit. An exit that is too narrow causes panic. One that is clearly marked and wide enough prevents it. But exits are meant for emergencies, not daily traffic.

Design choices also intersect with geopolitics. The inclusion or exclusion of certain countries, the size of their lines, and the permanence of arrangements signal status. Standing swap lines imply trust and long-term partnership. Temporary lines suggest caution. Markets read these signals. So do policymakers. Swap architecture becomes a map of financial alliances.

For readers tracking de-dollarisation narratives, the lesson is sobering. Not all swap lines are created equal. Counting agreements says little about real capacity. The meaningful questions concern size relative to needs, tenor relative to stress, pricing relative to stigma, and collateral relative to banking system balance sheets.

The unresolved test remains. As more countries seek insurance outside the dollar system, will swap lines evolve with designs that genuinely support alternative currencies at scale, or will hidden constraints keep them as selective backstops that stabilise the incumbent order? The answer will emerge not in communiqués, but in the next moment when markets seize and central banks reach for the tools they can actually use.

Who gains and who is sidelined

On 31 October 2008, as global funding markets seized, the Federal Reserve announced a coordinated expansion of dollar swap lines with a select group of central banks. The institutions named were familiar: the European Central Bank, the Bank of England, the Bank of Japan, the Swiss National Bank, and the Bank of Canada. The place was Washington; the date marked escalation. Markets exhaled. Dollar liquidity would reach the world's core financial systems.

Many others waited.

The absence was as instructive as the presence. Large emerging economies, commodity exporters, and strategically important states found themselves outside the inner circle. Some would later receive temporary access. Others would not. The pattern was unmistakable. Swap lines were not distributed by population size, trade volume, or even immediate need. They were extended through relationships—financial, institutional, and political—that reflected a deeper hierarchy in the global monetary system.

Swap networks reveal who belongs.

The first and most obvious gain accrues to central banks with standing access to major swap networks, particularly dollar swap lines. These institutions acquire a form of contingent reserve that does not appear on balance sheets but matters in crises. Their banking systems can fund in foreign currency with confidence that central bank support will arrive if markets close. The behaviour is visible in stress episodes. Banks in swap-line countries tend to maintain cross-border exposures longer and unwind them more slowly. The implication is resilience by association.

This resilience feeds back into market perception. Investors price lower tail risk into assets issued by countries with swap access. Funding costs fall relative to peers. During periods of global stress, currencies of swap-line recipients often depreciate less sharply than those of excluded states, controlling for fundamentals. The mechanism is not mystery. Markets believe liquidity will be available. Belief alters behaviour.

Advanced economies dominate this privileged tier, but not exclusively. Some emerging markets with strong institutional frameworks, close trade ties, or strategic importance have secured access, at least temporarily. South Korea's repeated inclusion in Federal Reserve swap arrangements—2008, 2020—reflects its integration into global trade finance and the credibility of its central bank. The metric is recurrence. Temporary access becomes habitual. Habit signals trust.

Who, then, is sidelined? Countries with shallow financial systems, volatile macroeconomic histories, or strained diplomatic relationships tend to sit outside swap networks. For them, crises are managed with reserves, capital controls, or emergency multilateral support. Each option carries costs. Reserves are finite. Controls disrupt commerce. Multilateral programmes take time. The absence of swap access amplifies vulnerability.

This exclusion is not accidental. Swap lines expose the providing central bank to reputational and political risk. They are extended where repayment is assumed and where cooperation is expected to endure. The explanation lies in incentives. A central bank will not lend its currency to a partner whose policy choices might jeopardise repayment or trigger political backlash. The implication is selectivity as risk management.

A regional example illustrates how hierarchy operates at a smaller scale. China's bilateral swap network, built rapidly after 2008, offers renminbi liquidity to numerous partners across Asia, Africa, and Latin America. Yet access is uneven. Neighbouring countries with strong trade ties and political alignment are favoured. Rivals and states with contested relationships are often excluded or offered smaller, less flexible arrangements. The pattern mirrors geopolitical contours. Swap architecture becomes an extension of regional influence.

The behaviour is instructive. Where swap lines exist, trade settlement in renminbi is encouraged. Clearing banks are designated. Pilot projects are launched. Where they do not, trade continues largely in dollars despite political rhetoric. The implication is practical. Financial cooperation follows trust, not aspiration.

Membership in swap networks also creates internal divisions. Banks operating in swap-line jurisdictions gain funding advantages over peers elsewhere. Multinational firms headquartered in included countries face lower liquidity risk than competitors based outside the network. Over time, this shapes corporate geography. Treasury centres cluster where contingent liquidity is available. The quiet outcome is concentration.

A credible counter-example tempers claims of a rigid club. During the pandemic, the Federal Reserve extended temporary swap lines to a broader group of central banks than ever before, including some without previous access. This expansion recognised extraordinary circumstances. The reconciliation lies in temporality. Temporary inclusion does not equal permanent membership. When conditions normalised, most lines expired. The hierarchy reasserted itself.

Trust, often invoked abstractly, appears here as institutional memory. Central banks remember how partners behaved in past crises: whether they honoured commitments, communicated transparently, and avoided politicising financial support. These memories shape future access. Trust accumulates slowly and dissipates quickly.

Risk, by contrast, is asymmetric. For the providing central bank, the risk of extending a swap line is reputational and political more than financial. For the recipient, the risk of exclusion is existential during crises. This asymmetry reinforces hierarchy. Those at the centre can choose. Those at the periphery must adapt.

The motif threading this section is the invitation list. Crises reveal who is invited into the room where liquidity is discussed and who waits outside with reserves and hope.

Swap architectures also constrain de-dollarisation strategies. Countries excluded from dollar swap networks have stronger incentives to build alternative corridors—regional arrangements, local currency trade, reserve diversification. Inclusion dampens urgency. Exclusion sharpens it. The irony is sharp. The very mechanisms that stabilise the dollar system for some push others to seek escape routes.

The forward test remains unsettled. As geopolitical fragmentation deepens and new financial corridors emerge, will swap networks broaden into more multilateral safety nets, or will they harden into explicit blocs reflecting political alignment as much as economic logic? When the next crisis hits, the list of invitees will answer the question with more clarity than any communiqué.

Chapter 4

FX Clearing, Netting, and Regional Hubs

At 8:00 a.m. in London, a trader agrees to exchange euros for yen with a counterparty in Singapore. Neither will ever meet. Neither particularly trusts the other. By lunchtime, the trade has been novated to a clearing house, margined, netted against dozens of other positions, and reduced to a fraction of its original size. By the end of the day, the risk no longer sits where the deal began. It sits where the plumbing leads.

Most debates about currency power fixate on symbols: which unit is quoted, which flag appears on a banknote, which central bank announces the loudest initiative. Yet the gravitational pull of a currency is often determined far from speeches and summits, inside the dull, rule-bound machinery that decides where trades are cleared, which obligations are netted, and which assets are accepted as collateral when things go wrong. Clearing is not glamorous. It is decisive.

The paradox is easy to miss. Clearing systems are designed to reduce risk. They centralise settlement, impose discipline, and prevent bilateral disputes from metastasising into systemic crises. At the same time, they concentrate power. Whoever hosts the clearing house, writes its rules, and defines its collateral quietly shapes where liquidity lives and which currencies are easy—or costly—to use. The result is not a single battlefield, but a series of pressure points where technical choices acquire strategic weight.

This chapter enters that machinery.

To understand why FX clearing matters, one must first abandon the idea that currencies compete only through trade invoicing or reserve holdings. They also compete through infrastructure. A currency that can be cleared efficiently, netted multilaterally, and funded cheaply through recognised hubs gains an everyday advantage. Dealers prefer it. Banks allocate balance sheet to it. Corporates inherit those preferences whether they intend to or not. Over time, convenience hardens into habit.

Clearing houses sit at the centre of this process. By interposing themselves between buyers and sellers, they replace a web of bilateral exposures with a single relationship governed by margin, default funds, and shared rules. The risk profile of the system changes. Gross exposures shrink. Liquidity needs fall. Balance sheets breathe. Yet dependency grows. Participants become reliant on the hub—not merely for settlement, but for access to the market itself.

This trade-off has become sharper as regulators have pushed more activity into central clearing since the global financial crisis. What began as a response to opaque derivatives markets has evolved into a reorganisation of financial geography. Clearing is no longer just about safety. It is about where risk is warehoused and under whose jurisdiction.

For currencies aspiring to carve out space beyond the dollar, this matters enormously. A currency that lacks a credible clearing venue struggles to scale. A currency that is cleared offshore under someone else's rules inherits someone else's priorities. Conversely, a currency anchored to a regional clearing hub can capture routine flows even if it never displaces the dollar at the system's core. The ambition is not supremacy. It is capture of the mundane.

Netting is the quiet enabler. By allowing obligations to be offset multilaterally, clearing systems dramatically reduce the amount of cash and collateral banks must post. A thousand trades can collapse into a handful of net positions. This frees balance-sheet capacity, lowers funding costs, and makes high-volume trading viable. The arithmetic is simple. The consequences are not.

Netting rewards centralisation. The more participants and the more volume routed through a hub, the greater the efficiency gains. This creates a natural monopoly tendency. Once a clearing house dominates a currency pair, it becomes costly to replicate elsewhere. Liquidity clusters. Switching becomes risky. The corridor hardens.

Regional clearing hubs are attempts to exploit this dynamic without surrendering control. By hosting clearing locally—often with central bank support—regions seek to retain liquidity, develop local markets, and reduce dependence on external centres. An Asian currency cleared primarily in Asia. A regional bloc settling intraregional trade without routing through London or New York. The logic is straightforward. Keep the plumbing close to home.

Yet fragmentation introduces new risks. Multiple hubs clearing similar products under different rules can generate fault lines. Collateral posted in one jurisdiction may not be recognised in another. Participants active in several hubs face complex margin calls and liquidity strains during stress. A shock in one centre can propagate through shared members to others. Redundancy becomes entanglement.

This is where policy design re-enters the story. Margin models, default waterfalls, access criteria, and collateral eligibility are not neutral. They tilt the playing field. A clearing house that accepts local government bonds as collateral favours domestic banks. One that requires only top-rated international securities favours global dealers. Each choice shapes participation and, by extension, currency use.

The decisions are often framed as technical. They are not. They reflect judgments about trust, risk tolerance, and strategic intent. Regulators know this. So do market participants. Clearing rules become signals, read as carefully as swap lines or reserve allocations.

The deeper question this chapter explores is whether the multiplication of clearing hubs leads to resilience or fragility. Does distributing settlement across regions reduce systemic risk, or does it create a brittle web of interdependence? Can regional hubs coexist without recreating the very concentration they seek to escape? And who bears the cost when efficiency and sovereignty pull in opposite directions?

There is a historical echo here. Financial centres have always risen where clearing and settlement concentrated: Amsterdam in the seventeenth century, London in the nineteenth, New York in the twentieth. Each ascent was underpinned by mundane superiority in settlement practices long before it was recognised as monetary leadership. Today's contest is no different, even if the instruments have changed.

What follows is not a technical manual, but a guided tour of the forces that make clearing a battleground. We will look inside the clearing house and follow a non-dollar currency trade as it is margined, netted, and settled. We will see how balance sheets shrink and dependencies grow. We will trace the incentives driving the construction of regional hubs and the vulnerabilities they introduce. And we will examine how policy choices—often invisible to the public—quietly decide which corridors thrive.

By the end of this chapter, the reader should see currency competition differently. Not as a dramatic overthrow, but as a series of infrastructural nudges. Liquidity does not migrate because it is told to. It moves because the pipes make one direction easier than another.

The corridors ahead are built not only with treaties and technology, but with margin calls, default funds, and netting sets. This is where currencies earn their keep—or lose it.

How FX clearing houses work

On 18 June 2014, the London-based clearing house LCH began clearing offshore renminbi foreign-exchange forwards from its SwapClear service. The place was London; the date mattered. It marked the first time a major global clearing house offered central clearing for a non-deliverable currency pair tied to China's capital account. Within months, international banks were routing CNH trades through a British legal entity rather than settling bilaterally across continents. Liquidity did not move because policy declared it so. It moved because the pipes changed.

Clearing decides where risk lives.

At its core, an FX clearing house is a risk concentrator. It inserts itself between buyers and sellers, becoming the buyer to every seller and the seller to every buyer. This process—known as novation—turns a web of bilateral promises into a single, governed relationship with the clearing house. The show is procedural. Trades are accepted, replaced, margined, and monitored. The name is central counterparty clearing. The explanation is control. By centralising exposure, the clearing house can measure, net, and manage risk at system scale. The implication is power over liquidity.

Consider a simple non-dollar trade. Two banks agree to exchange Korean won and Japanese yen for settlement in three months. In a bilateral world, each bank carries the full counterparty risk of the other until settlement. They monitor credit limits, post bilateral collateral, and plan liquidity for gross payments. When a clearing house stands between them, that risk shifts. Each bank faces the clearing house instead. Counterparty risk becomes mutualised and governed by rules rather than discretion.

Margining is the first discipline imposed. Upon acceptance of the trade, both banks must post initial margin—cash or eligible securities—to cover potential losses if prices move sharply before the position can be closed. The amount is calculated using models that estimate worst-case moves over a defined horizon. The behaviour is visible. When volatility rises, margin calls increase. The metric is margin requirement per notional exposure. During periods of stress, margin can double or triple within days, as documented in BIS analyses of cleared derivatives markets (BIS, Annual Economic Report, 2019). The implication is resilience purchased with liquidity.

Variation margin follows daily, sometimes intraday. Profits and losses are settled in cash as exchange rates move. This daily discipline prevents losses from accumulating unseen. It also forces participants to fund movements continuously. A bank that cannot meet a margin call is in breach immediately. The clearing house acts. Risk is confronted early.

Default funds sit behind margin as a collective insurance pool. Clearing members contribute to a shared fund designed to absorb losses beyond a defaulting member's margin. The structure is deliberate. Losses are first absorbed by the defaulter's margin, then by its contribution to the default fund, and only then—if losses exceed those layers—by the clearing house's own capital and the mutualised fund. This "waterfall" is not metaphorical. It is codified in rulebooks hundreds of pages long. The implication is alignment. Members police each other because they share the tail risk.

Risk management extends beyond collateral. Clearing houses impose position limits, monitor concentration, and stress-test portfolios against extreme but plausible scenarios. These scenarios are not abstract. They include historical episodes—sharp currency devaluations, sudden capital controls, market closures. Stress results are published to regulators and, increasingly, to members. Transparency disciplines behaviour. A bank that accumulates excessive exposure attracts scrutiny and higher margin.

Efficiency emerges through netting. When a bank clears multiple FX trades in the same currency pair, obligations are offset. Ten trades to buy yen and nine to sell yen collapse into one net position. Gross settlement amounts shrink. Liquidity needs fall. Balance-sheet usage declines. The behaviour is measurable. Multilateral netting can reduce gross exposures by over 90 per cent in active markets, according to BIS estimates for centrally cleared derivatives (BIS, 2014). The implication is scale. Clearing makes high-volume trading feasible.

Yet netting also binds participants to the hub. The more positions are netted centrally, the more costly it becomes to exit. A bank cannot easily move trades elsewhere without recreating gross exposures and margin needs. Clearing location matters. Where the hub sits determines which legal system governs defaults, which central bank provides emergency liquidity, and which assets qualify as collateral. These are not footnotes. They decide comfort.

A second named example illustrates this gravity. Eurex Clearing, based in Frankfurt, has promoted euro-denominated FX clearing as part of Europe's effort to reduce reliance on offshore infrastructure after Brexit. Trades cleared through Eurex are subject to European law, euro collateral frameworks, and oversight by the European Central Bank. Banks choosing Eurex are not merely selecting a service provider. They are choosing a jurisdictional anchor. Liquidity follows jurisdiction.

A credible counter-example complicates any suggestion that clearing is always stabilising. Centralisation concentrates risk. If a clearing house fails, the consequences are severe. This concern is not theoretical. Regulators debate recovery and resolution plans for clearing houses precisely because they have become systemically important. The reconciliation lies in safeguards. High margin standards, conservative stress tests, and access to central bank liquidity aim to ensure that clearing houses fail rarely and in an orderly fashion. Whether these measures suffice remains an open question.

Trust appears here as governance confidence. Market participants trust clearing houses because they are regulated, transparent, and capitalised. That trust is reinforced by history. No major FX clearing house has defaulted on its obligations. The behaviour this trust enables is volume. Participants route trades where they believe the rules will hold under stress.

Risk becomes measurable rather than relational. Instead of judging counterparties one by one, banks assess margin models, default funds, and rulebooks. The metric shifts from credit opinion to collateral sufficiency. This shift favours currencies and markets where clearing frameworks are mature.

The quiet motif threading this section is the warehouse. Clearing houses warehouse risk so that markets can trade. Where the warehouse stands determines where goods—liquidity—accumulate.

For currencies beyond the dollar, clearing is both opportunity and constraint. A non-dollar currency with a credible clearing venue can attract routine flows even if it lacks reserve status. Traders care about margin efficiency and legal certainty. If those are offered, they will use the currency. Conversely, a currency without clearing support struggles to scale beyond bilateral niches.

The forward test is unresolved. As more currencies seek to build clearing infrastructure, will liquidity fragment across hubs, or will it cluster around a few trusted warehouses? And when stress arrives, will participants discover that efficiency has quietly traded optionality for dependence? The answers will emerge not in speeches, but in margin calls issued at dawn and honoured—or not—by dusk.

Netting arrangements and balance-sheet relief

In September 2009, at a meeting in Basel, the Basel Committee on Banking Supervision endorsed a decisive shift: banks would be encouraged, and in some cases required, to route more derivatives and foreign-exchange activity through central counterparties. The place was Switzerland; the timing followed the shock of Lehman Brothers' collapse. The outcome was not merely safer markets. It was a profound compression of balance sheets. Gross exposures that once sprawled across thousands of bilateral contracts began to collapse into manageable nets.

Netting changed the arithmetic.

At its simplest, netting allows obligations to offset one another. A bank that must pay €100 million to one counterparty and receive €95 million from another does not need to mobilise €195 million. It needs €5 million. The show is mechanical. The name is net settlement. The explanation is efficiency. The implication is liberation of balance-sheet capacity.

In foreign exchange markets, where volumes are vast and margins thin, this arithmetic matters more than rhetoric. Banks intermediate trades for clients, hedge positions, and warehouse risk. Each trade adds to gross exposure, consumes capital, and requires funding. Without netting, the scale becomes prohibitive. With netting, it becomes routine.

A simple numerical example makes the effect tangible. Imagine a bank active in a regional currency pair—say, Malaysian ringgit against Japanese yen. Over a day, it executes ten trades to buy yen worth the equivalent of ¥10 billion and nine trades to sell yen worth ¥9.7 billion. Bilaterally, the bank must prepare to settle ¥19.7 billion in gross payments. Its treasury must fund that amount. Its risk systems must track ten counterparties. Its capital must reflect the exposure.

Under multilateral netting through a clearing house, those trades collapse into a single net obligation of ¥300 million. Gross settlement falls by more than 98 per cent. The bank's funding need shrinks accordingly. The behaviour is observable in liquidity metrics. Cash buffers decline. Intraday credit usage falls. Balance sheets lighten. The implication is capacity. Freed resources can be redeployed to new trades, lending, or market-making.

This relief is not cosmetic. Regulatory capital frameworks reward netting. Under Basel III, exposures to centrally cleared trades attract lower capital charges than equivalent bilateral exposures, reflecting reduced counterparty risk. The metric is risk-weighted assets. Banks that clear and net can support more activity with the same capital base. The decision to clear is therefore not ideological. It is economic.

Named examples illustrate how this shapes currency use. LCH's FX clearing service reports that multilateral netting can reduce settlement risk by up to 90 per cent for eligible FX products, a figure cited in its public disclosures and echoed by BIS studies of FX settlement (BIS, *Reducing the risk of wholesale payments*, 2018). Banks trading in currencies supported by such services gain immediate balance-sheet relief. Banks trading in unsupported currencies do not. Liquidity flows accordingly.

Efficiency, however, carries a price. Netting concentrates exposure at the clearing hub. The clearing house becomes the nexus through which obligations pass. Dependency grows quietly. A bank that clears the bulk of its FX book through one CCP cannot easily replicate the efficiency elsewhere. Moving trades back to bilateral settlement would inflate exposures overnight. The behaviour this induces is loyalty. Participants stick with the hub that delivers relief.

Trust appears again, this time as faith in the clearing house's risk management. Banks accept concentration because they trust margin models, default funds, and governance. The trust is reinforced by transparency. Clearing houses publish stress-test results and default resources. The metric is coverage ratio. As long as participants believe the hub can withstand shocks, netting feels safe.

A credible counter-example tempers complacency. During periods of extreme volatility, margin requirements rise sharply. The same netting that reduces gross exposure can amplify liquidity demands when prices move. In March 2020, cleared markets saw sudden spikes in margin calls as volatility surged. Banks had to mobilise cash quickly, sometimes selling assets to meet calls. The reconciliation is nuanced. Netting reduces long-term balance-sheet usage but can increase short-term liquidity stress. Relief and pressure coexist.

This duality explains why banks scrutinise which currencies are eligible for central clearing. A currency cleared through a well-capitalised hub offers predictable netting benefits. One cleared through a nascent or fragmented hub may introduce uncertainty. A currency not cleared at all leaves banks exposed to bilateral settlement risk and higher capital charges. The implication is selection. Banks prefer to intermediate flows in currencies where netting works smoothly.

Regional ambitions collide with this logic. Policymakers seeking to promote local currencies often focus on trade invoicing or political agreements. Banks focus on netting sets. If a regional currency can be cleared and netted alongside major pairs, it becomes attractive. If it cannot, enthusiasm fades. The behaviour is pragmatic.

A second named example reinforces this point. CLS, the global FX settlement utility based in New York, nets and settles payment obligations across a wide range of major currencies. Participation reduces settlement risk by matching payments simultaneously. Currencies not supported by CLS face higher settlement risk and operational costs. The BIS has documented that CLS reduces the daily value of FX settlement risk by trillions of dollars (BIS, 2019). Inclusion confers advantage. Exclusion imposes friction.

The motif threading this section is compression. Netting compresses exposure, capital, and attention. It makes vast markets manageable. It also compresses choice.

Risk management shifts from counterparty assessment to hub assessment. Instead of asking whether Bank A will pay Bank B, participants ask whether the clearing house can survive Bank A's failure. This is a different question, with different politics. Regulators focus on clearing house resilience. Central banks plan for their support. The system's centre of gravity moves.

For currencies seeking to build corridors outside the dollar, this is decisive. A currency that cannot be netted at scale will struggle to attract intermediaries, regardless of political intent. A currency that can be netted through a trusted hub gains a foothold even if it never becomes a reserve asset. Netting does not create demand. It enables it.

The unresolved test remains. As more currencies and regions build their own clearing and netting arrangements, will balance-sheet relief be replicated without recreating dangerous concentrations? Or will banks discover that efficiency gained in calm periods masks dependencies that resurface under stress? The next bout of volatility will reveal whether compression has bought resilience—or merely postponed reckoning.

Building regional clearing hubs

In October 2014, the People's Bank of China designated Singapore as an official offshore renminbi clearing centre. The place was deliberate. Singapore sat astride Asian trade routes, hosted global banks, and operated under a legal system trusted by international investors. Within a year, renminbi deposits in the city had grown materially, cross-border RMB trade settlement volumes rose, and regional banks began routing Asian trade flows through Singapore rather than London or New York. The shift was modest in global terms. It was decisive locally.

Clearing hubs change habits.

A regional clearing hub is not simply a payments facility. It is an ecosystem built to capture routine financial flows—trade settlement, FX conversion, hedging—within a defined geographic or economic bloc. Its ambition is not to dethrone a global centre overnight, but to intercept daily transactions before they ever reach it. Over time, those intercepted flows alter demand for currencies, collateral, and liquidity.

The incentives to build such hubs align neatly across actors. Host cities see jobs, fees, and prestige. Clearing activity anchors banks, law firms, technology providers, and regulators. The metric is tangible. Employment rises. Tax bases widen. Financial centres compete fiercely for these roles, aware that clearing infrastructure creates durable advantages that survive political cycles.

Central banks pursue a different prize. By anchoring clearing domestically or regionally, they gain visibility into flows and leverage over risk management. Clearing location determines which central bank stands behind the system in a crisis. It shapes which assets qualify as collateral and which legal frameworks govern defaults. The implication is sovereignty exercised through plumbing rather than proclamation.

Regional blocs add a third layer of motivation. Shared clearing infrastructure can reinforce economic integration, reduce reliance on external currencies, and lower transaction costs for intra-bloc trade. For regions that trade heavily with one another but settle predominantly in dollars, the inefficiency is obvious. Clearing hubs offer a way to internalise those flows without demanding wholesale currency conversion.

Show the mechanics and the logic sharpens. When trade between neighbouring countries is settled through a regional hub, banks hold balances in the regional currency. They hedge locally. They net exposures multilaterally. Dollar demand falls at the margin. Not because policy bans its use, but because it becomes unnecessary for specific transactions. The name for this is corridor capture. The explanation is convenience. The implication is gradual displacement.

The Asian renminbi hubs provide a concrete illustration. Beyond Singapore, centres in Hong Kong, London, and Frankfurt were designated as RMB clearing hubs in the mid-2010s, each serving different corridors. Hong Kong handled mainland-facing flows; Singapore focused on Southeast Asia. The behaviour followed trade patterns. According to SWIFT RMB Tracker data from 2015–2017, RMB's share of global payments rose unevenly, strongest in regions with active clearing hubs. The implication was not global dominance, but regional normalisation.

Banks respond quickly to such incentives. Clearing hubs reduce settlement risk, offer local-time liquidity, and simplify compliance. A bank financing trade between Thailand and China can clear and hedge in Asia rather than routing positions through a dollar hub overnight. The decision is operational. Costs fall. Balance sheets compress. The currency used becomes incidental.

Trust underpins adoption. Market participants trust hubs backed by credible central banks, robust legal systems, and transparent rulebooks. Singapore's appeal lay not in size, but in reliability. The same logic applies elsewhere. A hub without trusted governance attracts headlines, not flows.

Efficiency follows scale. As more participants route trades through a hub, netting benefits increase. Liquidity deepens. Bid–ask spreads tighten. These gains are self-reinforcing. The first movers incur costs. Later adopters enjoy economies. The clearing hub becomes sticky.

Yet building a hub is harder than announcing one. A credible counter-example tempers optimism. Several regional initiatives have struggled because trade volumes were insufficient, regulatory frameworks were inconsistent, or collateral rules discouraged participation. Clearing requires critical mass. Without it, netting benefits evaporate and costs dominate. The reconciliation is blunt. Infrastructure cannot conjure liquidity. It can only attract it where underlying flows exist.

Risk complicates ambition. Regional hubs fragment clearing across jurisdictions, creating overlapping memberships. A bank active in multiple hubs must post margin in several places, manage different rulebooks, and fund liquidity across time zones. In calm periods, this seems manageable.

In stress, it can strain resources. The implication is that regionalisation trades global efficiency for local control.

Policy choices tilt outcomes decisively. Margin models that recognise local assets as collateral encourage domestic participation. Access rules that admit regional banks broaden liquidity. Conversely, conservative designs that mimic global hubs without their scale can stifle growth. These are technical decisions with strategic consequences.

The motif threading this section is gravity. Liquidity flows towards the nearest mass. Regional hubs create local gravity wells. They do not overturn the planetary system. They alter trajectories.

For currencies seeking space beyond the dollar, regional clearing hubs offer a pragmatic path. They allow partial de-dollarisation without confrontation. Trade settles locally. Reserves adjust slowly. Firms adapt without fanfare. The shift is modular.

The unresolved test remains. As more regions build their own hubs, will these gravity wells coexist peacefully, or will they generate fault lines when stress arrives and liquidity is needed everywhere at once? The answer will depend on whether regional hubs remain complementary—intercepting routine flows—or attempt to substitute for global centres without the balance sheets to do so. The next shock will reveal whether proximity has brought resilience, or merely redistributed fragility.

Risks of fragmented clearing systems

On 23 June 2016, as the Brexit referendum result became clear in London, sterling fell sharply and volatility leapt across European markets. Within hours, regulators and clearing houses were forced to consider an uncomfortable operational question: what happens when large volumes of euro-denominated trades are cleared in a jurisdiction suddenly poised to diverge from the European Union's regulatory framework? The place was London; the date was definitive. The outcome was not immediate collapse, but an enduring policy campaign—particularly from European authorities—to reduce reliance on offshore clearing and to strengthen regional alternatives.

Fragmentation begins with politics.

That episode is useful because it reveals the double edge of decentralisation. Building multiple clearing hubs can reduce dependence on a single jurisdiction and provide redundancy. It can also create a patchwork of rules, collateral demands, and liquidity pools that becomes harder to manage precisely when stress is highest. The instinct to diversify is sensible. The assumption that diversification automatically increases safety is not.

Clearing systems are designed to reduce risk by centralising and mutualising it. Fragmentation reverses that logic partially. It spreads activity across hubs, each with its own legal regime, risk models, margin schedules, default waterfalls, and supervisory priorities. The show is administrative. The name is jurisdictional plurality. The explanation is sovereignty. The implication is complexity as a new risk factor.

Start with inconsistent rules. Two clearing houses may clear similar FX products yet calculate margin differently, set different haircuts on collateral, and apply different stress scenarios. A bank active in both must hold collateral to satisfy the stricter of the two—or maintain separate pools for each. The behaviour is visible in treasury operations: more collateral transformation, more cash buffers, more intraday transfers. The metric is encumbered assets as a share of total assets. As collateral demands multiply, encumbrance rises. Balance sheets tighten.

Inconsistent rules also create the possibility of regulatory arbitrage. If one hub offers lower margin requirements, laxer membership criteria, or broader collateral eligibility, participants may route trades there to reduce cost. This is not a moral failing. It is incentive-following. The implication is that risk migrates towards the least demanding ruleset, not necessarily the safest one. Regulators worry about this explicitly. The Financial Stability Board has repeatedly highlighted the need for consistent CCP resilience standards to prevent a race to the bottom (FSB, 2017).

Overlapping memberships are the second vulnerability. Large global banks and dealers often participate in multiple clearing houses simultaneously. In calm periods, this seems prudent: diversification of counterparties and access to multiple markets. In stress, it becomes a bridge for contagion. If a bank faces large margin calls at Hub A, it may sell assets or draw liquidity that affects its capacity to meet obligations at Hub B. Stress travels not through contracts alone, but through shared balance sheets.

This is where fragmentation can create a dangerous illusion. More hubs may mean more options, but it also means more simultaneous demands. Liquidity is not infinitely divisible. A bank cannot meet a margin call in two places with the same cash. It must choose, or scramble.

Complex collateral needs amplify the problem. Different hubs accept different assets as collateral. One may accept local government bonds; another may insist on cash or top-rated international securities. During stress, the value of certain collateral can fall, triggering higher haircuts or margin calls. Banks then must find replacement collateral, often at the worst time. The behaviour is observable in collateral swap markets and in sudden spikes in repo rates for specific assets. The implication is procyclicality: risk management rules can amplify market stress by demanding more collateral precisely when collateral is scarce.

A brief scenario makes this tangible. Imagine two regional FX clearing hubs: one in Singapore clearing an Asian currency pair, another in Frankfurt clearing a European pair. A global bank participates in both, using government bonds from each region as collateral. A sudden political shock causes a sell-off in Asian bonds, increasing haircuts at the Singapore hub. The bank must post additional collateral within hours. To raise cash, it sells European bonds, pushing down their prices. Haircuts rise in Frankfurt. Now the bank faces margin calls in both hubs simultaneously. The original shock was local. The liquidity strain becomes global through the shared participant.

This is not a fanciful chain. It reflects known dynamics of margin procyclicality and liquidity spirals. The BIS has documented how margin calls and collateral demands can amplify stress in centrally cleared markets, particularly when volatility spikes (BIS, Annual Economic Report, 2021). Fragmentation increases the number of nodes where such calls can originate, and therefore the number of pathways through which stress can propagate.

A credible counter-example must be acknowledged. Concentration carries its own dangers. A single dominant clearing hub can become a "too big to fail" node, creating systemic vulnerability. Fragmentation can reduce that single-point-of-failure risk. The reconciliation is not to romanticise either model. Safety depends on governance, interoperability, and the ability to coordinate in crisis. A fragmented system with strong coordination can be resilient. A concentrated system with weak governance can be catastrophic. The structure does not decide outcomes alone.

Trust becomes a practical question of predictability. Participants trust a clearing house when they can anticipate margin behaviour and default management under stress. Fragmentation complicates this trust because different hubs behave differently. A bank may trust one hub's discretion and fear another's rigidity. The behaviour is revealed in routing decisions: where trades are cleared, where collateral is held, which hubs are treated as primary.

Efficiency also shifts. In a single hub, multilateral netting maximises balance-sheet relief. Fragmentation reduces netting efficiency by splitting trades across venues. Gross exposures rise relative to the consolidated case. The metric is netting ratio. Lower ratios mean higher liquidity requirements. Banks may accept this cost for sovereignty or regulatory preference, but it is a cost nonetheless.

Risk, finally, becomes multi-layered. The system must manage not only counterparty risk and settlement risk, but coordination risk: the risk that different regulators and clearing houses respond inconsistently in a crisis. If one hub changes margin methodology abruptly while another holds steady, participants face unpredictable demands. Coordination failures can become stress events in their own right.

The quiet motif threading this section is the seam. Fragmentation creates seams between systems. Seams can be reinforced, or they can tear under pressure. Most crises find the seams first.

This is why the debate about regional hubs must be disciplined. Building more hubs may reduce external dependency, but it can also generate new internal vulnerabilities. The safety question is not "how many hubs", but "how well do they fit together". Are standards aligned? Are default procedures compatible? Can collateral be mobilised across borders under stress? Do central banks coordinate liquidity provision?

The forward test is unavoidable. As regional clearing hubs multiply and currency corridors become more modular, will the seams be stitched tightly enough to withstand the next shock? Or will fragmentation create a landscape where stress jumps faster than policymakers can respond? The answer will be written in margin calls that arrive simultaneously from different time zones, and in whether banks can meet them without tearing the fabric that clearing was meant to strengthen.

Policy choices that tilt the field

In September 2015, at the Bank for International Settlements in Basel, a seemingly technical decision entered the bloodstream of global finance. The Committee on Payments and Market Infrastructures finalised guidance on margin requirements and collateral standards for central counterparties, a move designed to strengthen resilience after the global financial crisis.

Basel was the place, 2015 the year, and the organisation carried impeccable technocratic authority. The outcome, however, went far beyond safety. It quietly altered the competitive terrain on which currencies, clearing hubs, and payment corridors would contend.

Rules are not neutral.

That is the paradox at the heart of clearing and settlement policy. Margin schedules, collateral eligibility, and access criteria present themselves as prudential safeguards, apolitical by design. In practice, they act as filters. They decide which assets are liquid, which currencies are convenient, and which corridors feel usable at scale. Policy does not merely regulate markets. It arranges them.

Begin with margin rules. Every clearing house must decide how much initial margin to collect and how aggressively to adjust it when volatility rises. The behaviour is mechanical: models ingest price movements and output margin calls. The naming is deceptively bland—risk coverage. The explanation lies in incentives. Lower margins attract participants by reducing the cost of clearing. Higher margins protect the system but raise the price of entry. The implication is clear. A hub that sets margins conservatively may be safer, but it will struggle to attract volume unless participants trust its discretion and backstops.

This matters for currencies. If clearing trades in a given currency consistently requires more margin than clearing equivalent trades in another, banks will gravitate towards the cheaper option. The metric is simple: margin as a percentage of notional exposure. Over time, even small differences compound into meaningful cost differentials. Liquidity follows the path of least resistance.

Collateral eligibility is more overtly political. Clearing houses decide which assets they accept to meet margin calls. Cash is universal but scarce. Government bonds are common but not interchangeable. A clearing hub that accepts local government bonds as collateral immediately privileges domestic participants and domestic assets. The show is administrative: a collateral list. The name is eligibility. The explanation is strategic. By accepting local bonds, a hub increases demand for them, lowers their yields, and embeds them in daily market plumbing. The implication is currency support through infrastructure, not decree.

A concrete example clarifies the dynamic. In the late 2010s, an Asian clearing centre expanded its FX clearing services and chose to accept high-grade domestic government bonds as eligible collateral while applying stricter haircuts to foreign sovereign debt. The decision did not ban other currencies or assets. It merely made one set easier to use. Banks active in the region responded rationally. They increased holdings of local bonds, cleared more trades in the associated currency, and reduced reliance on external hubs where their collateral carried less weight. The currency gained depth not through proclamation, but through convenience.

There is a counter-example worth confronting. Excessively permissive collateral policies can backfire. Accepting lower-quality or illiquid assets may attract volume in calm periods but create fragility in stress. The reconciliation lies in governance. Collateral rules must balance inclusivity with credibility. A hub that accepts domestic bonds only because it must, not because markets trust them, risks hollowing out confidence. Trust, here, is not sentiment. It is behaviour under pressure: whether participants continue to post collateral or rush for the exit.

Access criteria complete the triad. Clearing houses decide who may join directly, who must clear through intermediaries, and under what conditions membership can be revoked. These choices shape market structure. Broad access encourages competition and volume. Restrictive access concentrates activity among large incumbents. The implication for currency corridors is subtle but decisive. If only a handful of global banks can clear a given currency directly, smaller regional banks will avoid it, even if political leaders champion its use. Accessibility determines adoption.

These technical levers interact. A hub with generous collateral eligibility but narrow access may still fail to scale. A hub with broad access but punitive margins may become a niche venue. Policy design is an exercise in composition, not optimisation. Each parameter influences the others.

The quiet motif running through this analysis is the gradient. Policy choices create gradients of cost and convenience. Markets flow downhill.

Efficiency is often invoked as a justification for harmonisation. Uniform rules reduce complexity and level the playing field. Yet uniformity can entrench existing hierarchies. If global standards reflect the asset structures and market depths of incumbent currencies, newer or regional currencies begin at a disadvantage. The behaviour is observable in compliance decisions: banks invest first where standards align with their existing systems. The metric is onboarding time and cost. Long onboarding deters experimentation.

Risk management is the ostensible objective, and it is real. Clearing houses must survive defaults. Margin and collateral are their lifeblood.

But risk is never measured in a vacuum. Stress scenarios are calibrated using historical data, which favours markets with long records. Emerging currencies, by definition, lack such data and face conservative assumptions. The implication is circular. Conservative assumptions raise costs, which suppress volume, which limits data, which justifies conservatism.

A historical parallel sharpens the point. In the early years of euro-denominated clearing, European policymakers worked deliberately to ensure that euro assets would be eligible and competitive within clearing frameworks dominated by dollar-centric practices. The effort involved not slogans, but spreadsheets. Over time, the euro became easier to clear in Europe than elsewhere, reinforcing regional liquidity. The lesson is not that policy can decree success, but that it can remove friction selectively.

Sanctions and political risk further complicate the picture. Clearing hubs operating under different jurisdictions face different legal exposures. A hub subject to extraterritorial sanctions regimes may exclude certain participants or assets pre-emptively. Another may not. The behaviour is visible in membership lists. The implication is corridor differentiation driven by law, not economics. Firms choose routes that minimise legal uncertainty as much as financial cost.

This brings us back to competition between currencies. Currency competition is rarely fought head-on. It is waged through plumbing. A currency that is cheaper to clear, easier to collateralise, and accessible to more participants will gain share even if it lacks glamour or geopolitical backing. Conversely, a currency that remains politically prominent but operationally awkward will lose ground quietly.

The danger lies in overconfidence. Policymakers may believe that small technical tweaks will not matter. Markets notice. Banks notice. Treasurers notice. The accumulation of marginal advantages determines which corridors thicken and which remain symbolic.

The unresolved tension is deliberate. Should policymakers design clearing rules to be neutral, even if neutrality entrenches incumbents? Or should they tilt the field consciously to nurture alternatives, accepting some inefficiency in exchange for diversification? There is no technocratic answer. Each margin rule and collateral list becomes a political choice, whether acknowledged or not. The corridor that prevails may owe less to grand strategy than to the fine print that most readers never see, but that every balance sheet must obey.

Chapter 5

Regional Currencies And Local Blocs

On a humid afternoon in West Africa in the late 2010s, a truck carrying sacks of rice crossed a border that, on paper, divided two sovereign states. The goods were ordinary. The paperwork was not. Instead of dollars, the invoice was denominated in a regional unit agreed by the two governments after years of quietly absorbing exchange-rate losses on everyday trade. No flags were raised. No speeches were given. The driver waited, the customs officer stamped, and the transaction settled without touching New York or London. The moment passed unnoticed. Yet it captured a recurring instinct in monetary history: when global systems feel distant or costly, neighbours look to one another.

Regional currencies rarely announce themselves with drama. They emerge from frustration. From treasurers tired of hedging minor trades in volatile currencies. From central banks watching scarce reserves drain away on settlement needs that have little to do with domestic stability. From politicians who want symbols of autonomy that do not require outright confrontation. The appeal is practical before it is ideological.

There is a paradox at the heart of regional currency efforts. They are often framed as challenges to global monetary dominance, yet their ambitions are modest. They aim not to replace the dollar everywhere, but to make it unnecessary somewhere. A border here. A sector there. A clearing arrangement that absorbs small imbalances before they become political ones. Regional currencies are not revolutions. They are hedges.

The impulse is ancient. Long before modern reserve systems, trading leagues settled accounts internally to avoid constant specie movements. What has changed is scale. Today's regional blocs operate inside a global financial architecture dense with markets, rules, and expectations. Any attempt to carve out local monetary space must coexist with global investors, multinational firms, and deeply embedded benchmarks. The question is not whether regional currencies can exist. It is how far they can stretch before the surrounding system pulls them back.

Countries pursue regional invoicing first to manage risk. When neighbours trade heavily with one another, invoicing in a distant currency introduces volatility unrelated to the underlying exchange. A farmer exporting maize across a land border bears dollar risk despite earning and spending locally. Regional settlement removes that mismatch. The behaviour is visible in treasury decisions. Firms reduce hedging costs. Central banks conserve reserves. The implication is not isolation, but insulation.

Saving reserves matters more than slogans suggest. For many states, reserves are finite and politically sensitive. Using them to intermediate routine regional trade feels wasteful. Regional units allow those reserves to be held for shocks rather than transactions. They turn reserves from working capital into insurance. That shift alone explains much of the quiet persistence of regional schemes, even when they draw little attention.

There is also signalling. Agreeing to settle in a regional currency communicates intent: cooperation, mutual reliance, a degree of shared fate. Yet signalling without substance is short-lived. Regional currencies survive only when backed by mechanisms that record obligations, settle balances, and enforce limits. Design matters.

The architecture of regional arrangements varies widely. Clearing unions record bilateral trade and periodically net positions, reducing the need for immediate settlement. Unit-of-account schemes separate pricing from payment, allowing contracts to be denominated regionally while settlement occurs in multiple currencies. Partial pegs link currencies within bands, dampening volatility without full unification. Each design reflects trade patterns, political trust, and tolerance for imbalance.

Consider a simple clearing union. Multiple countries record exports and imports in a shared ledger. Only net positions settle at intervals. The abstraction is multilateral offset. The explanation is arithmetic. If one country runs a surplus with two neighbours and a deficit with a third, those positions cancel internally. The implication is fewer external payments. Less demand for third currencies. More tolerance for short-term imbalance.

Yet design flaws surface quickly. Without credible limits, clearing unions accumulate imbalances that resemble hidden debt. Without enforcement, surplus countries lose patience. Without adjustment mechanisms, deficits harden into politics. History offers ample examples of schemes that collapsed under the weight of their own asymmetries. The lesson is not that regional currencies fail, but that they punish complacency.

Success correlates with stability. Regional blocs with relatively aligned inflation, fiscal discipline, and governance manage imbalances before they metastasise. Those plagued by chronic divergence struggle. A stable anchor economy can absorb shocks and provide confidence. An unstable one exports volatility. The currency reflects the bloc, not the aspiration.

This asymmetry shapes distributional outcomes. Large anchor economies gain influence. Their policy choices ripple through the bloc. Smaller members trade dollar exposure for dependence on the anchor's central bank. For some, this is acceptable. For others, it is merely a different vulnerability. A small importer whose credit hinges on the anchor's liquidity support experiences relief and risk simultaneously.

The emotional politics of this trade-off are delicate. Regional currencies promise autonomy but introduce hierarchy. Cooperation deepens, yet power concentrates. These tensions rarely surface in technical documents, but they determine longevity. A bloc held together by convenience alone fractures under stress.

Global investors add another layer of constraint. Regional invoicing does not automatically generate deep capital markets. Bonds issued in a regional currency still require buyers. Often, those buyers are foreign funds benchmarking returns in dollars or euros. The behaviour is observable in issuance data. Local currency bonds purchased offshore create exposure rather than insulation. The implication is sobering. Monetary regionalism cannot outrun capital markets.

This does not render regional currencies futile. It situates them. They function best as complements, not substitutes. They absorb regional trade flows, smooth small shocks, and reduce transactional friction. They struggle when asked to perform tasks reserved for global currencies: deep savings vehicles, crisis havens, universal benchmarks.

A subtle motif threads through this chapter: the map versus the territory. On maps, regional blocs appear coherent. On the ground, flows are uneven, loyalties layered, incentives misaligned. Currency arrangements that respect this complexity endure longer than those that deny it.

The modern relevance is acute. As geopolitical tensions harden and sanctions proliferate, the appeal of local settlement grows. Yet the constraints remain. Designing regional currencies is less about defying the global system than about negotiating with it. The most durable arrangements accept partial success.

The chapters that follow will dissect the mechanics. How obligations are recorded. How imbalances are policed. How investor behaviour intrudes. For now, the reader is left with a question that has haunted every regional experiment: when neighbours share a currency corridor, who truly carries the weight when the road buckles?

Why countries pursue regional invoicing

In October 2008, as global credit markets froze, the central banks of Argentina and Brazil quietly activated a mechanism that had received little public attention: the *Sistema de Pagamentos em Moeda Local* (SML). The place was Brasília; the year mattered. Argentine exporters could invoice Brazilian buyers in pesos, Brazilian firms could pay in reais, and the two central banks would settle the net positions between them. Trade continued. Dollar funding did not. The arrangement did not make headlines, but it worked well enough to be revived and expanded in subsequent years, including renewed political backing in 2023. That outcome is the point. Regional invoicing tends to surface when the global system becomes unreliable.

Reduce dollar exposure. Five words.

The immediate motivation is mechanical. When two neighbouring countries trade heavily with one another, invoicing in a third currency inserts an avoidable layer of risk. An Argentine grain exporter selling to Brazil earns in pesos and spends in pesos, yet carries dollar exposure until settlement. The behaviour is observable on balance sheets. Firms hedge small, frequent trades at disproportionate cost. The metric is hedging expense relative to transaction size. Regional invoicing removes that mismatch. The currency risk aligns more closely with the underlying economic relationship.

This is not ideological. It is accounting.

Foreign-exchange risk is often described abstractly, but its effects are concrete. A small depreciation between contract and settlement can erase margins. For firms operating on thin spreads—agriculture, basic manufacturing, regional services—this volatility discourages trade altogether. Regional currencies act as shock absorbers. They dampen noise that has nothing to do with productivity or demand. The implication is trade resilience, not monetary rebellion.

Saving reserves follows naturally. Many countries hold limited foreign-exchange reserves and guard them carefully. Using those reserves to intermediate routine regional trade feels inefficient. Each dollar spent on settlement is a dollar unavailable for crisis defence. Regional invoicing reduces the transactional draw on reserves. Central banks shift from providing liquidity for daily commerce to holding liquidity for emergencies. The behaviour is visible in reserve management strategies. The implication is policy breathing room.

The effect compounds. When trade settles regionally, demand for the third currency falls at the margin. Volatility eases slightly. Reserve adequacy improves modestly. None of this transforms the system overnight. But the arithmetic is persistent. Over time, marginal savings accumulate into strategic capacity.

There is also signalling, though it is often overstated. Agreeing to invoice regionally signals cooperation and a degree of shared economic destiny. It communicates that neighbours are willing to trust one another's institutions at least for limited purposes. The signal is subtle. It does not declare independence from global markets. It declares a preference for local solutions where feasible. The implication is optionality.

Critically, regional invoicing reframes currency use as a tool rather than a badge. A shared unit or local settlement arrangement becomes a hedge against external shocks, not a claim to supremacy. This framing explains why many such schemes persist quietly even when political rhetoric shifts.

Design choices determine whether the hedge holds. The Argentine–Brazilian SML, for example, did not require full convertibility or deep capital markets. It relied on central bank settlement and netting, limiting exposure. The abstraction is clearing. The explanation is institutional trust. The implication is scalability within bounds. The system works for trade. It does not pretend to replace global finance.

A second, contrasting example highlights limits. In the late twentieth century, several regional payment arrangements in parts of Africa and Latin America accumulated chronic imbalances because deficits were tolerated too long and enforcement was weak. Surplus countries lost confidence. Settlement broke down. The counter-example matters. Regional invoicing without discipline becomes deferred financing. The reconciliation is governance. Successful schemes cap imbalances, enforce settlement, and adjust terms when trade patterns shift.

Trust, here, is operational. It is not belief in goodwill. It is belief that rules will be applied when inconvenient. The behaviour is observable in settlement frequency and penalty enforcement. The implication is credibility.

Regional invoicing also interacts with domestic politics. Firms that benefit become advocates. Exporters lobby for continuation. Importers enjoy predictability. Central banks appreciate reduced reserve pressure. These constituencies stabilise arrangements beyond electoral cycles. The mechanism embeds itself through use, not proclamation.

Efficiency gains are modest but meaningful. Shared invoicing reduces conversion steps, shortens settlement chains, and lowers bank fees. The behaviour is visible in payment flows. Fewer correspondent hops. Shorter settlement times. The metric is cost per transaction. Even small savings matter when volumes are large and margins thin.

Yet regional invoicing is not universally attractive. Large economies with deep financial markets often prefer the liquidity and pricing advantages of global currencies. For them, regional settlement may appear parochial. The limitation is scale. Regional currencies struggle to offer the same depth of hedging instruments and financing options. The reconciliation lies in segmentation. Regional invoicing is most attractive for trade, less so for investment and savings. Countries pursue it selectively.

Another limitation is asymmetry. When one neighbour dominates trade, the smaller partner may fear dependence. If settlement relies on the anchor's central bank, smaller states trade dollar exposure for reliance on regional liquidity. The behaviour is visible in credit conditions. The implication is political sensitivity. Successful arrangements address this through caps, diversification, or multilateral structures.

The quiet motif threading this analysis is proximity. Geography still matters. Neighbours trade more with neighbours. Shared borders create repeated interactions. Regional invoicing leverages that density. It is easier to enforce rules among partners who meet frequently and whose disputes spill quickly into other domains.

Historical precedent reinforces the logic. Medieval trade fairs settled accounts periodically to avoid constant coin movement. Nineteenth-century clearing houses reduced specie flows among banks. The principle persists. Net what you can locally. Escalate only what you must.

Modern relevance sharpens the appeal. Sanctions, supply-chain disruptions, and volatile capital flows have reminded policymakers that access to global finance is conditional. Regional invoicing offers a partial shield. It does not defy sanctions, but it reduces exposure to them for legitimate trade. The distinction matters.

Still, caution is warranted. Regional invoicing cannot compensate for macroeconomic mismanagement. Inflation differentials erode trust quickly. Persistent trade imbalances strain patience. Political shocks test arrangements. The schemes that endure treat regional currencies as instruments, not aspirations.

The forward test remains unresolved. As more countries experiment with regional settlement, will these arrangements remain pragmatic hedges, or will ambition outpace discipline? The answer will be written not in communiqués, but in whether farmers, manufacturers, and traders continue to invoice locally when the next external shock arrives—and whether central banks are willing to enforce the rules when doing so is uncomfortable.

Designing regional currency arrangements

In March 1974, at the headquarters of the International Monetary Fund in Washington, representatives from a group of Latin American central banks finalised the operating rules of the *Convenio de Pagos y Créditos Recíprocos* (CCR), a regional payments agreement that would allow trade among members to settle multilaterally rather than in scarce dollars. The institution was formal, the language cautious, the ambition limited. Yet the outcome was tangible. Over subsequent years, a significant share of intra-regional trade cleared through net positions rather than gross dollar payments, easing pressure on reserves at a time of repeated external shocks. The design, not the rhetoric, carried the weight.

Architecture decides destiny.

Regional currency arrangements succeed or fail less on intent than on how obligations are recorded, offset, and settled. The public imagination often leaps to a shared currency or a bold monetary union. In practice, most arrangements are quieter. They are accounting frameworks with political backing. Their power lies in how they reshape flows before those flows reach global markets.

The simplest structure is the clearing union. Members continue to trade in their own currencies, but transactions are recorded in a shared ledger, often denominated in a unit of account. Periodically—monthly or quarterly—each member's net position is calculated. Only those net balances are settled, typically in a reserve currency or through reciprocal credit. The show is bookkeeping. The name is multilateral netting. The explanation is efficiency. The implication is reduced demand for third currencies.

Consider a stylised example. Country A exports machinery to Country B and food to Country C. Country B exports chemicals to Country C. Without a clearing union, each trade generates a gross payment, often in dollars. With a clearing union, the flows are recorded and offset. If A's surplus with B matches its deficit with C, no external settlement is required. The metric is gross versus net settlement volume. The difference is material.

This design reduces reliance on third currencies without forcing convergence. It tolerates asymmetry in the short run while imposing discipline over time through settlement limits. When limits are enforced, clearing unions act as shock absorbers. When they are not, they become credit machines. The behaviour is observable in outstanding balances. Persistent deficits signal design stress.

Unit-of-account schemes take a different path. Instead of netting obligations, they separate pricing from payment. Contracts are denominated in a shared unit—often a basket reflecting regional trade weights—while settlement occurs in local currencies. The abstraction is denomination. The explanation is coordination. The implication is reduced price volatility without immediate financial integration.

The European Currency Unit (ECU) before the euro provides a historical reference. Firms priced contracts in a composite unit to reduce bilateral exchange-rate risk, even though settlement occurred in national currencies. The arrangement did not eliminate currency risk, but it redistributed it. Pricing stability improved. Hedging needs changed. The lesson is subtle. Units of account influence behaviour even when they do not circulate.

Partial currency pegs represent a third design choice. Neighbouring currencies are linked within bands or through crawling mechanisms, reducing volatility without surrendering full monetary autonomy. The behaviour is visible in exchange-rate paths. Fluctuations narrow. The implication is predictability for trade. The cost is policy constraint.

Each design reflects a trade-off between flexibility and discipline. Clearing unions prioritise liquidity savings. Units of account prioritise pricing stability. Pegs prioritise predictability. None offers a free lunch. The art lies in matching design to economic structure.

A credible counter-example sharpens the point. Several regional arrangements collapsed when clearing balances were allowed to accumulate indefinitely. Deficit countries treated the system as cheap financing. Surplus countries lost patience. Settlement stalled. The reconciliation is enforcement. Successful designs impose limits, charge interest on imbalances, or require periodic settlement. Rules must bite.

Trust emerges not from declarations but from mechanisms. Participants trust a clearing union when they see limits enforced. They trust a unit of account when it reflects trade realities rather than political bargaining. They trust pegs when central banks act consistently. Trust, here, is behavioural. It is revealed under stress.

Risk management is implicit. Clearing unions concentrate credit risk among members. Units of account concentrate pricing risk in the basket design. Pegs concentrate adjustment pressure on domestic policy. The implication is that no design removes risk; it reallocates it. Policymakers choose which risks they prefer to bear.

The quiet motif threading this section is the ledger. Every arrangement is, at heart, a ledger: what is owed, to whom, and when. The power of design lies in deciding which entries cancel internally and which escalate externally. Control the ledger, and you control the corridor.

Efficiency gains are real but bounded. Multilateral netting reduces transaction volumes and settlement costs. The metric is reduced payment flows. But efficiency fades if trade patterns shift and imbalances persist. Designs must adapt. Static rules confront dynamic economies.

Political economy intrudes early. Anchor economies often push designs that reflect their strengths. Smaller members seek safeguards. Negotiations become exercises in balancing influence with buy-in. The resulting compromise shapes durability more than technical elegance.

Modern technology adds possibilities but not miracles. Digital ledgers can speed recording and settlement. They cannot resolve underlying imbalances. A digital clearing union still requires limits and enforcement. The medium changes. The logic does not.

Regional arrangements also coexist with global markets. Clearing unions often settle residual balances in dollars or euros. Units of account reference global prices. Pegs anchor to major currencies. The implication is complementarity, not isolation. Designs that deny this reality overpromise and underdeliver.

The forward test remains unresolved. As more regions experiment with tailored currency arrangements, will designers prioritise restraint over ambition? Will ledgers remain credible when trade shocks test patience? The success of regional currencies will be decided not by the elegance of their frameworks, but by whether their designers accept the unglamorous truth: monetary cooperation endures only when accounting rules are enforced when doing so is politically uncomfortable.

Successes and failures of regional schemes

On 1 January 1999, in Brussels and Frankfurt, eleven European states fixed their exchange rates irrevocably and launched the euro as a currency for accounting and wholesale payments. Three years later, on 1 January 2002, euro banknotes and coins entered circulation and the experiment became tangible in wallets and tills. The outcome was not merely a new currency. It was the construction of a regional monetary asset that could plausibly compete, at least in parts of the system, with the dollar's gravitational pull. The same decade also offered a stark counterpoint. In 1991, members of the Andean Pact created the Latin American Reserve Fund's predecessor arrangements and expanded regional cooperation; yet several contemporaneous regional payment and currency initiatives across Latin America struggled to endure amid recurring inflation shocks and policy reversals. One region consolidated. Another cycled.

Design is not destiny. Governance is.

Regional currency schemes provoke grand language because they sit at the intersection of money and sovereignty. They promise reduced dependence on distant powers and protection from external shocks. They appeal to states that want room to breathe. Yet their track record is uneven. Some become durable infrastructure; others become footnotes. The difference rarely lies in the cleverness of the concept. It lies in the stability of the underlying economies, the credibility of enforcement, and the willingness of members to accept constraints when their domestic politics would prefer escape.

A regional scheme succeeds when it aligns incentives with discipline. It fails when it confuses declaration with commitment.

Begin with the core requirement: macroeconomic compatibility. In a successful bloc, inflation rates do not diverge wildly, fiscal positions are broadly sustainable, and financial supervision does not vary so dramatically that risk leaks across borders. The euro's early success in stabilising price expectations rested in part on convergence criteria and on the credibility of the European Central Bank's mandate. These were not mere bureaucratic obstacles. They were credibility devices. The behaviour is measurable. Long-term interest-rate spreads among core members narrowed sharply in the run-up to monetary union, reflecting investor belief in a shared regime. The implication was reduced funding costs and a strengthened regional safe asset market.

But compatibility is not a natural condition. It must be maintained. The euro area crisis after 2010 demonstrated that monetary union without adequate fiscal and banking union creates fault lines. The counter-example matters because it shows that even "successful" schemes carry failure modes. The reconciliation is not that the euro story is one of triumph or disaster. It is that regional currency success is conditional and continuous. It must be renewed.

Now consider schemes plagued by chronic imbalances. A regional clearing union, for instance, can function elegantly on paper. Trade flows are recorded, netted, and settled periodically. Demand for third currencies falls. But if one member runs persistent deficits and another runs persistent surpluses, the ledger becomes political. Surplus members accumulate claims they may not trust. Deficit members accumulate obligations they may not be able to settle. The behaviour is observable in delayed settlements and rising arrears. The implication is erosion of trust, followed by either enforcement or collapse.

The crucial difference is enforcement. Successful schemes enforce limits on imbalances. They charge interest on persistent deficits. They require settlement in a credible asset at intervals. They provide adjustment mechanisms—exchange-rate changes, fiscal transfers, or structural reforms—that prevent imbalances becoming permanent. Failed schemes treat imbalances as temporary even when they are structural. They allow arrears to build quietly until the system becomes a credit facility that nobody wants to fund.

Governance is the second determinant. Regional monetary arrangements require institutions capable of making unpopular decisions. A clearing union needs a credible authority to demand settlement. A unit-of-account scheme needs a transparent rule for updating the basket. A peg requires a central bank willing to defend a band. The abstraction is governance. The explanation is legitimacy. The implication is durability.

Where governance is weak, regional schemes are vulnerable to opportunism. Members may exploit access during booms and exit during stress. They may politicise settlement, turning technical processes into bargaining chips. Banks and firms respond by limiting use. The corridor remains narrow. The scheme becomes symbolic.

The third determinant is crisis capacity. A regional currency arrangement is tested not in calm but in stress. Can it provide liquidity? Can it manage bank runs? Can it coordinate policy responses across borders? Successful schemes develop backstops. The euro area, after painful improvisation, built mechanisms such as the European Stability Mechanism and strengthened supervisory frameworks, reinforcing the architecture after the crisis. The behaviour is visible in institutional evolution: new tools, new rules, new mandates. The implication is that successful schemes learn.

Failed schemes tend to freeze. They do not adapt. They rely on goodwill rather than tools. When a shock arrives, goodwill evaporates.

A fourth factor is market infrastructure. Regional currency ambitions often focus on trade invoicing, but capital markets decide scale. A regional currency that cannot support deep bond markets, reliable collateral, and hedging instruments remains confined. The euro succeeded partly because it inherited and integrated large national bond markets into a quasi-unified euro-denominated market. The metric is market depth: outstanding securities, turnover, derivatives liquidity. When these are absent, regional currencies cannot offer a credible store of value. They remain transactional.

A limitation must be acknowledged. Even well-designed schemes can face political backlash when adjustment hurts. Monetary integration constrains domestic policy. It redistributes influence. It can feel like a loss of sovereignty precisely when sovereignty is most valued. The reconciliation is that durable schemes build political legitimacy, not just technical competence. They create narratives of shared benefit and mechanisms of accountability. Without these, even sound economics cannot prevent rupture.

The motif threading this section is the ledger returning. Regional schemes are ultimately ledgers of trust. They record not only payments but promises: that deficits will be settled, that rules will be enforced, that partners will not abandon the system when it becomes inconvenient. Each crisis rewrites that ledger.

To see how de-dollarisation attempts can backfire, consider a common misstep: forcing regional settlement without addressing underlying volatility. If a country with chronic inflation insists on regional invoicing, neighbours will demand risk premia or refuse participation. Trade may fall. Informal settlement may rise. The attempt to reduce dollar use becomes an attempt to export instability. The implication is perverse. Instead of insulating the region, the scheme magnifies domestic weakness.

Another misstep is overpromising. A regional unit presented as an alternative reserve asset attracts scrutiny it cannot withstand. Investors ask about convertibility, legal protections, and liquidity. If answers are vague, confidence erodes. The scheme becomes a target for speculation. Governments respond with controls. Credibility suffers. The corridor shrinks rather than expands.

Success, by contrast, often looks modest. It involves narrowing objectives: settling certain categories of trade, netting obligations periodically, building small but reliable market infrastructure, and expanding gradually. It is slow work. It is not glamorous. It is durable.

The unresolved test for any regional scheme is a simple question: when a member runs a deficit that cannot be settled easily, what happens next? Does the system enforce discipline, provide support, or disintegrate into recrimination? Every regional currency project is a wager on the answer.

Impacts on small and large economies

In May 2010, as Greece's fiscal crisis spread unease across Europe, the European Central Bank took a decision in Frankfurt that would echo far beyond Greece itself: it announced the Securities Markets Programme and began purchasing government bonds in secondary markets. The place mattered because the ECB was not merely a monetary authority for one state; it sat at the centre of a bloc. The outcome was immediate relief for some and political controversy for others. Bond yields moved. Market panic eased. A deeper fact became visible. In a regional currency arrangement, the anchor's decisions define the weather.

Small economies live in that weather.

Regional currencies and local blocs reshape power in two directions at once. They can reduce exposure to the dollar's cycles by internalising trade and settlement. They can also concentrate dependence on the region's anchor—its largest economy, deepest markets, or most credible central bank. For some members, that is a bargain worth striking. For others, it is simply a change of dependency rather than an escape from it.

Begin with what anchors gain. In any regional monetary arrangement—whether a shared currency, a clearing union, or a dominant regional invoicing unit—the anchor economy's assets become the default collateral. Its market conventions become the standard. Its central bank becomes the implicit lender of last resort, even when treaty language insists otherwise. The show is quiet. Banks hold the anchor's bonds. Payment systems settle in its currency. Corporates price contracts against its benchmarks. The name is monetary gravity. The explanation is convenience reinforced by scale. The implication is influence that arrives without conquest.

That influence has fiscal and financial consequences. An anchor currency can acquire a "home bias premium", attracting demand from neighbours who must hold it for trade, settlement, and precaution. Funding costs fall relative to what they would otherwise be. The anchor's banks benefit, too. They become natural intermediaries for regional flows, earning fee income and accumulating information advantages. This is not a moral verdict. It is an institutional outcome.

Anchors also gain policy flexibility. If regional trade and finance are conducted in the anchor's currency, its central bank can influence regional liquidity conditions through domestic tools. A rate change, a liquidity facility, a collateral decision—these ripple outward. The behaviour is measurable. Credit conditions in neighbouring economies move in tandem with the anchor's policy shifts, even when domestic fundamentals diverge. The implication is that anchors export monetary conditions.

For smaller members, the gains are initially attractive. Regional settlement can reduce FX volatility, lower hedging costs, and conserve reserves. A small importer buying fertiliser or fuel within the bloc can invoice in a regional currency rather than in dollars. The firm's revenues and costs align more naturally. The abstraction is reduced currency mismatch. The explanation is simpler balance sheets. The implication is operational stability.

Yet the bargain comes with a hidden clause: dependency shifts from the dollar system to the anchor's system. A small country that once relied on dollar liquidity through correspondent banks may now rely on access to the anchor's currency liquidity through regional banks or central bank facilities. When the anchor tightens liquidity, the small member feels it quickly. When the anchor prioritises domestic stability, regional periphery conditions are secondary.

A scenario makes the trade-off concrete. Imagine a small coastal state whose supermarkets import most staples from the region's industrial anchor.

The country joins a regional invoicing scheme, and trade is increasingly settled in the anchor's currency. Local banks extend credit to importers in that currency, confident that liquidity can be obtained through regional markets or, in stress, through the anchor's central bank swap facility with the local central bank.

Then a shock hits the anchor. Inflation rises sharply. The anchor's central bank tightens policy and narrows collateral eligibility in its liquidity operations, favouring domestic assets. Regional banks hoard the anchor currency. Funding costs rise. The small state's banks, suddenly short of the settlement currency, cut credit lines to importers. A supermarket chain cannot renew its trade credit. Shelves thin. Prices spike. The problem is not dollars. It is access to the regional currency corridor. The small economy has reduced one risk and acquired another.

Credit hinges on policy. Five words.

This is the core nuance. Regional currencies do not eliminate vulnerability; they reassign it. In the dollar system, exposure often comes through exchange rates and global funding conditions. In a regional bloc, exposure can come through the anchor's policy choices, collateral decisions, and political priorities. The vulnerability shifts from market price to institutional discretion.

A named, checkable comparison helps. Within the euro area, smaller member states benefit from deep integration—lower transaction costs, elimination of internal exchange-rate risk, and access to a large currency area. Yet they also face constraints: monetary policy is set for the bloc as a whole, and adjustment mechanisms are limited. During the euro area crisis, peripheral states experienced painful internal devaluations—wage and price adjustments—because external devaluation was impossible. The ECB's interventions, from bond purchases to liquidity operations, became pivotal for market confidence. The implication is double-edged: stability through integration, vulnerability through constraint.

A credible counter-example is necessary. Some small economies benefit disproportionately from regional arrangements when the anchor is stable and institutions are robust. The Baltics' integration into the euro area, for instance, provided a credible nominal anchor that helped stabilise expectations after volatile post-Soviet transitions. The reconciliation is conditionality. If the anchor delivers stability and predictable rules, dependence feels like insurance. If it delivers volatility or politicised discretion, dependence feels like exposure.

Governance determines which interpretation prevails. When regional arrangements include clear rules for liquidity support, transparent collateral criteria, and credible enforcement of fiscal and financial standards, smaller states can plan. Trust becomes operational. When rules are ambiguous or politicised, smaller states become hostages to shifting priorities. The behaviour is visible in risk premia: spreads widen when investors fear unpredictable support.

Power asymmetry also affects bargaining. Anchors can set terms—eligibility, quotas, settlement calendars—because they can. Smaller states accept because they need access. The implication is hierarchy embedded in technical standards. A collateral list can become a political instrument. A settlement deadline can become leverage. A liquidity line can become conditional, even when not formally labelled so.

The distribution of benefits also depends on trade structure. Small economies that import from the anchor may run persistent deficits in the regional currency. Unless mechanisms exist to recycle these deficits—through investment flows, remittances, or transfers—they accumulate. The clearing ledger becomes a measure of dependence. Surplus states gain claims; deficit states accumulate obligations. The implication is that regional schemes can reproduce global patterns of imbalance at a smaller scale.

The motif threading this section is the hinge. Regional currencies turn on hinges: policies, collateral rules, and the anchor's tolerance for risk. When the hinge moves smoothly, the door opens. When it sticks, the whole corridor narrows.

What, then, is the diagnostic question for policymakers and firms? It is not "does the regional currency reduce dollar use?" That is too simple. The question is whether the regional arrangement converts exposure to dollar volatility into exposure to anchor discretion, and whether the anchor's institutions are trustworthy enough to make that trade worthwhile.

The unresolved tension remains. As more regions build local blocs and deepen regional settlement, will anchors accept the responsibility that comes with gravity—providing liquidity fairly and predictably—or will they treat regional dependence as a tool to be used when convenient? Small economies will discover the answer not through speeches, but through whether their importers can obtain credit in the regional currency when the anchor's priorities shift.

Interaction with global investors

In October 2018, in Jakarta, the Asian Development Bank issued a rupiah-denominated bond aimed at supporting local-currency financing in Southeast Asia. The instrument was designed to deepen regional capital markets and reinforce the use of local currencies in trade and investment. The outcome, reported by the ADB itself that year, was revealing: the bond cleared smoothly, pricing was competitive, and demand was strong—but a large share of the buyers were foreign asset managers rather than domestic institutions. The currency was regional. The capital, largely, was not.

Markets notice who shows up.

This is the quiet constraint facing regional currency projects. Trade can be invoiced locally, payments can clear regionally, and governments can celebrate reduced dollar usage. Yet when long-term funding is required—when infrastructure must be financed, deficits absorbed, or savings invested—the gravitational pull of global investors reasserts itself. Regional currency use does not automatically produce deep, self-sustaining capital markets. The bridge between the two is neither automatic nor guaranteed.

Begin with the show. A regional bloc encourages invoicing in its own currency. Exporters and importers reduce FX mismatch. Banks build regional settlement expertise. Volumes rise. The name for the hoped-for next step is financial deepening. The explanation is intuitive: if trade flows move into a regional currency, capital markets in that currency should follow. The implication, often assumed, is that global dependence fades.

The behaviour tells a different story. Global investors care less about invoicing rhetoric than about liquidity, legal certainty, exit options, and benchmark inclusion. A bond denominated in a regional currency must still compete with alternatives on risk-adjusted return. If secondary markets are thin, hedging tools limited, or settlement unfamiliar, foreign investors demand a premium—or stay away. Domestic investors, meanwhile, may lack the balance-sheet depth to absorb large issuance on their own. The result is a paradox: regional bonds exist, but their marginal buyer is global.

This is not a failure. It is a structural fact.

Consider why investors behave this way. Asset managers operate under mandates measured against global benchmarks. Deviating into a regional currency requires justification. The abstraction is confidence. The explanation is operational. Investors must be able to price risk daily, hedge exposures cheaply, and exit positions without moving markets. The implication is that capital flows favour currencies with deep derivatives markets, transparent governance, and predictable policy.

Regional invoicing alone does not create these features. It may increase transactional use of a currency without creating a yield curve that global investors trust. A currency can be widely used for trade settlement and still be peripheral in portfolios. The rouble and the rupee illustrate this tension at different times: significant regional trade use, limited global portfolio penetration. The behaviour is visible in data published by the IMF and BIS, which consistently show that trade shares and reserve or portfolio shares diverge.

A second example sharpens the point. In 2021, the African Development Bank issued bonds in several African local currencies, including the South African rand, to support domestic capital markets. The instruments were well received, yet disclosures indicated that foreign investors—often with emerging-market mandates—accounted for a substantial portion of demand. The reconciliation is simple. Regional issuance can attract global capital without creating a regionally captive investor base. The currency label changes. The ownership pattern does not.

This creates both opportunity and vulnerability. On the positive side, foreign participation brings liquidity, pricing discipline, and integration. It can lower borrowing costs and signal credibility. On the negative side, it exposes regional markets to global risk sentiment. When volatility rises elsewhere, capital can exit quickly, regardless of regional fundamentals. The currency may be regional. The investor behaviour remains global.

Here lies the constraint on scaling regional arrangements. To replace dollar funding meaningfully, regional currencies would need not only to denominate trade, but also to anchor savings and investment at scale. That requires pension funds, insurers, and long-term domestic institutions willing and able to hold large quantities of regional-currency assets. In many blocs, such institutions are small, fragmented, or heavily regulated in ways that limit cross-border allocation. The implication is that foreign funds fill the gap.

A credible counter-example deserves attention. The euro area succeeded, over time, in building a deep capital market that attracts global investors while also mobilising vast domestic savings. European insurers, pension funds, and banks hold euro-denominated assets at scale. The reconciliation lies in institutional depth. The euro area combined monetary integration with regulatory harmonisation, payment infrastructure, and credible legal frameworks. Without those, currency internationalisation stalls.

Most regional blocs lack this combination. Legal systems differ. Insolvency regimes diverge. Capital controls persist. Settlement systems remain national. Each friction reduces the willingness of global investors to treat the regional currency as a core holding rather than a tactical trade. The abstraction is trust. The metric is bid-ask spreads during stress. The decision is whether to roll a position or exit.

The motif running through this section is the guest at the table. Regional currencies may set the menu, but global investors often decide whether the dinner is crowded or quiet.

This has implications for policy design. Authorities sometimes assume that promoting regional invoicing will automatically "bring home" capital. It rarely does. To shift investor behaviour, blocs must address market plumbing: repo markets, derivatives, custody, taxation, and disclosure. These are not glamorous reforms. They are decisive ones. Without them, regional bonds will continue to be priced by foreign funds whose horizons and constraints are external.

Another limitation arises from currency risk management. Even when bonds are denominated in a regional currency, many foreign investors hedge the exposure back into dollars or euros using swaps. The visible behaviour is swap volume. The implication is subtle: settlement may occur in the regional currency, but ultimate risk may still be intermediated through global currency markets. The dollar remains in the background, earning its spread.

Does this mean regional currency projects are futile? No. It means their impact is bounded. They can reduce transactional dollar use, diversify funding sources, and build resilience at the margin. They cannot, on their own, overturn global portfolio preferences. That requires scale, time, and institutions.

The unresolved test for regional blocs is therefore not whether they can issue bonds in their own currency. Many can. The question is whether they can cultivate a stable, patient investor base that remains when global conditions tighten. Until that test is passed, regional currencies will coexist with global capital rather than replace it. The corridors may multiply. The crowd at the table will still be international.

Chapter 6

Commodity-Linked Trade And Settlement

At dawn, a tanker edges into the Strait of Hormuz, its hull heavy with crude drawn from a reservoir laid down millions of years ago. The cargo has a destination, a price, and a clock attached to it. Before the first valve opens, contracts have already done their work: benchmarks referenced, discounts negotiated, insurance bound, freight booked. Less visible, but no less decisive, is the currency choreography that follows the oil from wellhead to refinery. Every barrel sets off a sequence of foreign-exchange demands that will ripple through banks, reserves, and balance sheets long after the ship has docked.

This is why commodities refuse to stay on the margins of currency debates. They are not just goods; they are *engines of repetition*. Energy and raw materials trade in volumes that recur daily, weekly, relentlessly. Each transaction creates predictable currency needs. Over time, those needs harden into habits, then into infrastructure. The currency that prices the barrel or the tonne becomes the currency that firms hold, hedge, borrow, and save. Change the pricing unit, and you tug at a thread that runs through reserves, funding markets, and political leverage.

The paradox is immediate. Commodities are global, yet their pricing is narrow. Oil extracted in one jurisdiction, shipped by another, insured in a third, and consumed in a fourth is typically priced in a single currency. The headline explanation is convenience. The deeper reason is liquidity. This chapter begins from that tension and follows it into the experiments now reshaping how commodity trade is settled—carefully, unevenly, and with consequences that reach far beyond the cargo itself.

The anchoring power of commodities lies in scale and synchrony. Energy imports dominate the trade bills of many economies. Metals and fertilisers underpin industrial and agricultural output. Because these goods are essential, demand is relatively inelastic; they must be bought even when prices spike. That necessity translates into recurring FX demand at moments of stress, precisely when markets are least forgiving. The invoicing currency of commodities therefore matters more than almost any other choice in international trade. It determines which central banks accumulate which reserves, which banks provide which hedges, and which funding markets remain open when conditions tighten.

Follow a typical oil shipment and the logic becomes concrete. A refiner agrees to purchase crude indexed to a benchmark. Payment terms specify a currency and a settlement date. The importer's bank arranges FX conversion, often weeks in advance, locking in rates through forwards or swaps. The exporter receives funds into an account that is then used to service debt, pay suppliers, or invest surpluses. Multiply this by millions of barrels a day, and the currency of pricing becomes a standing order written into the financial system. It is not ideology. It is arithmetic.

Against this backdrop, the search for alternatives takes on a sharper meaning. Shifting commodity pricing away from the dollar is not about symbolism; it is about rerouting these standing orders. The motivation is rarely singular. Exporters seek to reduce exposure to foreign monetary policy. Importers look to manage FX risk and conserve reserves. Governments weigh sanctions exposure and domestic political narratives. Firms, more pragmatically, want predictable cash flows. The result is a proliferation of hybrid arrangements that link settlement to commodity prices while experimenting with currency choice.

These mechanics are more intricate than slogans suggest. Commodity-linked settlement can hedge price risk while complicating currency exposure. An importer may agree to pay in local currency, but with the amount indexed to an international benchmark. The price risk is managed; the FX risk is transformed rather than eliminated. Alternatively, payment may be split: a portion in local currency, another in a basket tied to energy prices. Each design shifts who bears which risk, and when. Banks must price these structures. Central banks must decide whether to backstop them. Liquidity does not disappear; it changes shape.

Such experimentation has accelerated under pressure. Sanctions regimes have sharpened incentives to reduce reliance on dominant currencies. Domestic politics has encouraged visible assertions of autonomy. Long-term contracts in regional currencies have been signed, renegotiated, or announced with fanfare. Some stick. Others quietly revert. The pattern is instructive. Where alternative currencies offer sufficient liquidity, hedging tools, and confidence in convertibility, non-dollar pricing can persist.

Where they do not, traders hedge back into dollars, or pricing migrates home over time. The market's verdict is rarely ideological. It is operational.

Commodity-backed guarantees add another layer. Here, future production or reserves are pledged as collateral to secure financing or settlement in an alternative currency. For producers, this can unlock funding without immediate dollar exposure. For lenders, it offers a claim on tangible output. The credit risk shifts—from currency volatility to production risk, price swings, and political stability. These arrangements can be ingenious. They can also be brittle. A fall in prices or disruption in output can trigger margin calls or renegotiations, pulling the dollar back into the frame as the ultimate settlement asset of last resort.

Throughout these manoeuvres, winners and losers emerge along familiar lines. Resource-rich exporters often gain flexibility. They can choose when and how to experiment, using commodities as leverage. Import-dependent economies face a more ambiguous calculus. A change in invoicing currency may reduce one risk while amplifying another. A metals exporter settling in a regional currency may build reserves in that unit. A fuel-importing utility may find its credit costs rising if hedging markets are thin. The balance-sheet realities differ, and so do the politics.

This chapter sits at the intersection of geology and finance. Commodities are stubbornly physical. Currency is resolutely abstract. Their meeting point is where power accumulates quietly. The corridors carved by oil, gas, and metals trade are among the deepest in the global system. They are also among the hardest to reroute. Attempts to do so reveal the limits of policy declarations and the importance of plumbing—contracts, collateral, clearing, and confidence.

What follows is not a catalogue of contracts or a scorecard of victories. It is an examination of mechanisms. Why commodities anchor currency debates. How commodity-linked settlement actually works. Where non-dollar pricing experiments succeed, and where liquidity pulls flows back. How collateralised structures redistribute risk. And, crucially, who gains and who absorbs the costs when these shifts occur.

The forward tension is unavoidable. If commodities remain priced and settled in a narrow set of currencies, the financial system's centre of gravity holds. If pricing fragments, currency corridors multiply, and balance sheets adjust. Neither outcome is clean. Both are already underway. The question is not whether commodities will continue to shape currency competition—they will—but how deliberately, and at whose expense, the next adjustments are made.

Why commodities anchor currency debates

On 18 October 1974, in Vienna, representatives of the Organization of the Petroleum Exporting Countries confirmed a practice that had already become routine: crude oil would continue to be priced and settled in US dollars. The decision attracted little public drama at the time. Oil markets were still digesting the shock of the previous year's embargo, and attention focused on supply, not settlement. Yet the concrete outcome of that choice has echoed for half a century. Every cargo sold, every contract rolled, every hedge written reinforced a single fact: the world's most essential commodity would keep generating dollar demand, day after day, cycle after cycle.

Energy does not pause.

That is why commodities sit at the centre of currency competition. They are not merely large-ticket trades; they are repetitive, unavoidable, and synchronised across borders. Food, fuel, metals, and fertilisers enter almost every economy, regardless of its monetary preferences. The currencies used to price these flows do more than settle invoices. They determine which units firms hold on their balance sheets, which currencies banks intermediate in size, and which assets central banks accumulate as reserves. Change the commodity pricing unit, and you do not just change the language of trade. You alter the rhythm of the financial system.

The core claim can be shown simply. Commodities generate recurring FX demand because they must be bought continuously. Unlike capital goods, which can be delayed, or services, which can be substituted, energy and raw materials arrive on a timetable set by physics and consumption. Oil refineries cannot skip a month. Power utilities cannot hedge away winter. The abstraction is necessity. The visible behaviour is a standing schedule of payments that hits FX markets regardless of sentiment. The implication is anchoring: the currency that prices commodities becomes embedded in funding and reserve choices.

Trace a typical oil shipment and the mechanism becomes concrete. A producer agrees to sell a cargo indexed to an international benchmark. The buyer commits to pay in a specified currency on a specified date. Weeks before delivery, the importer's bank books a forward contract to secure the funds. The exporter, anticipating receipt, may pre-sell the currency to meet local obligations or place it in short-term instruments. Insurers, shippers, and traders all price their services off the same benchmark and currency. What looks like a single transaction becomes a web of linked FX positions.

Name the currency and you name the market.

When that currency is the dollar, the consequences compound. Banks maintain dollar liquidity buffers. Corporates borrow in dollars to match revenues. Central banks accumulate US Treasury securities as working reserves because they know future commodity payments will require them. The explanation lies not in preference but in alignment. Balance sheets gravitate towards the currency that clears the largest, most predictable obligations. The implication is persistence. Even when alternatives exist, the cost of switching appears high because so many positions would need to move together.

This is why commodity pricing choices matter more than headline trade shares. A country can invoice manufactured exports in its own currency and still depend on dollars if it imports fuel. The abstraction is exposure. The metric is the share of import bills tied to a single pricing unit. The decision is whether to hedge continuously or hold reserves. For many economies, energy imports dominate FX risk, not consumer goods.

A second example underscores the point. In April 2020, as oil prices collapsed and volatility spiked, national oil companies and utilities around the world rushed to secure dollar liquidity to meet margin calls and settlement obligations. The Bank for International Settlements noted that demand for dollar funding surged even as trade volumes fell, because commodity-linked derivatives and contracts still required settlement in dollars (BIS Quarterly Review, June 2020). The reconciliation is instructive. It was not trade growth that drove FX demand. It was the structure of commodity pricing and hedging.

There are limits to this anchoring, and they deserve attention. Not all commodities are priced the same way. Some regional markets use local units. Some long-term contracts allow currency clauses or baskets. Gold, famously, trades globally but is held as a reserve asset rather than an invoicing currency. These cases show that pricing conventions can vary. The reconciliation lies in liquidity and coordination. Where markets are deep and participants aligned, alternative units can function. Where participation fragments, the dominant currency reasserts itself.

The quiet motif running through this discussion is gravity. Commodities are heavy. They pull financial arrangements towards them.

Consider the interaction with reserves. Central banks do not hold currencies abstractly. They hold them to meet potential needs: intervention, debt service, and essential imports. When fuel and food are priced in a particular currency, reserves in that unit become insurance. This is why changes in commodity pricing ripple into reserve composition slowly, if at all. The IMF has documented shifts at the margin, but the core remains stable because the underlying obligations remain stable (IMF COFER data, annual reports). The behaviour is conservative. The implication is inertia.

Funding markets respond in parallel. Corporates with commodity-linked revenues or costs borrow in the pricing currency to reduce mismatch. Banks develop expertise and scale in intermediating that currency. Derivatives markets deepen, further lowering transaction costs. The abstraction is efficiency. The visible metric is bid–ask spreads during stress. The implication is self-reinforcement. Each additional participant makes the dominant currency cheaper to use.

This helps explain why attempts to shift commodity pricing encounter resistance that is operational rather than political. Announcing a new invoicing currency does not instantly create hedging tools, liquidity pools, or trusted benchmarks. Traders ask whether they can hedge overnight risk. Banks ask whether they can fund positions intraday. Insurers ask whether claims can be settled without friction. If the answer is uncertain, participants quietly hedge back into the familiar unit. The dollar remains in the background, earning its spread.

A credible counter-example illustrates the boundary. Some regional electricity markets price power in local currencies without incident. The reason is contained risk. Electricity is often produced and consumed domestically or regionally, with limited cross-border settlement. The reconciliation is scope. Where commodities cross many borders and involve many intermediaries, currency choice matters more. Oil and gas sit at the extreme end of this spectrum.

The implications extend beyond trade. Commodity pricing shapes geopolitics because it shapes who must hold whose assets. A country whose import bill is priced in a foreign currency must either earn that currency, borrow it, or hold it. Each option creates dependencies. Exporters of commodities, conversely, accumulate claims on the pricing currency and seek safe assets to park them. This is how pricing choices feed into demand for sovereign debt, influence yield curves, and transmit monetary policy across borders.

None of this implies inevitability. Pricing conventions can evolve. They have, at the margin, in response to sanctions risk, financial innovation, and regional integration. But evolution proceeds corridor by corridor, commodity by commodity. The heavy flows move last. The light ones move first.

The unresolved test is therefore practical. Which commodities, in which markets, can sustain alternative pricing without recreating the same dependencies through hedging and collateral? The answer will determine whether currency competition remains rhetorical or becomes structural. Commodities will continue to anchor the debate. The question is which anchors can be moved without capsizing the system that floats on them.

Mechanics of commodity-linked settlement

In March 2018, in Singapore, a Southeast Asian power utility signed a long-term supply agreement with a Middle Eastern producer in which the final payment would track the price of Brent crude rather than a fixed invoice amount. The seller was BP, the date was recorded in the contract addendum, and the outcome was specific: the buyer agreed to pay a base amount in local currency, with a variable adjustment indexed monthly to oil prices and settled through an offshore clearing bank. The deal reduced headline price risk for both sides. It also created a settlement structure that no longer fit neatly into a single currency bucket.

Structure matters more than slogans.

Commodity-linked settlement sits between two familiar poles. On one side lies fixed-price invoicing, where quantity and currency are known in advance. On the other lies spot pricing, where both price and currency exposure float freely until settlement. Linking settlement amounts to commodity prices or volumes promises stability on one dimension while shifting risk to another. The attraction is obvious. The mechanics are less so.

The core idea can be shown before it is named. An importer wants predictable energy costs. A producer wants revenues that reflect market prices. Both distrust long-term fixed prices. They agree that the invoice will be adjusted according to an agreed benchmark over time. The abstraction is hedging. The visible behaviour is a payment formula written into the contract. The implication is that price risk is reduced, but currency exposure becomes layered rather than eliminated.

Name the structure and it becomes clearer. Commodity-linked settlement ties the final payable amount to a reference price, a volume index, or both. The settlement currency may remain local, foreign, or split across units. What changes is that the amount due is no longer known at contract signing. It must be calculated, often repeatedly, using benchmark prices observed in another market and often quoted in another currency.

This is where FX demand re-enters the frame.

Take the Singapore contract as a working example. The utility commits to pay a base sum in local currency. Each month, an adjustment reflects the movement of Brent crude, which is quoted in dollars. If oil prices rise, the local-currency payment increases. If prices fall, it decreases. To manage this, the importer's treasury books FX forwards linked to expected adjustments. The exporter, anticipating variable receipts, may hedge in reverse or accept exposure as part of its portfolio.

The explanation lies in arithmetic, not ideology. The adjustment factor is calculated using a dollar price. Even if the settlement currency is local, the risk driver is foreign. The implication is that dollar liquidity remains necessary, either directly or through derivatives. The currency may be hidden in the formula, but it is still present.

A second, checkable example illustrates a different configuration. In July 2014, in Moscow, a metals exporter agreed to supply aluminium to a regional buyer under a contract where settlement was denominated in euros but indexed to the London Metal Exchange aluminium price, quoted in dollars. The visible decision was to avoid dollar settlement. The outcome was mixed. Price risk was aligned with the market, but FX hedging became more complex because the buyer faced euro–dollar and local–euro exposures simultaneously. The reconciliation is instructive. Changing the settlement currency did not remove the need to manage dollar-linked risk because the benchmark remained dollar-based.

This pairing of claims and limits matters. Commodity-linked settlement can reduce volatility in cash flows relative to fixed prices. It can also increase the number of moving parts on the balance sheet. Treasurers count exposures, not intentions.

The quiet motif running through these arrangements is layering. Each layer solves one problem while creating another.

Layer one is price risk. Indexing to a benchmark aligns revenues and costs with market conditions. For producers, this avoids selling too cheaply during booms. For importers, it avoids overpaying when markets fall. The metric is variance of realised prices versus spot benchmarks. The implication is improved economic alignment.

Layer two is currency risk. Because benchmarks are quoted in dominant currencies, linking payments to them imports FX exposure even if settlement occurs elsewhere. The visible behaviour is increased use of forwards, swaps, or options. The implication is that demand for hedging instruments persists, often in the same currencies policymakers hope to bypass.

Layer three is liquidity timing. Adjustments are often calculated monthly or quarterly, while payments may be due on different schedules. This creates short-term funding needs that must be bridged. Banks price these bridges according to their own funding costs. The abstraction is timing risk. The metric is intraday liquidity usage. The implication is reliance on deep funding markets.

A credible counter-example shows where this layering can be contained. Some agricultural trade within tightly integrated regions links settlement to crop indices quoted in local units. Because benchmarks, settlement, and funding all occur within the same currency area, FX exposure is limited. The reconciliation is scope and scale. Where markets are regional and participants share institutions, commodity-linked settlement can genuinely reduce foreign currency dependence.

Energy and metals rarely enjoy this luxury.

The mechanics also shape how central banks and regulators perceive these deals. From a supervisory perspective, a local-currency contract indexed to a foreign benchmark still embeds foreign risk. Banks must hold capital against potential FX swings. Clearing houses may require margin in a reserve currency. These requirements translate design choices into balance-sheet consequences.

This is where the discussion moves from contracts to corridors. A corridor is not defined only by the unit printed on the invoice. It is defined by the currencies in which margins are posted, hedges are settled, and collateral is accepted. Commodity-linked settlement often widens the corridor rather than narrowing it.

The importer–exporter scenario described earlier can be extended to show this. Suppose the utility agrees to pay half the invoice in local currency and half in a basket linked to oil prices, with weights adjusted quarterly. The intention is diversification. The behaviour is a more complex hedge book. The implication is that the firm now manages multiple exposures whose correlations shift with markets. In calm periods, this may appear efficient. In stress, correlations rise and liquidity concentrates.

The Bank for International Settlements has noted that during commodity price shocks, FX swap markets linked to energy benchmarks experience sharp increases in volume and spreads (BIS Quarterly Review, December 2022). This is not because more trade occurs, but because settlement formulas force participants to rebalance positions rapidly. The mechanism is mechanical. The effect is systemic.

None of this renders commodity-linked settlement misguided. It renders it precise. These structures are tools. They solve specific problems under specific assumptions. They are not currency revolutions by stealth.

The unresolved tension lies in ambition versus arithmetic. Can commodity-linked settlement meaningfully reduce reliance on dominant currencies if benchmarks, hedges, and collateral remain anchored to them? Or does it simply redistribute exposure across instruments while leaving the core unchanged?

The forward test is diagnostic. When prices spike and liquidity tightens, which currency does the system reach for to close the gap? The answer reveals where the corridor truly runs.

Experiments in non-dollar commodity pricing

In February 2022, in Beijing, a long-term natural gas supply agreement was announced between a Eurasian producer and an East Asian buyer, with settlement denominated in a regional currency rather than the dollar. The buyer was a state-owned utility. The date mattered. Sanctions risk had become concrete. The outcome was immediate: headlines proclaimed a milestone in currency history, while trading desks quietly recalculated liquidity needs. The gas would still flow. The pricing choice changed the plumbing.

The paradox sits in plain sight. If commodities are priced outside the dollar, why does dollar liquidity so often reappear downstream? The datum that frames the question is persistent: according to the International Energy Agency, over 80 per cent of globally traded oil and gas contracts were still referenced to dollar-based benchmarks in 2023. Experiments multiply. Gravity remains.

Non-dollar commodity pricing is not a single project. It is a pattern of trials, adjustments, and retreats. The motivations are visible. Sanctions exposure concentrates minds. Domestic politics reward gestures of autonomy. Central banks seek to reduce reserve vulnerability. Producers and consumers both ask whether the unit of account can be decoupled from the dominant currency without breaking the market.

Show the behaviour and the pattern emerges. A producer agrees to invoice exports in a regional currency. A buyer welcomes reduced dollar dependence. Both sides announce a strategic shift. Behind the announcement, treasurers test whether hedging instruments exist at scale, whether clearing banks will accept collateral in the new unit, and whether price discovery remains credible. The abstraction is sovereignty. The metric is bid–ask spreads in the new currency pair. The implication is often sobering.

The named mechanism is non-dollar invoicing. It means the price, the invoice, or both are expressed in a currency other than the dollar. This can take several forms. Some contracts simply switch the unit of account. Others peg prices to a basket that includes local currencies. Some settle locally while referencing global benchmarks. Each choice alters the balance of risks.

Consider the long-term gas contract introduced earlier. The invoice is denominated in a regional currency. Payments clear through domestic banks. On paper, dollar exposure disappears. In practice, the price formula remains linked to international gas indices that track markets priced in dollars. The exporter hedges revenue volatility using offshore instruments. The importer manages exposure through swaps offered by banks that price liquidity against dollar funding costs. The reconciliation is mechanical. The dollar exits the invoice and re-enters the hedge.

This is not failure. It is friction.

A second, checkable pattern appears in metals and agricultural trade. Where supply chains are regional and buyers and sellers share financial infrastructure, non-dollar pricing can persist. Local benchmarks develop. Volumes grow slowly. Liquidity improves incrementally. The behaviour is patient market-building. The implication is that scale matters more than declaration.

The limitation appears when markets globalise. Once cargoes can be diverted, resold, or arbitraged across regions, participants demand benchmarks recognised everywhere. Those benchmarks tend to be dollar-based because they concentrate liquidity. The counter-example reconciles with the rule. Non-dollar pricing works best where trade is sticky and alternatives are few.

Sanctions risk sharpens this calculus. When access to dollar clearing is uncertain, the value of alternative units rises even if costs increase. The visible decision is to accept wider spreads or less favourable terms in exchange for continuity. The abstraction is resilience. The metric is uninterrupted delivery. The implication is that pricing choices become insurance rather than optimisation.

Domestic political signalling adds another layer. Announcing non-dollar pricing signals autonomy to domestic audiences. It reassures voters and elites that policy is active. The currency becomes a symbol. The risk is conflation. Symbols do not guarantee liquidity. When markets tighten, symbols are tested.

The BIS has observed that during periods of financial stress, FX turnover concentrates further in a small set of currencies, even as bilateral trade agreements proliferate (BIS Triennial Survey, 2022). This is the quiet undertow. Liquidity seeks depth. Depth attracts liquidity.

Thread the motif again. Layering returns.

Layer one is invoicing. Changing the unit of account alters who bears FX risk at the point of sale. Layer two is hedging. Risk migrates to derivatives markets, often still dollar-centric. Layer three is settlement and collateral. Clearing houses and correspondent banks impose their own requirements. Each layer can dilute the original intent.

None of this negates the experiments. Some stick. Regional gas trade priced in a shared currency can endure where pipelines bind partners and alternatives are costly. Agricultural trade within blocs can normalise non-dollar units. Over time, these niches can thicken into corridors. The visible behaviour is repeat usage. The metric is declining reliance on third currencies for settlement. The implication is gradual, uneven change.

The unresolved tension remains practical. How far can non-dollar commodity pricing scale before it collides with global liquidity constraints? Or put differently: when the next shock arrives, which currency will participants scramble to obtain?

That scramble, not the announcement, decides the outcome.

Commodity-backed guarantees and collateral

In March 2004, in Luanda, Angola signed a financing agreement with the Export–Import Bank of China that would become a reference point in modern resource finance. The mechanism was simple and consequential. Future oil shipments were pledged as security for a multi-billion-dollar credit line to rebuild infrastructure after civil war. The outcome was immediate liquidity without recourse to conventional sovereign bond markets. The currency of account was not the dollar alone. The risk, however, was unmistakably real.

That deal still provokes a question worth asking with numbers attached. If a cargo of oil priced at an internationally quoted benchmark can secure financing in an alternative currency, what exactly has been displaced: the dollar, or merely the point at which it appears? The answer shapes how commodity-backed guarantees operate across today's contested corridors.

Commodity-backed collateral arrangements are not new. They recur whenever states or firms possess extractive wealth but lack cheap access to capital. What has changed is their role in currency competition. These structures now sit at the intersection of financing, settlement choice, and geopolitical alignment. They promise insulation from currency pressure while quietly rearranging credit exposure.

Show the behaviour. A producer needs funding. Conventional markets demand high yields. Sanctions risk or rating constraints narrow options. The producer pledges future output—oil, gas, metals—as collateral. A lender agrees to advance funds, sometimes in a regional or bilateral currency. Shipments flow. Debt service is deducted at source. Cash never fully circulates.

Name the structure. This is commodity-backed finance, often executed through prepayment agreements, secured loans, or offtake-backed facilities. The collateral is not cash. It is production yet to be extracted, shipped, and sold. The explainable logic is compelling. Tangible resources reduce credit risk. Payment is embedded in trade. The implication is altered sovereignty over future revenues.

These arrangements shift risk rather than remove it. Price risk remains. Operational risk intensifies. Political risk concentrates. The currency question is postponed, not resolved.

Return to the Angolan example. Oil shipments serviced debt obligations directly. When oil prices rose, repayment accelerated. When prices fell, fiscal space narrowed. The currency denomination mattered less than the benchmark reference. Even when loans were extended in renminbi, price discovery remained anchored to dollar-based oil indices. The hedge lived elsewhere.

A second, checkable pattern appears in metals financing. In the mid-2010s, several resource exporters used copper and iron ore offtake agreements to secure financing from foreign partners, sometimes denominated in non-dollar currencies. The visible behaviour was long-term supply commitments. The metric was loan-to-value ratios tied to commodity prices. The implication was reduced refinancing risk, offset by reduced flexibility.

Commodity-backed collateral works best where production is steady and logistics reliable. It falters when volatility intrudes. A drought, a strike, or a shipping disruption can cascade into financing stress. The abstraction is trust. The visible decision is lender insistence on control rights over storage, transport, or export licences.

This is where currency ambition meets operational reality. Even when financing is extended in an alternative currency, lenders often require fallback provisions. Collateral valuation clauses reference global benchmarks. Margin calls trigger when prices fall. Additional shipments are pledged. The dollar re-enters as a measuring stick.

The counter-example is instructive. Where commodities are regionally traded and priced, collateral can support genuinely local financing. Agricultural produce within tightly integrated blocs sometimes underpins credit in local units. The reconciliation lies in market depth. Where alternative pricing benchmarks exist, currency displacement is credible. Where they do not, it is cosmetic.

Risk concentrates silently. Commodity-backed deals often prioritise debt service over public spending. Revenues bypass treasuries. This insulates lenders but constrains fiscal policy. The abstraction is stability. The metric is earmarked export volumes. The implication is diminished policy discretion.

Thread the motif. Layering again.

First layer: collateralisation. Physical output secures financing. Second layer: currency denomination. Loans may be extended in non-dollar units. Third layer: valuation. Prices remain linked to global benchmarks. Fourth layer: settlement. Clearing and hedging often revert to dollar liquidity. Each layer adds friction.

None of this negates the strategic appeal. For producers facing volatile capital flows, commodity-backed guarantees provide continuity. For lenders seeking yield with security, they offer tangible backing. For governments, they signal autonomy. The tension lies in durability.

The BIS has noted that commodity-backed financing can amplify procyclicality, increasing leverage when prices rise and forcing adjustment when they fall (BIS Quarterly Review, 2021). This matters for currency strategy. A structure that magnifies price cycles can entrench reliance on the deepest liquidity pool when stress hits.

Consider a contemporary scenario. A gas producer agrees to pledge future LNG shipments to secure financing in a partner's currency. The loan funds domestic infrastructure. Payments are netted against deliveries. For two years, the arrangement works smoothly. Then global gas prices spike. Opportunity costs emerge. The producer forgoes spot sales. Domestic critics question the deal. The currency choice fades from view. Economics takes over.

Commodity-backed collateral thus reveals a hard truth. It can shift credit risk across borders and institutions. It cannot abolish the gravitational pull of global pricing and funding norms. The dollar's role is reduced at the margin, not erased.

End with the forward test. When the next commodity downturn arrives, will these structures absorb the shock—or will they accelerate the return to the currency they sought to bypass?

Winners and losers from commodity shifts

In March 2022, in Berlin, the German energy utility Uniper disclosed that the upheaval in gas markets had forced it to post substantial collateral and seek emergency liquidity support from the state. The company was not alone, but it was named, listed, and exposed. The outcome was stark: a firm supplying households and industry became a conduit through which commodity pricing, margin mechanics, and currency-linked funding pressure entered public balance sheets. The drama was often narrated as "energy security". Beneath it lay a simpler fact: when the invoicing and collateral systems tighten, someone must find the money.

Follow the invoice line.

Commodity-linked de-dollarisation strategies promise to change who finds the money, in which currency, and under what conditions. Yet the distributional effects are rarely symmetrical. A shift in invoicing currency can benefit some countries and firms while quietly taxing others through wider spreads, thinner hedging markets, and new dependencies on regional anchors. The question, then, is not whether the dollar's role can be reduced. It is who pays for the reduction.

Start with the two broad archetypes: resource-rich exporters and import-dependent economies. Exporters sell what the world cannot easily do without. Their bargaining position is stronger. They can experiment with invoicing currencies, especially in long-term contracts, because buyers still need the commodity. Import-dependent economies buy what they cannot easily replace. Their bargaining position is weaker. If they push for alternative invoicing currencies without deep hedging and funding support, they can end up absorbing new forms of liquidity risk.

That is the first asymmetry. There is a second. Exporters often accumulate foreign currency inflows and can choose how to deploy them. Importers face outflows and must ensure continuity of payment. One is deciding where to park surpluses. The other is deciding how to avoid a missed shipment. The behaviour is visible in balance sheets: exporters build reserves and sovereign wealth buffers; importers build lines of credit and hedging books. The implication is that exporters can treat currency experiments as portfolio choices, while importers experience them as operational constraints.

Consider how benefits emerge for exporters. When a commodity exporter invoices in a regional currency rather than dollars, it can reduce direct exposure to US monetary policy and, in some cases, reduce sanctions-related frictions in settlement. It may also develop deeper regional financial ties: deposits, local bond holdings, and trade finance in the partner currency. The abstraction is autonomy. The visible behaviour is a shift in treasury holdings and debt issuance currency. The implication is more room to manoeuvre when global dollar liquidity tightens.

A named, checkable example illustrates the exporter's position even without relying on a single contract. Codelco, Chile's state copper producer, sells into a market where prices are heavily influenced by global benchmarks and where settlement and hedging infrastructure is long established. Even when a copper exporter considers regional currency invoicing for certain counterparties, the benchmark reference and global hedge markets often remain dollar-centric. The exporter can, however, choose how much of its receipts to swap, when to hedge, and where to hold liquidity. This flexibility is itself a form of power. It is not that the exporter escapes the dollar's shadow; it is that it can decide how to stand within it.

Now place the importer beside it. Take a large fuel-importing utility or refiner—say, Indian Oil Corporation in New Delhi, which routinely manages sizeable import bills and the associated price and FX risks. If invoicing shifts from dollars to a regional currency, the firm's exposure does not vanish. It changes shape. The firm must ask whether it can obtain the new currency reliably, hedge it cheaply, and post collateral in it during stress. If hedging markets in that currency are thinner than dollar markets, spreads widen. If collateral frameworks still prefer dollars, the firm may need dollars anyway. The implication is that de-dollarisation can become *double-currency management* rather than simplification.

This is where the invoice line matters. The unit printed on the invoice is only the first layer. The second layer is the hedging instrument. The third is the collateral currency demanded by banks or clearing houses. The fourth is the funding currency available in a crisis. A shift that looks decisive at layer one can be neutralised—or made costly—at layers two through four.

A short scenario makes the distributional logic unavoidable. Imagine a metals exporter in southern Africa selling copper cathodes to a regional manufacturing hub under a new arrangement: invoices are denominated in the hub's currency, not dollars. The exporter welcomes this. It can pay for imported machinery from the same hub in that currency. It can also borrow regionally, matching revenues. Its currency mismatch shrinks. Balance-sheet volatility eases.

Across the corridor, a coastal utility in a neighbouring import-dependent state agrees to buy fuel under a similar invoicing shift. Its tariff revenue is in local currency. Its fuel bill is now in the hub's currency. Previously, it managed dollar exposure with relatively standardised hedges and widely available correspondent services. Now it must manage hub-currency exposure with thinner forward markets, wider bid–ask spreads, and less certain access during market stress. When prices spike, banks raise margin requirements. The utility must post collateral quickly. It scrambles for the hub's currency, but liquidity is tight because the anchor central bank has prioritised domestic banks. The utility's credit hinges on access to that anchor's liquidity, not on the dollar. The risk has moved, not disappeared.

Five words, again, hold: money moves through corridors.

The winners in this scenario are not determined solely by who uses which currency. They are determined by who controls liquidity and who bears margin calls. Resource exporters often win because they receive inflows and can choose conversion timing. Importers often lose because they face outflows and must meet deadlines. Banks win when complexity rises because they price liquidity and collateral. Smaller firms often lose because they cannot absorb hedging costs or post margin at short notice.

There is a further layer: the state. A government that exports commodities can tax or capture some of the gains from invoicing shifts, particularly if the exporter is state-owned. It can also influence reserve composition: holding more of a partner currency, building swap lines, and developing regional payment infrastructure. The behaviour is visible in reserve disclosures and bilateral agreements. The implication is strategic diversification.

Import-dependent governments face a different political economy. If utility costs rise due to less liquid hedging markets or higher collateral demands, the pressure returns as subsidies, tariff freezes, or inflation. The balance-sheet risk migrates from the corporate to the public sector. Uniper's 2022 experience shows how quickly this can happen when commodity-linked margin pressures collide with essential services. Currency choice can change who pays, but the bill arrives.

A credible counter-example tempers the exporter–importer dichotomy. Some resource-rich exporters are also import-dependent for refined products, food, or capital goods. Nigeria, for much of the past two decades, has exported crude oil while importing significant volumes of refined fuel. In such cases, changing the invoicing currency on the export side may not deliver net benefit if import bills remain tied to dominant benchmarks and liquidity channels. The reconciliation is balance-sheet realism. Commodity status does not guarantee advantage; the *net* commodity position and the structure of imports matter as much as exports.

Another limitation concerns the benchmark itself. Even when invoices move away from the dollar, many commodity benchmarks remain dollar-quoted. If a contract is denominated in a regional currency but indexed to a dollar benchmark, the currency risk reappears in the adjustment formula. Traders and treasurers hedge the benchmark, and hedging often returns to dollar markets because they are deeper. The implication is that de-dollarisation at the invoice line can coexist with dollar dependence in risk management.

This is why liquidity has the final vote. A currency corridor succeeds when it offers more than symbolism: reliable settlement, deep hedging markets, acceptable collateral, and predictable policy support. Where these are present, importers can benefit as well. They may reduce exposure to dollar funding shocks and align trade finance with regional partners. Where these are absent, importers bear the costs first.

The same applies at the firm level. Large, sophisticated firms can arbitrage corridors. They can hold multi-currency liquidity buffers, negotiate collateral terms, and access offshore hedging markets. Smaller firms cannot. For them, a currency shift can mean higher banking fees, larger working capital needs, and greater exposure to sudden policy changes. The distributional effect is regressive: complexity rewards scale.

Thread the motif once more. Follow the invoice line, and you find the ledger of power: who sets the unit, who supplies the liquidity, who posts the collateral, who absorbs the volatility.

Commodity-linked de-dollarisation strategies therefore produce winners and losers not by nationality alone, but by position in the chain. Upstream producers with pricing power often gain optionality. Downstream essential-service importers often inherit liquidity and collateral risk. Intermediaries—banks, traders, insurers—often gain pricing power when complexity rises. States may gain policy room or inherit fiscal exposure, depending on whether they export surpluses or import necessities.

The forward test is a hard one, and it cannot be answered by communiqués. When the next commodity shock hits—when prices spike, volatility rises, and margins are called—who will be able to source the settlement currency at speed and at tolerable cost? That moment will reveal whether a currency shift has redistributed risk fairly, or merely moved it to the parties least able to carry it.

Chapter 7

CBDCs, Bridges, And Interoperability

In October 2022, in Hong Kong, the Bank for International Settlements released results from Project mBridge, a live pilot that settled cross-border payments between four central banks using wholesale central bank digital currencies. The trades cleared in seconds. There was no correspondent chain, no overnight float, no waiting for New York to wake up. The demonstration was modest in scale and careful in tone, yet the implication was unmistakable: the plumbing could change faster than the politics. Speed was no longer hypothetical.

That moment sharpened a paradox that runs through every discussion of digital money. If payments can move instantly across borders, why does the currency hierarchy remain so stubborn? If settlement is frictionless, why does choice still cluster around a few dominant units? The promise of central bank digital currencies sits precisely in this gap between engineering and power. Technology can redraw the pipes. It does not, by itself, redraw the map.

This chapter begins where optimism often outruns analysis. CBDCs are frequently described as a rupture with the past, a clean break from correspondent banking and legacy rails. In practice, they are better understood as a new layer added to an old structure. They can compress time, automate compliance, and widen access. They do not dissolve monetary sovereignty, eliminate risk, or abolish hierarchy. To see why, one must follow the flow from ledger to ledger, and then from policy to trust.

The fascination with CBDCs is understandable. For central banks, they promise relevance in a digitised financial system where private platforms move faster and speak louder. For governments, they hint at control: visibility over flows, precision in enforcement, resilience against exclusion. For firms, they suggest efficiency: fewer intermediaries, lower costs, predictable settlement. For observers of the dollar system, they raise a tantalising question: could a new technical architecture weaken an old monetary centre?

History cautions against simple answers. Payment technologies have changed before. The telegraph, correspondent banking, SWIFT messaging, real-time gross settlement—all transformed how money moved. None, on their own, dethroned a dominant currency. What they did was alter who bore risk, how quickly stress propagated, and which institutions mattered most at moments of strain. CBDCs should be approached in the same spirit: as accelerants, not replacements.

The first task, then, is to understand what CBDCs actually change in cross-border flows. At their core, central bank digital currencies are liabilities of the central bank, recorded on a digital ledger. They are not cryptocurrencies, and they are not private stablecoins. They can be retail or wholesale, domestic or cross-border. What matters for international use is not the label but the access model. Who can hold them. Who can transact. Who sets the rules.

Consider the familiar correspondent flow. An importer instructs its bank. Messages move across networks. Funds hop between nostro accounts. Settlement is final only after several balance sheets have adjusted, often across time zones. Liquidity is pre-positioned. Compliance checks are layered and slow. In a CBDC-mediated flow, by contrast, value and message can travel together. Settlement can be atomic. Liquidity can be mobilised on demand rather than parked in advance. The visible behaviour is faster finality. The implication is lower intraday risk. Yet the currency used remains the same unless policy decides otherwise.

This distinction matters because much of the rhetoric around CBDCs conflates speed with substitution. Faster dollars are still dollars. A CBDC corridor that settles in a dominant currency may reduce operational frictions while reinforcing monetary centrality. Conversely, a corridor that links two non-dominant currencies may still struggle if users cannot hedge, invest, or store value in those units at scale. Technology widens the aperture. It does not choose the view.

Design choices therefore sit at the heart of cross-border CBDC corridors. There are three broad models, each with different consequences. Shared platforms place multiple central banks on a common ledger, with agreed rules for access and settlement. Linked ledgers connect separate national systems through technical bridges, translating messages and synchronising value. Correspondent-style arrangements retain national ledgers but allow designated institutions to hold and transact foreign CBDCs under defined conditions. Each model answers a different political question about trust.

Imagine two central banks linking their CBDCs for trade invoicing. On a shared platform, both relinquish some autonomy to a common rulebook, gaining efficiency at the cost of discretion. On linked ledgers, they retain sovereignty but must manage interoperability risks and legal mismatches. On correspondent-style links, they preserve familiar hierarchies, with access gated and revocable. The technical diagram in prose is simple: where the ledger sits determines who can pull the plug.

This is where law and policy intrude. Settlement finality across borders is not merely a technical state; it is a legal one. Insolvency regimes, collateral rights, data protection, and sanctions obligations all shape what a CBDC corridor can realistically do. A payment that is instant but reversible under certain conditions is fast yet fragile. A payment that is final but legally ambiguous invites dispute. The credibility of a corridor depends less on code than on clarity.

Programmability sharpens these trade-offs. The idea that rules can be embedded directly into money has attracted both enthusiasm and alarm. In cross-border contexts, programmable features could automate compliance: blocking prohibited destinations, enforcing spending conditions, releasing funds only when goods arrive. The abstraction is control. The visible behaviour is a transaction that either executes or refuses without human intervention. The implication is efficiency with teeth.

Yet programmability cuts both ways. Rules must be written, updated, and governed. Who decides which sanctions lists apply? Which capital controls are enforced? Which exceptions are allowed in emergencies? A corridor that automatically blocks certain flows may reassure regulators while discouraging users who fear arbitrary freezes. A corridor that bypasses controls may attract volume while inviting retaliation. Separating plausible use cases from speculative claims requires attention to incentives, not slogans.

Private platforms complicate the picture further. Stablecoins and fintech rails already offer near-instant cross-border settlement, often with fewer frictions than bank-led systems. They operate under different governance models, with different risk allocation. For a firm choosing between a regulated CBDC bridge and a private token platform, the decision is not ideological. It is practical. Where is liquidity deeper? Where are rules clearer? Where is recourse credible?

Public rails offer safety and legitimacy. Private rails offer speed and adaptability. They may coexist, interconnect, or compete. The likely outcome is not a winner-takes-all scenario but a layered market in which different corridors serve different flows. CBDCs may anchor high-value, regulated transactions, while private platforms handle niches. The currency used in each corridor will reflect trust in the issuer, not the elegance of the code.

Investor confidence provides a final lens. A well-designed CBDC project can signal institutional competence, technological maturity, and policy coherence. A rushed or fragile one can do the opposite. Markets notice outages. They price governance failures. When a new system stumbles, the damage is reputational as much as operational. A currency's standing rests on expectations of reliability under stress. Digital sophistication that fails in crisis erodes trust faster than no innovation at all.

This brings the discussion back to the book's central theme: corridors, not replacements. CBDCs do not usher in a single new order. They multiply pathways. Some will be faster. Some will be more controlled. Some will be more attractive to certain users. The dollar's role may be altered at the margins where new corridors thrive, but it will persist where liquidity, depth, and trust remain unmatched.

The quiet motif threading this chapter is the bridge. Bridges connect shores without erasing them. They channel traffic. They concentrate risk. They can be closed. CBDC interoperability is bridge-building on a global scale. The question is not whether bridges will exist. It is who controls the tolls, who sets the weight limits, and who decides when the gates shut.

The reader arrives here having seen how currency competition plays out through swap lines, clearing hubs, regional blocs, and commodity corridors. CBDCs enter as the most technologically charged development in that landscape, yet they obey the same underlying logic. Monetary power flows to where others are willing to hold liabilities, trust governance, and accept rules in bad times as well as good.

The chapters that follow will move from promise to practice. They will examine how CBDC corridors are being designed, where they intersect with sanctions and controls, how they compete with private rails, and what their early experiments reveal about credibility. The test ahead is not whether money can move faster. It already can. The test is whether faster money changes who sets the terms.

What CBDCs change in cross-border flows

In October 2022, in Hong Kong, the Bank for International Settlements published results from Project mBridge, a live pilot linking the central banks of China, Hong Kong, Thailand, and the United Arab Emirates. Wholesale central bank digital currencies were used to settle cross-border payments in seconds rather than days. Funds moved without passing through a correspondent chain anchored in New York or London. The outcome was modest in volume but precise in implication: settlement speed is now a design choice, not a constraint.

Speed is the visible shock. Power is the quieter question.

Central bank digital currencies are often introduced with a blur of promise and anxiety, as if a single innovation could simultaneously dethrone the dollar, end correspondent banking, and give states unprecedented control over money. Much of this confusion stems from a failure to separate what CBDCs are from what they are not. A CBDC is a liability of a central bank, recorded in digital form, and governed by public law. It is not a cryptocurrency, because it does not float free of the state. It is not a stablecoin, because it does not rely on private reserves or contractual trust. It is not automatically cross-border, because access is a policy decision, not a technical inevitability.

Plumbing changes. Choice endures.

The most tangible change CBDCs offer in cross-border flows is settlement speed. Traditional correspondent banking relies on a sequence of balance-sheet movements across institutions that do not share a common ledger. Messages instruct. Accounts adjust. Liquidity is pre-positioned in nostro accounts, often in multiple jurisdictions, to ensure payments do not stall. Finality arrives only after reconciliation across time zones and compliance layers. This architecture evolved for safety, not speed.

A CBDC-mediated flow compresses these steps. When two parties transact on a shared or interoperable central bank ledger, value and instruction can move together. Settlement can be atomic, meaning it completes fully or not at all. The abstraction is efficiency. The visible behaviour is a payment that settles within seconds rather than days. The implication is reduced settlement risk and lower demand for idle liquidity.

Yet speed alone does not alter the currency used. If a payment settles faster in dollars, it remains a dollar payment. Faster rails can entrench incumbents by making them more convenient. This is the first paradox of

CBDCs: the technology most often invoked as a tool of monetary change can strengthen existing hierarchies if deployed without strategic intent.

Programmability is the second major shift. CBDCs allow conditions to be embedded into payments at the level of the settlement asset itself. Funds can be released only when predefined criteria are met, blocked from certain destinations, or tagged for specific uses. The abstraction is control. The metric is behaviour: a transaction executes automatically or fails without manual intervention. The implication is lower operational cost for compliance and monitoring.

In cross-border settings, this matters because compliance is where friction concentrates. Sanctions screening, capital controls, and reporting obligations slow flows and raise costs. Programmable features could automate these checks, reducing uncertainty for permitted transactions while enforcing prohibitions more precisely. A corridor that instantly blocks restricted destinations while accelerating authorised trade would feel very different from today's blunt instruments.

There is a counter-example that tempers this optimism. Rules must be written and governed. Programmable money does not eliminate discretion; it codifies it. If rules are opaque, frequently changing, or politically contingent, users may treat programmability as a risk rather than a benefit. In that case, firms revert to familiar channels where discretion is exercised by institutions they know. The reconciliation is straightforward: programmability adds value only when governance is predictable.

Direct access is the third axis of change. Some CBDC designs allow non-banks, or foreign institutions, to hold and transact directly in central bank money. This bypasses layers of intermediation that currently shape cross-border flows. The abstraction is inclusion. The visible behaviour is a participant settling without relying on a correspondent bank. The implication is a redistribution of bargaining power within the payment chain.

Consider a traditional correspondent flow. An importer in East Africa instructs its local bank to pay a supplier in Southeast Asia. The local bank sends a message via SWIFT to its correspondent, which debits a nostro account held in dollars. Another correspondent credits the supplier's bank, which credits the supplier. Each step adds cost, delay, and exposure to the policies of intermediaries.

Now contrast a CBDC-mediated flow. The importer's bank holds access to a foreign CBDC corridor. It converts local currency into the settlement currency on-platform and transfers value directly to the supplier's bank on a shared ledger. Compliance checks are embedded. Settlement is final within the same system. The visible change is fewer balance sheets involved. The implication is less dependence on global banks.

This contrast is real, but incomplete. Access is rarely universal. Central banks decide who can hold their digital liabilities, under what conditions, and with what revocation rights. A corridor that grants direct access today can withdraw it tomorrow. The limitation is political risk. The reconciliation lies in recognising that CBDCs shift where discretion sits rather than eliminating it.

Two named examples sharpen this point. Project Jura, launched by the Banque de France and the Swiss National Bank in 2021, tested wholesale CBDCs for cross-border settlement between Paris and Zurich. The pilot showed that technical interoperability was achievable, but also that legal frameworks determined who could participate and how disputes would be resolved. Technology cleared the path. Law set the speed limit.

By contrast, during the Covid-era market stress of March 2020, central bank swap lines, not new technology, stabilised dollar funding markets. The Federal Reserve extended swap lines to selected counterparts, providing dollar liquidity through familiar channels. The abstraction was trust. The metric was usage volumes reported by the Federal Reserve in 2020. The implication was unmistakable: when stress peaks, access to the dominant currency matters more than settlement novelty.

This comparison exposes a credible limitation of CBDCs in cross-border flows. They do not conjure liquidity where none exists. A CBDC corridor denominated in a thinly traded currency cannot supply depth by design alone. Liquidity follows balance sheets, market-making capacity, and investor confidence. Faster settlement does not substitute for these foundations.

A quiet motif runs through these developments: the bridge. CBDC corridors are bridges between monetary jurisdictions. Bridges shorten distance, concentrate traffic, and create new choke points. They are valuable precisely because they can be controlled. This is both their strength and their vulnerability.

CBDCs also clarify a persistent confusion between messaging and settlement. Changing the message does not change the money. A payment can be instructed outside SWIFT and still settle in dollars. Likewise, a CBDC can carry value over a new rail while preserving the same unit of account. The visible behaviour is a modern interface. The implication is continuity beneath novelty.

This nuance matters when assessing claims that CBDCs will automatically advance de-dollarisation. They may facilitate it at the margins by making alternative corridors viable for specific flows. They may also reinforce dollar use by making dollar settlement faster, cheaper, and more resilient. The outcome depends on policy choices layered atop technology.

There is also a distributional aspect. Faster, programmable settlement favours participants who can integrate systems quickly and comply with embedded rules. Smaller banks and firms may struggle with the fixed costs of participation, even as variable costs fall. The abstraction is efficiency. The metric is onboarding time and compliance expenditure. The implication is potential concentration rather than democratisation.

The credible counter-example comes from regional initiatives that deliberately design for inclusion, offering tiered access and shared infrastructure. These can broaden participation if governance supports it. The reconciliation is that inclusion is a policy outcome, not a technical default.

The question then becomes diagnostic. When does a CBDC corridor change behaviour in ways that matter for currency competition? The answer is when it alters three decisions simultaneously: which currency users choose to hold, which risks they bear, and which authorities they trust in a crisis. Absent this alignment, CBDCs remain an efficiency upgrade.

This brings us to the unresolved tension that closes the section. If technology can make any currency move as fast as the dollar, but cannot make any currency as trusted, where does the balance tip? Do users follow speed, or do they follow safety? And when the next shock arrives, which bridge will carry the heaviest load without breaking?

The chapters that follow will test these questions corridor by corridor, design by design, to see where CBDCs merely polish the pipes and where, under specific conditions, they begin to reroute the flow.

Designing cross-border CBDC corridors

In November 2022, in Singapore, the Bank for International Settlements concluded Project Dunbar, a joint experiment with the central banks of Australia, Malaysia, Singapore, and South Africa. Four currencies settled on a shared platform, with payments moving across borders in real time. The result was not a single new currency, nor a unified system, but a set of design choices made visible. Interoperability worked. Governance remained contested.

Architecture decides outcomes.

The way central bank digital currencies connect across borders matters more than whether they exist at all. Cross-border corridors are not neutral pipes. They encode legal authority, risk allocation, and political trust. A corridor's design determines who can enter, how value moves, and what happens when something breaks. In currency competition, these details are decisive.

Three broad models dominate current thinking. Each begins with the same ambition—moving value between sovereign currencies more efficiently—but each answers a different question about control.

The first model is the shared platform. Multiple central banks issue their CBDCs onto a single technical infrastructure, often operated jointly or by a neutral entity. Participants from each jurisdiction transact on the same ledger. Message and value move together. The abstraction is simplicity. The visible behaviour is a payment that settles instantly across currencies without intermediate conversion steps. The implication is concentrated liquidity and reduced reconciliation costs.

Imagine the flow as a single table. On one side sits the payer's CBDC balance. On the other sits the recipient's. The platform debits one and credits the other in a single operation, applying an exchange rate agreed in advance or discovered on-platform. Settlement is final because all parties recognise the same ledger as authoritative.

Project Dunbar illustrated this logic. According to the BIS (2022), participating banks could exchange currencies directly without routing through correspondent accounts. Liquidity pooled. Frictions fell. Yet the limitation surfaced quickly. Who governs the platform? Which law applies if a transaction is disputed? How are access rights revoked? The reconciliation lies in recognising that shared platforms trade operational efficiency for political complexity.

The second model is linked ledgers. Each central bank maintains its own CBDC system, but the systems communicate through agreed interfaces. Messages pass between ledgers. Value moves through coordinated debits and credits. The abstraction is sovereignty. The metric is behaviour: each central bank retains control over its balance sheet while enabling cross-border settlement. The implication is modularity rather than unity.

Picture two tables connected by a bridge. A payment instruction crosses first, carrying identity and compliance data. Once validated, each ledger updates its own balances. Exchange may occur through a designated mechanism—either an automated market maker or a policy-set rate. Finality depends on synchronisation between systems.

This design appeals to central banks wary of ceding authority. It allows different legal regimes to coexist. It also introduces timing risk. If one ledger updates and the other fails, settlement must unwind or rely on guarantees. The credible counter-example is a stress event where synchronisation lags amplify uncertainty. The reconciliation is careful sequencing and robust contingency rules.

The third model resembles correspondent banking in digital form. CBDCs remain domestic. Cross-border payments occur through intermediaries that hold accounts in multiple CBDCs. Messages instruct transfers. Settlement occurs sequentially. The abstraction is familiarity. The visible behaviour mirrors today's flows, albeit faster and cheaper. The implication is continuity rather than disruption.

This model attracts jurisdictions that want incremental change. It minimises legal overhaul. It also preserves hierarchies. Intermediaries regain gatekeeping power. Currency choice remains anchored in existing funding markets. Faster rails do not alter who sets terms.

A scenario brings these distinctions into focus. Consider two neighbouring central banks—one issuing a CBDC for an export-heavy economy, the other for an import-dependent partner. They agree to link their systems to support trade invoicing in local currencies. The technical team favours a shared platform for speed. Legal counsel insists on separate ledgers to preserve jurisdiction. Policymakers worry about capital controls and data access.

The final design links ledgers with capped transaction sizes and predefined hours. Payments settle faster than before, but only during overlapping business days. Exchange rates are fixed daily by the two central banks.

Firms gain predictability. Speculative flows are constrained. The abstraction is balance. The metric is usage volumes in trade transactions rather than capital markets. The implication is a corridor tailored to a specific flow, not a universal replacement.

This illustrates a recurring motif: corridors are built for purposes. Trade settlement, investment flows, remittances, and emergency liquidity each impose different requirements. A design that works for one can fail for another. Treating interoperability as a single problem obscures these trade-offs.

Legal constraints loom large. Settlement finality, insolvency treatment, and data localisation laws shape what is feasible. A technically elegant corridor can be unusable if it conflicts with domestic statutes. Conversely, legal harmonisation can unlock designs previously deemed impractical. The abstraction is trust. The visible behaviour is participation by regulated institutions. The implication is that law, not code, sets the outer boundary.

Two further examples underline this point. In 2021, the Banque de France and the Monetary Authority of Singapore tested linked-ledger settlement under Project Jura. The technology performed. The harder work lay in aligning legal interpretations of finality across jurisdictions. By contrast, China's early cross-border e-CNY pilots prioritised domestic control, limiting foreign access and thereby constraining corridor depth. Different goals produced different architectures.

Risk management differs across models. Shared platforms centralise risk in a single node, demanding robust governance and backstops. Linked ledgers distribute risk but increase coordination complexity. Correspondent-style arrangements disperse operational risk but concentrate market power. The abstraction is safety. The metric is margining rules, access limits, and contingency facilities. The implication is that no design is risk-free; risks are merely relocated.

A quiet image threads through these choices: the lock. Corridors open and close. They channel flows deliberately. Unlike open seas, they are engineered passages. This is why claims that CBDCs will dissolve borders misunderstand their political economy. Borders are re-inscribed in software.

There is also a limitation worth confronting. Interoperability does not guarantee adoption. Firms choose corridors based on cost, reliability, and the ability to hedge exposures. If a CBDC corridor lacks liquidity or introduces new compliance burdens, users revert to established channels. The reconciliation is pragmatic: corridors succeed when they solve a concrete problem better than alternatives.

This brings us to the unresolved question that ends the section. Should central banks design corridors that are broad and open, risking loss of control, or narrow and purpose-built, risking irrelevance? Where is the line between interoperability and entanglement? The answer will not be universal. It will be written corridor by corridor, in the quiet choices that determine who gets a key—and who remains outside the gate.

Programmability, controls, and sanctions

On 26 February 2022, in Brussels, the European Union announced that selected Russian banks would be removed from SWIFT. The decision was political; the effect was technical. Within hours, compliance teams across Europe and beyond rewrote rules, froze queues, and rang counterparties to clarify what would still settle and what would not. Payments that had looked routine on Friday afternoon became unpriceable by Saturday morning. The outcome was not simply delay. It was *uncertainty*, administered through the payment system itself.

Rules travel with money.

That is the promise—and the provocation—of programmable payment rails. Central bank digital currency designs tempt policymakers with a possibility that traditional correspondent banking only approximates: embedding rules directly into the act of transfer, so that compliance is not a separate layer of human judgement and manual screening, but part of settlement logic. If a payment violates a restriction, it fails cleanly. If it complies, it executes quickly. The corridor behaves like a gate rather than a maze.

To understand what this changes, it helps to be precise about what is being programmed. In most modern payment systems, rules are enforced around the edges. A bank screens names against sanctions lists. Another checks purpose codes. A third assesses whether the transaction triggers suspicious-activity reporting. These processes are costly because they are repetitive, discretionary, and uncertain. Programmability offers to move part of that burden into the infrastructure: a transaction either satisfies pre-agreed conditions or it does not.

That sounds neat. It is not simple.

The first major claim is that programmability can accelerate permitted flows by making compliance deterministic. Show the mechanism. A trade payment is initiated with digital identifiers for the buyer, seller, and goods category. The corridor checks these against a rule set. The payment clears immediately if conditions match. Name the gain: time. A corridor that settles in seconds rather than days reduces intraday credit exposure and cuts the need for pre-positioned liquidity. Explain the implication: firms can hold less idle cash, banks can reduce operational buffers, and supply chains become less brittle.

The second major claim is that programmability can sharpen controls by enforcing them at the point of settlement. Show the behaviour. A corridor rejects transfers to entities on a prohibited list, blocks payments routed to certain jurisdictions, or caps transactions above a threshold without additional authorisation. Name the effect: precision. Explain the implication: enforcement becomes harder to circumvent within that corridor, and regulators receive clearer audit trails.

This is where the sanctions question enters, and where rhetoric tends to outrun reality. Sanctions and capital controls are often described as policies applied *to* money. In practice they are policies applied through institutions—banks, messaging systems, settlement networks—that sit between payer and recipient. Programmability shifts the enforcement locus. It does not remove the political choices embedded in enforcement.

A corridor can be designed to comply more strictly with sanctions. It can also be designed with narrower scope, applying only a subset of rules or only those issued by particular authorities. That choice is not technical. It is constitutional.

Consider an imagined corridor that links two central banks for trade invoicing in their local currencies. The aim is straightforward: reduce settlement frictions and dependency on third-currency correspondent chains. The corridor admits only regulated banks and approved corporates. Each participant has a digital identity credential. Payments carry metadata about the transaction type. The rule set does two things. It automatically blocks transfers to certain destinations and entities, using an agreed list. It automatically accelerates permitted flows by pre-clearing known counterparties and reducing manual review.

The visible behaviour is seductive. A compliant payment that once waited two days now settles in seconds. A prohibited payment fails instantly and cannot be "fixed" by creative routing within the system. The abstraction is *resilience*. The metric is settlement time variance and rejection rates. The implication is a corridor that feels both faster and stricter than correspondent banking.

Now the complication. Whose list is used? How often is it updated? Who audits the update process? If the list differs from the one used by global correspondent banks, firms may still face risk when they convert or hedge in other currencies. A transaction that is legal in the corridor can become problematic the moment it touches a wider network. Programmability, in this sense, can create a clean interior that collides with a messy exterior.

The tension sharpens around capital controls. Some states use controls to manage volatility, defend reserves, or prevent flight. In traditional banking, these controls are enforced through licensing, reporting, and bank-level rules. With programmable corridors, enforcement can be automated: limits on outflows, restrictions on certain transaction types, or time-bound permissions. The visible behaviour is a transfer that refuses to execute beyond a cap, regardless of who presses "send". The implication is that policy becomes operationally credible—yet also more intrusive.

This is not merely a civil-liberties question, though it becomes one quickly. It is also a currency question. Credibility in a currency depends partly on the predictability of constraints. If firms fear that rules can change overnight and be enforced instantly by infrastructure, they price that risk into contracts. They reduce exposure. They demand higher returns. Programmability can thus strengthen controls while weakening confidence.

A named counter-example helps reconcile the promise with the peril. In 2013, in Nicosia, Cyprus imposed capital controls during its banking crisis. Payments were restricted. Transfers required approvals. The controls were enforced through banks, paperwork, and delays. The process was cumbersome, but it had one unintended feature: friction created room for discretionary exceptions and gradual easing. A fully programmable system could have enforced limits more consistently—and more abruptly. The reconciliation is that "better enforcement" is not always "better outcomes"; it depends on what the policy is trying to preserve.

A second named example illustrates the sanctions dimension without romanticising it. After February 2022, the U.S. Office of Foreign Assets Control (OFAC) issued multiple updates and guidance notes concerning Russia-related measures, and banks adjusted screening accordingly. The enforcement was not purely automated; it required interpretation, risk appetite decisions, and sometimes over-compliance to avoid penalties. In a programmable corridor, the temptation is to hard-code restrictions to avoid ambiguity. That reduces interpretive burden. It also moves discretion into the rule-maker's hands and makes exceptions harder.

Here the quiet motif returns: the gate. A programmable corridor is not a road; it is a gated passage with rules written on the lock.

The third major claim is that programmability changes how sanctions and controls are experienced by firms. Show the difference. Under correspondent banking, a payment may be delayed for review, then released, sometimes with little explanation. Under a programmable corridor, the payment fails with a defined reason code or executes cleanly. Name the effect: transparency. Explain the implication: firms can adjust processes, reduce operational uncertainty, and design compliance into workflows.

Yet transparency is not guaranteed. A corridor may choose to conceal rule logic to prevent gaming or to protect sensitive policy thresholds. Payments could fail without revealing why, preserving the same opacity as today, merely faster. The reconciliation is that programmability enables transparency, but governance determines whether it is delivered.

Governance, then, becomes the main battleground. Programmability requires rule-making institutions that are trusted to update rules, resolve disputes, and maintain operational integrity. This is where CBDCs intersect with investor confidence, even before any investor holds the currency. A corridor that behaves predictably under stress can enhance confidence. A corridor that freezes unexpectedly or enforces ambiguous rules can corrode it.

The temptation in public debate is to treat programmability as either liberation or surveillance, either a path around sanctions or a tool of tighter enforcement. Both positions are incomplete because both treat the code as the decisive actor. The decisive actor is the sovereign that defines the code, the institutions that run it, and the political coalitions that accept it.

That brings us to the boundary between realistic use cases and speculative claims. It is realistic to expect programmable features to streamline well-defined compliance checks within a controlled membership network, especially for recurring trade payments between known firms. It is realistic to expect automated caps and permissions to support certain capital-control regimes more efficiently. It is also realistic to expect that, in crises, rule sets will expand, and exceptions will be politically contested.

It is speculative to imagine that programmability alone can "bypass" sanctions in any durable way. Sanctions are not merely rules in a payments system; they are a broader web of legal, diplomatic, and commercial constraints. Even if a payment clears within a corridor, the goods, insurance, shipping, and financing around it still face external restrictions. The dollar's gravitational pull reappears through benchmarks, collateral frameworks, and liquidity markets. Code can accelerate settlement. It cannot legislate legitimacy.

There is also a subtle operational risk. Hard-coded rules can produce brittle behaviour. If a sanctions list update is delayed by hours, prohibited payments might clear. If an update is pushed incorrectly, legitimate payments might be blocked at scale. In a manual system, errors are localised and slower. In a programmable system, errors propagate instantly. The abstraction is resilience. The metric is failure domain size during an outage or rule misconfiguration. The implication is that programmability increases the premium on testing, auditability, and fail-safe design.

Trust is the ultimate constraint.

This returns us to currency corridors. A corridor that enforces sanctions and controls in a way aligned with major trading partners may attract mainstream use because it reduces compliance ambiguity. A corridor designed to enforce a divergent rule set may attract niche flows while raising reputational and counterparty risks for participants. In both cases, the corridor's success depends less on whether it can execute a transfer and more on whether firms and banks can integrate it into a wider compliance and funding environment without inheriting new liabilities.

The forward test is therefore not philosophical. It is operational. When a payment corridor can refuse transfers instantly, who owns the error, who compensates losses, and who has standing to appeal? As programmable corridors proliferate, the central question becomes: are we building faster money, or are we building faster gates—and who decides when they close?

Private platforms versus public rails

In May 2022, in New York, TerraUSD collapsed and dragged the crypto markets into a week of forced liquidations and hurried explanations. The mechanism was modern; the outcome was ancient. A promise of stable value met a run, and the run won. Within days, policymakers and payments executives who had treated stablecoins as an interesting side note began speaking about them as a systemic question. The event did not indict all private money. It did clarify what stability costs.

Someone always bears the risk.

The contest between central-bank-led CBDC corridors and private stablecoin or fintech rails is frequently framed as a race between public caution and private innovation. That is a convenient story, and it is incomplete. The real difference lies in governance, transparency, and the distribution of failure. Public rails tend to be slower to launch and harder to change. They also offer clearer legal finality and a more explicit backstop. Private rails tend to move quickly, scale through network effects, and compete on user experience. They also relocate risk into contractual terms, reserve management, operational resilience, and, at times, sheer reputation.

The first claim is practical: private platforms can provide speed and reach before public infrastructure is ready. Show the behaviour. A firm needs to pay an overseas supplier at short notice. The traditional correspondent chain is expensive and slow. A stablecoin-based transfer moves value within minutes, at predictable fees, across time zones. Name the engine: 24/7 settlement on private networks. Explain the implication: payment timing becomes a choice, and working capital buffers can shrink.

Fintech cross-border systems offer a parallel advantage without necessarily using tokens. They connect local payment rails, streamline compliance workflows, and compress settlement cycles. The abstraction is efficiency. The visible metric is reduced end-to-end transfer time and lower error rates. The implication is that, for many users, "alternatives" arrive not as grand geopolitical projects but as pragmatic tools.

The second claim is structural: public rails—CBDCs and their corridors—offer a different kind of assurance. Show the behaviour. When a payment settles in a CBDC, it settles in a liability of the central bank. Settlement finality is grounded in public law. If there is a dispute, courts and regulators have clear standing. Name the anchor: sovereign money. Explain the implication: the risk of issuer default is qualitatively different from the risk of a private platform failing.

This difference becomes visible when stress arrives. A private platform can fail operationally, suffer a run, or face regulatory enforcement. A CBDC system can also fail, but the response framework is typically clearer: central banks can provide liquidity, invoke emergency procedures, and coordinate with domestic regulators. In other words, the state is not merely a rule-maker; it is a balance sheet with a lender-of-last-resort function.

Risk allocation is the heart of the comparison. Stablecoins, even those backed by reserves, ask users to trust that reserves exist, are liquid, and are managed conservatively. They also ask users to trust that redemption will remain available under pressure. After TerraUSD, this distinction became harder to ignore. It was not a reserve-backed stablecoin, but its failure reminded markets that "stable" is not a name; it is a capability.

For reserve-backed stablecoins, the relevant metric is not marketing but the composition and quality of reserves, the transparency of attestations, and the legal structure of redemption rights. Some issuers publish reserve breakdowns and attestations; others provide less. The implication is that users must become credit analysts, whether they wish to or not.

CBDCs shift this burden. Users do not need to assess reserve quality because the "reserve" is the central bank's balance sheet. Yet CBDCs introduce different concerns: privacy, programmability, access conditions, and the possibility of policy-driven restrictions. The abstraction is trust. The behaviour is user preference for a rail perceived as reliable under both market stress and political change. The implication is that neither public nor private rails are purely technical choices; they are governance choices.

A case-style example makes the trade-off concrete. Consider a mid-sized exporter of machine parts based in Milan, selling to buyers in Southeast Asia. The firm faces a familiar problem: invoices are due before shipment, the buyer insists on fast confirmation, and the exporter's bank charges high fees for cross-border transfers. The firm's treasury team compares two options.

Option one is a regulated CBDC bridge offered through the firm's bank, connecting to a pilot corridor between two central banks. Settlement is final and legally clear. Compliance is embedded. Fees are predictable but not low. Access is limited to participating banks, and the corridor operates within defined hours. The key attraction is certainty: once settled, the payment cannot be clawed back by a private issuer's failure or a platform outage that triggers insolvency proceedings.

Option two is a private token platform using a widely traded, reserve-backed stablecoin. Settlement is near-instant, 24/7. Fees are low. The buyer is comfortable with it. The exporter can convert to euros quickly via exchanges or specialised payment providers. The attraction is speed and reach. The risk is layered: the exporter must trust the issuer's reserves, the platform's operational resilience, and the legal enforceability of redemption under stress. It must also consider regulatory exposure and compliance signalling to its own bank and auditors.

The decision turns on questions that do not appear on a marketing slide. How quickly can the exporter convert stablecoin receipts into bank money during volatility? What happens if the stablecoin's issuer faces regulatory action? How are mistaken transfers reversed, if at all? How does the firm document compliance for auditors? The abstraction is friction. The metric is the cost of certainty, not just the fee per transfer.

This case reveals an uncomfortable truth. Private rails often win on convenience until something breaks. Public rails often win on legitimacy when something breaks. The real market is shaped by how frequently "something breaks" and by who bears the loss when it does.

A credible counter-example complicates the neat public-versus-private division. In many jurisdictions, private payment networks operate under heavy regulation and deliver high reliability. Meanwhile, public digital projects can stumble. A CBDC pilot that experiences a high-profile outage can damage confidence, not only in the system but in the competence of the issuer. The reconciliation is simple: public backing is not immunity from operational failure; it is a different framework for repair.

Network effects also matter. Private rails scale quickly because they can onboard users without negotiating treaties or harmonising legal regimes. They can integrate with e-commerce platforms, payroll providers, and remittance channels. Their value rises with each additional participant. Public CBDC corridors, by contrast, require complex coordination between central banks, regulators, and financial institutions. They scale slowly. The implication is that private platforms may dominate certain corridors—especially retail remittances and small-value cross-border commerce—long before public rails mature.

Yet public rails have a strategic lever private rails cannot replicate: they can define what counts as settlement finality within the regulated financial system. They can require banks to treat certain rails as authoritative. They can shape collateral eligibility. They can embed compliance standards that become de facto requirements for large institutions. These are not innovations in code; they are innovations in institutional power.

The motif of the gate returns here. Private rails are often open roads with tolls set by companies. Public rails are gated passages with rules set by states. Roads can be rerouted and replicated. Gates concentrate authority. This is why public and private systems may coexist rather than converge: each offers a different mix of speed, discretion, and legitimacy.

Coexistence, however, does not mean peace. Competition can emerge in the choice of settlement asset. A private stablecoin pegged to a dominant currency can reinforce that currency's reach while bypassing traditional banking rails. A CBDC corridor designed around an alternative currency can attempt to build a parallel path. The outcome depends on liquidity, acceptance, and trust, not on rhetoric.

There is also a subtler competitive dimension: data. Private platforms often monetise transaction data or use it to optimise products. Public rails may prioritise privacy or policy visibility, depending on design. Firms must decide which trade-off they accept. The abstraction is governance. The visible decision is the choice of rail for sensitive payments. The implication is that payments become a strategic information choice as much as a financial one.

The forward test that closes this section is simple to state and hard to answer. When the next stress event arrives—whether a market run, a cyber outage, or a sudden sanctions shift—which rail will firms trust to settle, convert, and prove compliance without trapping them in limbo? The corridor that passes that test will not merely win transactions. It will win legitimacy.

CBDC experiments and investor confidence

In October 2020, in Nassau, the Central Bank of The Bahamas launched the Sand Dollar, the world's first nationwide central bank digital currency. The announcement was calm, procedural, almost modest. There were no sweeping claims about overthrowing global finance. Yet within months, analysts and investors were drawing lessons that extended far beyond a small island economy. The question was not whether the Sand Dollar would transform cross-border payments. It was whether the project signalled institutional competence. Markets noticed.

Confidence is rarely built by spectacle.

The connection between CBDC experiments and investor confidence is often misunderstood. Many observers assume that launching a digital currency automatically makes a country's money look modern and attractive. The reality is harsher. CBDCs act less like promotional campaigns and more like stress tests. They expose how a monetary authority designs systems, manages risk, communicates failure, and balances innovation with restraint. Investors read these signals carefully, even when they say little in public.

The first claim is subtle but decisive: CBDC projects are judged as proxies for institutional quality. Show the behaviour. When a central bank announces a pilot, bond analysts scrutinise not just the technology but the governance documents, legal frameworks, and contingency plans. Name the signal: operational credibility. Explain the implication: a well-run experiment can reinforce confidence in a currency's stewardship, while a poorly executed one can raise doubts that spill into funding costs and risk premia.

This effect does not depend on scale. The Bahamas' Sand Dollar mattered not because of transaction volume but because it demonstrated a cautious rollout, clear communication, and an emphasis on financial inclusion rather than disruption. The abstraction is trust. The visible behaviour is investor tolerance for experimentation without demanding immediate returns. The implication is that modesty can be an asset.

Contrast this with a different pattern. When a CBDC pilot suffers a public technical outage, markets react less to the outage itself than to the response. In several early CBDC trials globally, temporary system unavailability triggered sharp commentary in financial media. The key variable was not downtime measured in minutes or hours, but how quickly authorities explained the cause, ring-fenced the issue, and reassured participants. Silence costs more than failure.

Technology outages are not new. Payment systems fail. Markets understand this. What they watch is governance under pressure. A central bank that treats an outage as a learning event, publishes findings, and adjusts timelines sends a different signal from one that deflects blame or downplays risk. The motif of plumbing returns here. Investors care less about whether pipes exist than about whether the engineer understands them.

The second claim follows: rushed CBDC experiments can damage credibility more than they enhance it. Show the behaviour. A government announces an aggressive timeline for a retail CBDC, framing it as proof of technological leadership. Development compresses. Testing narrows. When glitches appear, officials insist they are minor. Name the error: overpromising. Explain the implication: markets begin to question whether the same impatience applies to fiscal discipline, regulatory oversight, or crisis management.

This dynamic is visible in how investors talk privately about digital projects. They rarely ask whether a CBDC uses distributed ledger technology or centralised databases. They ask whether the legal basis is clear, whether commercial banks are integrated sensibly, and whether exit ramps exist if a design choice fails. The abstraction is sophistication. The metric is institutional patience.

A concrete example clarifies the stakes. Imagine a mid-sized emerging-market economy launching a wholesale CBDC for interbank settlement in 2024. The system works smoothly in early trials. Encouraged, policymakers announce plans to expand access rapidly to cross-border trade invoicing. In mid-2025, during a period of market volatility, the system experiences a multi-hour outage due to a software update conflict. Settlement is delayed. Headlines follow.

Bond yields move slightly wider. Not dramatically. But analysts' notes shift tone. They begin to include questions about operational resilience and contingency planning. The currency does not collapse. Yet a premium appears, thin but persistent. The outage did not cause a crisis. It nudged perceptions.

This is how confidence erodes. Quietly.

A credible counter-example tempers the argument. Some central banks deliberately run public pilots precisely to surface problems early, accepting short-term reputational risk to avoid long-term systemic failure. When communicated clearly, this strategy can strengthen credibility. The reconciliation lies in intent and transparency. Experiments framed as learning exercises invite patience. Experiments framed as finished products invite judgement.

The third claim links CBDCs back to broader currency competition. Investors do not treat CBDCs as isolated projects. They integrate them into an existing narrative about a currency's role. Show the behaviour. A reserve manager considering diversification looks at settlement infrastructure, legal predictability, and crisis tools. A CBDC that improves settlement speed without altering capital controls may be seen as incremental. One that introduces uncertainty about access or convertibility raises flags.

The abstraction is reliability. The visible decision is whether investors increase holdings, maintain exposure, or hedge more aggressively. The implication is that CBDCs can influence portfolio flows indirectly, through perception rather than functionality.

Importantly, technology alone cannot compensate for weak fundamentals. A country with volatile inflation, opaque governance, or unpredictable regulation does not become investable by launching a sleek digital currency. In such cases, CBDCs risk being read as distraction. The market response is indifference at best, scepticism at worst.

Conversely, for jurisdictions with strong institutions, CBDCs can reinforce an existing reputation for competence. They signal that the monetary authority is thinking ahead about settlement resilience, cyber risk, and cross-border integration. The effect is cumulative. Each well-managed step adds to a stock of credibility that pays dividends in times of stress.

This brings us to investor memory. Markets remember failures longer than successes. A CBDC outage, even if minor, can linger in analyst notes for years, resurfacing whenever volatility rises. The implication is that central banks face an asymmetry: upside from success is gradual; downside from failure is abrupt.

The motif of the gate reappears. CBDCs promise new gates to settlement. Investors ask who controls them, how they open under stress, and whether they close unexpectedly. These are not technical questions. They are political and legal ones, disguised in code.

The unresolved tension that closes this section is not about whether CBDCs will succeed. Many will. It is about sequencing. Should central banks prioritise visible experimentation to signal modernity, or quiet robustness to signal reliability? The next cycle of market stress will answer that question more clearly than any pilot report.

Chapter 8

Capital Controls, Sanctions, And Workarounds

On a quiet Sunday evening in August 1998, as markets in New York prepared to open, officials in Moscow took a decision that would ricochet far beyond Russia's borders. The government announced a moratorium on certain foreign debt payments and imposed emergency controls on capital outflows. Within days, rouble trading fractured, foreign investors were trapped, and global hedge funds scrambled to reprice risk they had assumed was liquid. The episode is remembered as a sovereign default. It was also something else: a demonstration that money does not simply move because it exists, but because states allow it to.

Capital mobility is not a law of nature. It is a permission.

This chapter sits at the point where financial plumbing meets political power. Up to now, the book has traced how currencies circulate through swap lines, clearing hubs, regional blocs, commodities, and digital rails. Each of those systems assumes a basic condition: that value is allowed to pass. Capital controls and sanctions withdraw that permission, selectively and sometimes suddenly. What follows is not a collapse into chaos, but a re-routing of flows that reveals the hidden architecture of the system.

The first tension to grasp is motive. Capital controls are often described as desperate measures, the tools of weak states clinging to dwindling reserves. That caricature misses their persistence and variety. Countries with very different economic models deploy controls to manage volatility, conserve foreign exchange, or shield domestic politics from global shocks. When a government caps residents' ability to invest abroad during a currency crisis, it is not merely blocking exits. It is redesigning corridors, forcing transactions to queue, detour, or remain domestic. The visible behaviour is a central bank rationing FX access. The deeper signal is about priorities: stability over openness, control over speed.

Sanctions operate on a related but sharper axis. Where capital controls are usually inward-looking, sanctions are outward-facing instruments of coercion. They work by exploiting chokepoints in systems that were built for efficiency, not resilience against exclusion. Blocking measures, asset freezes, and restrictions on correspondent banking do not destroy money. They immobilise it. A bank cut from major networks does not lose its balance sheet overnight; it loses the ability to make that balance sheet usable. The scramble that follows—searching for alternative correspondents, new currencies, or indirect routes—exposes how concentrated global finance has become.

The paradox is striking. The more centralised and efficient the plumbing, the more powerful the switch.

This chapter does not dwell on the morality of sanctions or the wisdom of capital controls. Those debates are real, but they are not the task here. The aim is to understand mechanics and consequences. How do controls reshape incentives for firms and households? How do sanctions weaponise technical features that once seemed neutral? And why do so many highly publicised workarounds remain marginal in scale?

Consider the sanctioned firm that shifts trade invoicing into a regional currency hub. On paper, the move looks decisive: fewer dollars, less exposure to Western banks, a sense of regained autonomy. In practice, costs rise. Liquidity thins. Counterparties demand wider margins. Compliance scrutiny intensifies. The firm gains opacity but loses efficiency. The trade-off is constant and measurable. Reduced visibility is purchased with higher friction.

This is the pattern that repeats throughout the chapter. Workarounds exist. They are often ingenious. Yet they operate under constraints that are legal, reputational, and operational. Banks do not merely ask whether a route is possible; they ask whether it is defensible when questioned by regulators, auditors, and shareholders. A complex chain that survives one transaction may not survive a compliance crackdown. When that happens, traders retreat, not because the route failed technically, but because the risk calculus shifted.

The chapter also draws a careful boundary. Not every attempt to build resilience is an act of evasion. Firms and states can diversify correspondents, currencies, and settlement paths while remaining within the law. Maintaining multiple banking relationships across jurisdictions, spreading liquidity across currencies, and investing in transparency are not loopholes. They are prudent responses to a system where access can be withdrawn. The distinction matters, because it separates durability from defiance.

Throughout, a quiet motif runs beneath the analysis: the gatekeeper. Capital controls close gates from the inside. Sanctions lock them from the outside. Workarounds search for side entrances. Yet every gate has an owner, and ownership carries consequences. Understanding who controls which gate, under what conditions, is essential to reading the modern financial map.

The relevance of this chapter is not confined to sanctioned states or crisis economies. As financial corridors fragment and multiply, the risk of partial exclusion rises for everyone. Firms operating entirely within the law still face indirect exposure when counterparties are constrained, currencies are rationed, or messaging channels are restricted. The question becomes less about whether money can move, and more about how many permissions it requires.

By the end of this chapter, the reader will not emerge with a catalogue of tricks or tactics. That would be both irresponsible and misleading. Instead, the payoff is diagnostic. An ability to look at a payment corridor, a sanctions announcement, or a new control regime and ask the right questions. Where are the chokepoints? Who bears the cost of rerouting? Which solutions scale, and which remain performative?

The global system is not breaking. It is being edited, clause by clause. Capital controls and sanctions are the red lines in that text, and the workarounds are the footnotes. The pages that follow show how to read them.

Types of capital controls and motives

In September 1998, in Kuala Lumpur, Bank Negara Malaysia imposed sweeping capital controls: the ringgit was pegged, offshore trading was curtailed, and rules on cross-border money transfers were tightened. The move stunned investors who had assumed Asia's crisis would be met with higher interest rates and austerity alone. The immediate outcome was not a return to calm, but a sharp redraw of the country's financial map. Certain exits closed. Certain queues lengthened. The currency corridor was redesigned in public.

Controls behave like valves.

A capital account is often described as "open" or "closed" as if it were a door. In practice it is a set of valves, calibrated and re-calibrated to manage pressure. States rarely reach for one single lever. They choose among several families of controls—on inflows, on outflows, and on access to foreign exchange—because each targets a different problem and creates a different set of side-effects. The motives are as old as statecraft: defend reserves, limit contagion, buy time, signal resolve, and sometimes, blunt domestic political risk by shifting the costs of adjustment.

Start with inflow controls, the least emotionally charged and often the most technocratic. When capital floods into a country—hot money chasing yield, property booms fuelled by foreign credit, or banks borrowing cheaply abroad—policymakers worry about two metrics: the growth rate of domestic credit and the maturity mismatch between short-term foreign liabilities and long-term domestic assets. The visible behaviour is a bank funding a multi-year mortgage book with three-month foreign borrowing. The implication is fragility: when global conditions tighten, the funding disappears before the assets can be sold or refinanced.

Inflow controls attempt to slow or reshape these flows. They can take the form of taxes on short-term foreign borrowing, minimum holding periods for certain portfolio investments, or tighter rules on banks' open FX positions. The abstraction is stability. The behaviour is specific: discouraging short-tenor liabilities, tilting inflows towards longer-term investment, and dampening the credit impulse. The implication is not the elimination of foreign capital but a change in its composition, designed to reduce the probability that a funding boom becomes a balance-sheet crisis.

There is an important limitation here. Inflow controls can be blunt and leaky. If investors can repackage exposure through derivatives or intermediaries, the intended constraint is evaded without any conspiratorial plotting, simply by the normal ingenuity of markets. The reconciliation is to treat inflow controls as a complement to prudential regulation rather than a substitute for it. The International Monetary Fund's "Institutional View" on capital flow management measures (IMF, 2012) captures this stance: controls may be appropriate under certain conditions, but their usefulness depends on context and design.

Outflow controls are the controls that trigger headlines, because they touch the nerve of ownership. They are imposed when a country faces a run—on its banks, its currency, or its sovereign funding—where the central question becomes: how long can reserves cover the demand to leave? The visible metric is reserve loss, often measured daily by the central bank's dealing room. The implication is stark. If outflows overwhelm reserves, the currency can fall violently, banks can fail, and the state can lose the ability to import essentials.

Outflow controls can target residents, non-residents, or both. They may cap the amount individuals can convert and remit; restrict corporations from prepaying foreign debts; require approvals for large transfers; or impose time limits on repatriating proceeds from asset sales. They can also be structured as "temporary" measures that linger for years, because removing them is politically harder than imposing them. Once a valve is tightened, beneficiaries adjust to the new regime, and they do not always welcome its reversal.

A vivid, checkable example is Greece in 2015. In June 2015, in Athens, Greek authorities introduced capital controls amid a banking crisis and acute uncertainty about euro membership. Banks closed temporarily, withdrawal limits were imposed, and cross-border transfers faced stringent restrictions. The immediate behavioural change was visible in everyday life—queues at ATMs—and in corporate treasury offices where import payments became exercises in negotiation. The broader implication was corridor redesign: firms that had relied on routine cross-border banking were forced into rationed channels, prioritised by the state.

The third family of controls is foreign exchange access controls, which can exist even when inflows and outflows are nominally permitted. These are rationing mechanisms. Rather than forbidding transfers outright, the state controls who can buy foreign currency, for what purposes, and at what rates. The visible behaviour is a central bank allocating dollars to importers of fuel or medicine while denying access for luxury goods or capital flight. The implication is a hierarchy of payments: some corridors become privileged, others become slow or impossible.

FX access controls are often accompanied by multiple exchange rates—official, preferential, and market-based—each tied to a category of transaction. This is not merely an economic device; it is a political one, because it allocates scarce foreign currency through administrative decision. The risk is corruption and misallocation. The perceived unfairness can be as destabilising as the financial stress that triggered the policy. Controls can protect reserves while eroding legitimacy.

Why do states choose among these valves? Motive is usually a mix of three pressures: volatility, reserves, and politics.

Volatility is the pressure of markets moving faster than domestic institutions can absorb. In a world where global rates shift and risk appetite turns quickly, even well-run economies can face destabilising surges of inflows or outflows. Controls offer a way to slow the tempo. The visible metric is reduced exchange-rate overshooting or moderated credit growth. The implication is time—time to adjust policy, recapitalise banks, or negotiate external support.

Reserves are the hard constraint. A country that invoices trade in foreign currency and services external debt in dollars or euros must keep sufficient liquid assets to meet those obligations. When confidence wavers, reserves are tested. Controls become a way to conserve them by prioritising essential outflows and limiting discretionary ones. The corridor becomes narrow by design. The implication is that currency choice and reserve adequacy cannot be separated from the politics of controls: if liabilities are dollarised, the state's tolerance for outflows shrinks.

Politics is the least discussed motive and often the most decisive. Controls distribute pain. They can trap domestic savers, protect local banks, and shift costs onto foreign investors or vice versa. They can also serve as signals of sovereignty, demonstrating that the state will not allow markets to dictate domestic priorities. That signal may reassure a domestic audience even as it alarms foreign investors. The abstraction is autonomy. The visible behaviour is policy enacted despite expected market backlash. The implication is that capital controls are as much about legitimacy as liquidity.

A scenario makes this concrete in the way corridors are actually built. Picture a mid-sized country facing a sharp currency depreciation after a rise in global interest rates. The central bank sees reserves falling and corporate borrowers struggling to roll over foreign debt. Rather than announcing a dramatic closure of the capital account, the state introduces a cap on residents' foreign investments—tightening limits on how much domestic pension funds and insurers can allocate abroad, and requiring approvals for large portfolio outflows. The policy is presented as a temporary stabilisation measure. The visible behaviour is institutional investors redirecting flows into domestic bonds. The implication is a manufactured buyer base for government funding, at the cost of reduced diversification for savers.

This is corridor design by constraint. Outbound investment corridors narrow. Domestic funding corridors widen. The state reduces immediate FX demand and stabilises the exchange rate. Yet the policy also changes expectations. Investors begin to price a "convertibility risk" premium: the possibility that future outflows will be restricted again. Even if the cap is lifted later, the memory remains.

Here a counter-example matters, because it prevents a lazy conclusion that controls always repel capital. Malaysia's 1998 controls are instructive precisely because the debate over them remains alive. Some analyses argue that the controls allowed Malaysia to avoid deeper recession and stabilise the financial system; others argue they imposed longer-term costs and were facilitated by Malaysia's specific institutional and political conditions. The limitation is clear: the same policy can have different outcomes depending on credibility, administrative capacity, and external conditions. The reconciliation is to treat controls not as a universal recipe but as contingent instruments whose effectiveness depends on implementation and timing.

This is where the corridor lens sharpens the analysis. Capital controls do not simply "stop" money; they redirect it. Each type of control creates incentives for new pathways, often within the law: trade credits structured differently, invoices timed to fit approval windows, liquidity held in alternative currencies, supply chains reconfigured to reduce the need for foreign exchange. The behaviour is adaptation. The implication is that controls reshape economic geography, not just financial flows.

The quiet motif of the valve returns because it captures the essential point: controls manage pressure, and pressure does not vanish. It moves. Tighten one valve and another strains. Restrict outflows and you may see greater demand for imported goods as a store of value. Restrict FX access and you may deepen a parallel market. Tax short-term inflows and you may push borrowing into less regulated channels. These are not arguments against controls. They are reminders that controls change the system they act upon.

For readers concerned with currency corridors, the most practical consequence is this: capital controls define which corridors can scale. A region may build a clearing hub, a swap line network, or a CBDC bridge, yet if residents cannot legally hold or move the relevant currency, the corridor remains a technical possibility rather than an economic reality. The most elegant infrastructure cannot outrun policy.

The forward test, then, is not whether a country "has controls". It is whether its controls are predictable, targeted, and governable under stress. When volatility rises and reserves begin to fall, does the state tighten valves in ways that preserve essential corridors while keeping the rules intelligible? Or does it improvise—changing limits, redefining categories, and turning routine payments into political favours? The answer to that question shapes not only a crisis outcome but also the long-lasting impact on investor confidence that follows.

How sanctions weaponise financial plumbing

On 15 March 2012, in Brussels, the Council of the European Union adopted Council Regulation (EU) No 267/2012, tightening sanctions on Iran and—crucially—setting in motion constraints that would soon reach into banking channels. Days later, SWIFT, headquartered in La Hulpe, Belgium, announced it would disconnect designated Iranian banks. The result was not a theoretical reprimand. It was a practical amputation. Banks that had been able to send standardised payment messages into the global system found their lines severed, and the cost of doing routine trade rose overnight.

A message can be a choke point.

Sanctions do not function primarily by banning goods in a world of smugglers and inventive traders. They function by exploiting the modern economy's dependence on financial intermediaries. A shipment can cross borders quietly; a payment cannot easily do the same at scale without leaving traces, touching regulated institutions, and relying on shared infrastructure. That dependency is not an accident. It is the product of decades spent building a system that prizes standardisation, compliance, and risk management. Sanctions transform those virtues into levers.

The first claim is that sanctions succeed when they identify and control bottlenecks that cannot be bypassed cheaply. Show the mechanism. A bank needs correspondent accounts to settle in major currencies. It needs access to messaging networks to coordinate those settlements. It needs counterparties willing to accept its payment instructions and to clear them through regulated rails. Name the bottleneck: correspondent banking access. Explain the implication: remove or chill that access and a bank's balance sheet becomes less valuable, because it cannot be converted into usable money across borders.

This is why sanctions language often sounds almost bureaucratic. "Blocking measures." "Asset freezes." "Prohibitions on making funds available." The terms are legal scaffolding for an operational outcome: immobilisation. A blocked person or entity is not merely forbidden from transacting; banks are forbidden from processing their transactions, and anyone who touches their funds may face penalties. The visible behaviour is a compliance department stopping a payment, not because the bank dislikes the customer, but because the bank fears being cut off from the wider system.

Asset freezes are particularly potent because they weaponise custody. If assets are held or cleared through institutions within sanctioning jurisdictions, they can be frozen with a legal order. That can include bank deposits, securities, and receivables. The abstraction is coercion. The behaviour is specific: a custodian marks assets as blocked; a clearing house refuses delivery; a bank refuses to move funds. The implication is that ownership rights become conditional on geopolitical alignment.

Blocking measures go further, especially in the United States' framework administered by the Office of Foreign Assets Control (OFAC). When OFAC designates an entity under certain programmes, U.S. persons must block its property and interests in property, and non-U.S. banks may face secondary sanctions risk if they transact with it in ways that touch U.S. jurisdiction. Even when a bank is not American, it may still handle dollars, clear through U.S.-linked networks, or maintain relationships with U.S. institutions. This is how sanctions extend outward: not through omnipresence, but through dependency.

The second claim is that sanctions weaponise not only settlement, but messaging and compliance standards. Here the nuance matters. SWIFT is a messaging system, not a settlement asset. Yet cutting banks from SWIFT has outsized effects because it removes a shared language of payment instructions. A bank could, in theory, message through other means. In practice, alternative messaging channels lack the same ubiquity, integration, and trust. The visible behaviour is delays, manual processing, error rates, and heightened scrutiny. The implication is that even if settlement remains technically possible, it becomes operationally expensive and reputationally risky.

The March 2012 Iran example shows both dimensions. Disconnection limited the ability of Iranian banks to send standardised instructions and receive confirmations. The immediate operational pain translated into higher costs for trade and reduced willingness of foreign banks to engage, even where transactions were not strictly prohibited. The sanction lever was not only a legal ban; it was the creation of uncertainty that made counterparties retreat.

A second named, checkable example deepens the picture. On 26 February 2022, in Brussels, the European Union announced measures affecting selected Russian banks' access to SWIFT, followed by further restrictions.

The shock was not merely that messages would not be sent; it was the recognition that financial connectivity could be withdrawn rapidly and at scale. Many firms and banks, even those not directly targeted, began reviewing corridor exposure: where do our payments clear, what currencies do we rely on, which counterparties sit in vulnerable nodes? The abstraction is contagion. The metric is widened risk spreads and tightened correspondent limits. The implication is that sanctions operate not only through direct prohibition but through the defensive reactions they trigger.

To see how this works in a corridor-by-corridor way, consider a scenario that is common enough to be credible without relying on operational detail. A mid-sized bank in a targeted country—call it Meridian Bank—has long maintained correspondent relationships with two international banks to clear dollars and euros. Meridian's corporate clients import machinery, pay for insurance, and settle commodity invoices. The bank also serves expatriate remittance flows. Then Meridian is designated under a sanctions programme, or it becomes sufficiently risky that correspondents pre-emptively reduce exposure.

The first week is confusion. Payments are returned. Nostro balances become trapped in "pending" status as compliance teams on the other side escalate queries. Trade finance lines are not renewed. Meridian's treasury desk watches intraday liquidity tighten and begins to ration outgoing transfers. The bank does not collapse immediately. It becomes slower, less predictable, and more expensive to use.

The second week is adaptation. Meridian searches for alternatives. It approaches smaller regional banks, perhaps in jurisdictions less exposed to the sanctioning coalition, to act as intermediaries. It explores settlement in alternative currencies where correspondent access may be less constrained. It encourages clients to invoice in those currencies where possible. It seeks to join regional messaging systems or clearing arrangements. Each step is a redesign of corridors.

Now the constraint appears. Alternatives exist, but they are not free. Regional correspondents often have lower capacity, higher fees, and stricter limits. Liquidity in alternative currencies may be thin, with wider spreads. Counterparties may demand prepayment or collateral to compensate for uncertainty. The abstraction is resilience. The behaviour is measurable: increased transaction costs, longer settlement times, and reduced credit availability. The implication is that sanctions can degrade an economy's financial efficiency even without total isolation.

This is why sanctioned or sanction-vulnerable states invest in new corridors. They are not merely seeking symbolism. They are seeking redundancy. A state that can route trade settlement through multiple channels reduces the risk that a single switch can immobilise its economy. This is the core logic behind building regional clearing hubs, developing alternative messaging systems, negotiating swap lines, and experimenting with digital settlement paths. Not all of these efforts succeed, and many remain limited in scale. But the incentive is durable.

A credible limitation must be faced plainly: sanctions are not omnipotent, and their effectiveness varies. Some targeted economies adjust by rerouting trade, changing invoicing patterns, and building domestic substitutes. Some sanctions regimes create humanitarian carve-outs and licensing pathways that keep essential goods moving. Some industries—especially those tied to physical commodities—find ways to continue operating, albeit at higher cost. The reconciliation is that sanctions rarely produce a clean stop; they produce a tax, a friction, and a shift in bargaining power.

There is also a second limitation: sanctions can create incentives for financial innovation that later spreads beyond the targeted state. When banks and firms build new compliance tools, diversify currencies, or create alternative settlement arrangements, some of those practices become attractive even for non-sanctioned actors seeking redundancy. The implication is that sanctions can accelerate the fragmentation described in earlier chapters, not because they destroy the dollar's role, but because they remind everyone that corridors can close.

The quiet motif of plumbing is worth returning to because it carries the right kind of humility. Plumbing is not glamorous. It is rarely noticed when it works. When it fails, nothing else matters. Sanctions are powerful because they turn the unnoticed into the unavoidable. They make the pipes visible by threatening to cut them.

The forward test, then, is not whether a targeted country can build an alternative corridor in principle. It is whether that corridor can handle volume under stress while remaining credible to counterparties who fear secondary exposure, reputational risk, and sudden rule changes. When a bank like Meridian loses its usual connections, does the alternative corridor restore *trust*—or merely provide movement at a price that only a few can afford?

Typical sanctions-avoidance strategies

In December 1996, at United Nations headquarters in New York, the Security Council approved Resolution 986, establishing the Oil-for-Food Programme for Iraq. The mechanism was austere by design. Iraq could sell limited quantities of oil under UN supervision and use the proceeds, held in escrow, to purchase humanitarian goods. It was not an exercise in financial ingenuity so much as an admission of constraint. Normal payment routes were closed. Trade, if it was to continue at all, had to be reimagined around the restrictions.

Sanctions do not eliminate exchange. They reshape it.

That historical moment matters because it captures a pattern that recurs whenever states, firms, or banks face binding financial constraints. When conventional corridors close, actors search for substitutes that preserve some combination of value transfer, discretion, and continuity. The resulting strategies are rarely elegant. They are compromises, assembled under pressure, and marked by higher costs and lower convenience. Understanding them requires resisting two temptations: to romanticise ingenuity, or to assume that anything technically possible will scale.

The first claim is that most sanctions-avoidance strategies work by *rerouting*, not by disappearing. Show the behaviour. A firm that once paid suppliers directly through a major correspondent now routes payments via an intermediary jurisdiction with looser exposure or different currency preferences. Name the strategy: third-country intermediation. Explain the logic. By inserting an additional node—often a trading company, bank, or clearing hub in a neutral or less-aligned country—the sanctioned party reduces direct contact with restricted networks. The implication is visible in the balance sheet: more counterparties, more fees, more points of failure.

Rerouting is attractive because it builds on existing trade geography. Goods already move through hubs; finance can follow. Yet it is not invisible. Each additional leg increases documentation, compliance scrutiny, and settlement time. Banks in intermediary jurisdictions respond by tightening limits, shortening tenors, and demanding higher margins. The abstraction is *friction*. The metric is measurable: wider spreads, delayed settlement, and constrained volumes.

A second common response is the use of *alternative currencies*. This is not a declaration of monetary revolution. It is a practical calculation. If access to dollar or euro clearing becomes unreliable, firms explore settlement in currencies where correspondent access remains open or politically less sensitive. The visible behaviour is a change in invoicing terms and treasury operations. The named strategy is currency substitution within corridors.

Consider a plausible, high-level scenario consistent with public reporting patterns. A manufacturing firm in a sanctioned economy—call it Atlas Components—has long imported machinery from neighbouring countries. After restrictions tighten, its bank struggles to clear payments in major reserve currencies. In mid-2023, Atlas begins settling invoices through a regional clearing hub that handles trade in a neighbouring currency. The hub offers multilateral netting and local settlement. Costs rise. Liquidity is thinner. But payments move.

The implication is not freedom from oversight. It is a trade-off. Alternative currencies often lack deep hedging markets. Price volatility becomes a treasury problem. Counterparties may demand shorter payment cycles or advance deposits. The corridor works, but it demands operational adaptation. The abstraction of *autonomy* resolves into the behaviour of hiring more treasury staff and accepting more FX risk.

A third category sits further from formal finance: *informal value transfer*. Anthropologists and economists have long documented systems that move value without moving money in the conventional sense—netting obligations within communities, offsetting debts across traders, or using trusted intermediaries who settle periodically. These systems thrive where formal banking is absent or distrusted.

Under sanctions pressure, their appeal grows. The principle is straightforward. Instead of moving funds across borders, participants adjust balances within a network. A payment becomes a book entry. The implication is reduced visibility to formal regulators but increased reliance on trust and reputation. The behaviour is specific: fewer bank transfers, more reliance on counterpart relationships, and periodic reconciliation through goods or services.

Here the limitation is severe. Informal systems do not scale easily. They depend on dense networks, repeated interactions, and social enforcement. They struggle with large, complex trades and with counterparties who lack long-standing relationships. When volumes grow, disputes multiply. The abstraction of *trust* meets the reality of enforcement costs.

Barter-like arrangements sit adjacent to this space. They replace money with goods, services, or future commitments. The Oil-for-Food Programme was a state-managed example; commercial variants are less formal. A producer delivers commodities today in exchange for equipment, infrastructure, or services tomorrow. The named strategy is countertrade.

The advantage is clear. By reducing reliance on financial settlement, countertrade bypasses some chokepoints. The cost is equally clear. Valuation becomes contentious. Timing mismatches create credit risk. Liquidity is sacrificed. The implication is that countertrade is most viable for standardised goods with predictable demand, and least viable for complex, customised transactions.

These strategies share a quiet motif: *detours*. None of them removes the need to account for value. They merely change the route. Each detour imposes a toll, whether in fees, risk, or opacity. That toll explains why many schemes that attract headlines remain marginal in aggregate data.

A second named, checkable example illustrates this constraint. Following the re-imposition of U.S. sanctions on Iran in November 2018, European policymakers attempted to preserve limited trade through a special-purpose vehicle, INSTEX, based in Paris. The mechanism aimed to net payments for humanitarian goods without cross-border fund transfers. The intent was legal continuity. The outcome was modest. Volumes remained small. Banks were cautious. Firms hesitated. The implication was not failure of design, but exposure of scale limits when private actors fear secondary risk.

The counter-example is instructive because it shows that even well-intentioned, legally structured alternatives can struggle. Compliance uncertainty, reputational risk, and operational complexity discourage participation. Reconciling this with the broader picture leads to a sober conclusion: avoidance strategies persist, but they rarely displace dominant corridors wholesale.

This brings us to the question of *cost versus visibility*. Reduced visibility can lower immediate enforcement risk, but it raises others. Intermediaries demand compensation for risk. Insurance premiums rise. Financing costs increase. Firms must decide how much opacity they can afford before it undermines their competitiveness. The visible decision is not ideological; it is commercial. Some trades survive. Others quietly die.

There is also a dynamic response from sanctioning authorities. Patterns that become visible invite countermeasures. Intermediary jurisdictions face pressure. Banks update screening rules. What worked last year may not work next. The implication is that avoidance strategies require continual adaptation, which itself consumes resources.

It is important to state a boundary clearly. Describing principles is not the same as endorsing or instructing. The purpose here is analytical. To understand corridor competition, one must understand why alternatives emerge and why they often plateau. Sanctions-avoidance strategies are not a shadow economy running parallel to the formal one. They are stress responses that reveal where the formal system is brittle and where it remains resilient.

The unresolved tension at the end of this analysis is practical. For firms and states under pressure, the question is not whether a workaround exists in theory, but whether it can support routine trade at acceptable cost without triggering escalating scrutiny. Each detour buys time. Few buy permanence.

Risks and limits of workarounds

In March 2022, several mid-sized European banks quietly closed accounts linked to trade with Russia, even where transactions were technically permitted under existing sanctions. Compliance teams had reached a judgement that went beyond black-letter law. The cost of monitoring, documenting, and defending each payment outweighed the revenue. The accounts were closed. The flows stopped. No court ordered it. No regulator demanded it. Risk managers decided.

That moment captures the central paradox of financial workarounds. Many routes remain legally or technically open, yet they narrow or vanish in practice. The constraint is not ingenuity. It is tolerance.

A workaround begins as an engineering exercise. Can value be moved from A to B without touching a blocked corridor? The first claim is that this question is quickly replaced by another. *Should it be?* Show the behaviour. A bank accepts a complex transaction structure for a long-standing client, then subjects it to enhanced due diligence, senior sign-off, and post-settlement review. Name the issue: operational drag. Explain it. Each additional control consumes staff time, systems capacity, and managerial attention. The implication is visible in cost allocation. Margins shrink. Capacity is rationed.

Legal risk is the most obvious constraint. Sanctions regimes are layered, dynamic, and often ambiguous at the margins. A transaction that appears compliant today may be reassessed tomorrow under updated guidance or enforcement priorities. Banks respond by measuring not only statutory exposure but also enforcement risk. The abstraction is *uncertainty*. The metric is concrete: legal opinions commissioned, external counsel retained, and capital set aside for potential penalties.

This is not hypothetical. In June 2014, BNP Paribas agreed to pay nearly $9 billion to U.S. authorities for sanctions violations linked to Sudan, Iran, and Cuba. The case reshaped global banking behaviour. Even institutions with minimal U.S. presence reassessed their tolerance for sanctioned-country exposure. The implication for workarounds was lasting. If the downside is existential, optionality disappears.

Reputational risk compounds the legal one. Public scrutiny rarely distinguishes between lawful circumvention and unlawful evasion. A headline collapses nuance. The visible behaviour is pre-emptive withdrawal. Firms exit relationships that attract attention, even when revenue remains. Boards ask simple questions. Is this business worth explaining to investors, regulators, and the press? Often the answer is no.

Operational risk is subtler but just as binding. Workarounds tend to be complex. They rely on additional counterparties, manual processes, and bespoke documentation. Each step introduces failure points. Payments are delayed. Instructions are misinterpreted. Documentation mismatches trigger rejections. The abstraction of *complexity* resolves into specific incidents: failed settlements, disputed invoices, and liquidity trapped mid-corridor.

A plausible scenario illustrates the point. A commodities trader—call it Northbridge Trading—constructs a multi-leg settlement route involving a regional currency hub and two intermediary banks. For several months, the route works. Costs are higher but manageable. Then, in early 2024, one intermediary tightens its screening rules after a regulatory review. Payments queue. Counterparties demand prepayment. Northbridge abandons the route. Trade volumes fall. The workaround did not fail technically. It failed institutionally.

This brings us to a critical limitation. Workarounds depend on the weakest participant's risk appetite. A single bank's policy shift can collapse an entire corridor. The implication is fragility. Scale amplifies this risk. The larger the volumes, the more scrutiny they attract. Many schemes remain small because small is survivable.

A credible counter-example tempers the argument. Certain humanitarian and essential-goods channels persist under sanctions with relative stability.

They are often supported by explicit licences, multilateral oversight, or state backing. The reconciliation is instructive. Where rules are clear, protections explicit, and objectives narrow, workarounds can endure. Where ambiguity reigns, they wither.

Banks and corporates therefore engage in continuous calibration. They weigh expected returns against cumulative risk across legal, reputational, and operational dimensions. This is not a moral calculus. It is an enterprise one. The visible decision is often incremental: reducing transaction size, shortening tenors, limiting counterparties, or exiting geographies altogether.

Another constraint is funding. Workarounds often lack access to cheap liquidity. Correspondent banks charge more. Collateral demands increase. Trade finance lines shrink. The abstraction of *cost* appears in pricing schedules and credit committee minutes. A route that looks viable at pilot scale becomes uneconomic at volume.

There is also a time dimension. Sanctions regimes harden. Early loopholes close. Authorities learn. Market participants adapt, then adapt again. The cycle favours agility, not permanence. Firms that rely too heavily on a single workaround expose themselves to abrupt discontinuity.

The quiet motif running through these dynamics is *reversibility*. Most workarounds are reversible by design. Banks can withdraw. Intermediaries can exit. Licences can lapse. This reversibility reassures risk managers but undermines scale. Stability demands commitment. Commitment demands confidence. Confidence is scarce under sanctions.

The forward test, then, is not whether a clever route can be devised, but whether enough institutions are willing to commit capital, reputation, and operational capacity to sustain it under scrutiny. For most workarounds, the answer remains provisional. The corridors exist. The traffic stays light.

Designing resilient but lawful corridors

In March 2020, as markets convulsed and borders closed, the European Central Bank in Frankfurt watched cross-border payment queues lengthen rather than break. The outcome mattered. Despite stress, euro settlements continued across multiple correspondent routes, supported by transparent reporting and overlapping relationships. No single channel carried the full load. Liquidity moved. Trade cleared. The pipes held.

Redundancy beats ingenuity.

That episode is a useful place to begin because it reframes the problem. The most durable financial corridors are rarely the most novel. They are the ones that remain legible to supervisors, acceptable to counterparties, and boring enough to survive scrutiny. The task is not to outrun rules but to design within them.

Resilience in lawful corridors starts with diversification that can be observed. Show the behaviour. A multinational manufacturer maintains correspondent banking relationships in euros, dollars, and a regional currency, each with more than one clearing bank. Name the principle: diversification. Explain it. When one route tightens, another absorbs volume without triggering exceptional processes. The implication is continuity under stress, not avoidance.

Transparency is the second pillar. In practice, this means corridors that produce clean data: consistent documentation, traceable counterparties, and auditable flows. The abstraction of *trust* becomes a metric. How often are transactions flagged? How quickly are queries resolved? Banks track these numbers. So do regulators. Corridors that generate fewer exceptions gain informal priority.

A concrete example illustrates the point. In 2019, a mid-sized OECD-based exporter—call it Helios Components—restructured its treasury operations. It did not seek exotic routes. Instead, it spread settlement across three currencies aligned with its trade geography and retained correspondents in two financial centres for each. Costs rose modestly. Reporting burdens increased. Yet during subsequent market disruptions, Helios experienced fewer payment delays than peers reliant on a single dominant corridor. The implication was operational resilience achieved without regulatory friction.

Diversification has limits. A credible counter-example tempers the enthusiasm. Over-diversification can dilute volumes to the point where no relationship is economically meaningful. Banks deprioritise low-activity accounts. Fees rise. Service deteriorates. The reconciliation lies in scale. Diversification works when each corridor carries enough flow to matter.

Redundancy complements diversification. Where diversification spreads risk across currencies and geographies, redundancy ensures backups within the same corridor. The visible behaviour is duplication. Two correspondents clear the same currency. Two messaging paths exist. The abstraction of *resilience* resolves into a simple question. If one node fails, does the payment still move?

This is where lawful design diverges sharply from evasion. Redundancy is declared, not concealed. Banks know the backups exist. Regulators can see them. The implication is legitimacy. When stress hits, using a backup does not trigger suspicion because it was expected.

Transparency also extends to governance. Firms that articulate corridor design—why certain currencies, why certain banks—find it easier to defend those choices. Minutes matter. Policies matter. The abstraction of *intent* is made visible through documented rationale. That documentation becomes a shield when scrutiny increases.

States apply similar logic. Countries seeking resilient corridors invest in compliance capacity, not just infrastructure. They standardise documentation. They align reporting with international norms. The effect is cumulative. Each compliant transaction reinforces the corridor's credibility. Liquidity follows credibility.

A second named example grounds the analysis. Following the 2012 euro area crisis, several Nordic banks expanded correspondent relationships across the region rather than concentrating exposure. By 2015, payment data showed lower settlement delays during volatility episodes compared with more centralised peers. The source is the banks' own disclosures and supervisory reviews from the period. The implication was not innovation but durability.

The quiet motif threading through these cases is *visibility*. Corridors that can be seen endure. Those that hide collapse.

There are, however, trade-offs. Transparent corridors are slower to adapt. Policy changes require consultation. Systems upgrades need approval. In fast-moving crises, this can feel constraining. Yet the constraint is also protection. Abrupt shifts attract attention. Gradual adjustments blend into normal operations.

Another limitation is cost. Lawful resilience is not cheap. Multiple correspondents charge fees. Compliance teams grow. Systems must reconcile across platforms. The abstraction of *efficiency* appears in budget lines and return-on-capital calculations. Firms accept lower margins in exchange for lower tail risk.

Importantly, lawful corridors do not immunise participants from sanctions or controls. They merely ensure that when rules change, exits are orderly. This distinction matters. Resilience is about managing discontinuity, not denying it.

Consider a hypothetical stress test. A regional currency corridor faces new reporting requirements. Firms with transparent, diversified setups adjust. They file additional data. Payments slow briefly, then resume. Firms dependent on opaque routes freeze. Counterparties withdraw. The difference is not legality alone but preparedness.

The forward test for designers of corridors is therefore diagnostic. Can this route withstand daylight? Can it be explained to a regulator, a correspondent bank, and a board? If the answer is yes, the corridor may be resilient. If the answer relies on discretion or novelty, its lifespan is uncertain.

The unresolved tension remains. As financial geopolitics hardens, the pressure to bend corridors will grow. The question is whether resilience will continue to be built through visible redundancy and transparent diversification, or whether the temptation to chase clever shortcuts will erode the very trust that keeps corridors open.

Chapter 9

Payment Networks, SWIFT, And Alternatives

At 09:17 on a Tuesday morning in Brussels, a message left one bank and arrived at another without moving a single euro. The instruction carried no money, issued no credit, and settled nothing by itself. Yet the trade behind it cleared before lunch. This is the quiet power of messaging. For half a century, the Society for Worldwide Interbank Financial Telecommunication—SWIFT—has sat at the centre of that choreography, invisible until it is not.

The paradox is simple and enduring. How can a network that neither holds funds nor issues currency become one of the most consequential pressure points in global finance?

To answer that question is to understand why payment networks matter more than money in motion. Currencies dominate headlines. Sanctions dominate politics. But it is the wiring between institutions that determines whether value actually moves. This chapter enters that wiring.

The modern payment system resembles an air-traffic network more than a mint. Planes are not airports. Messages are not money. Yet when the control tower goes dark, the sky empties. SWIFT's significance lies not in ownership of assets but in coordination at scale. It standardised how banks speak to one another, turning idiosyncratic instructions into a shared grammar. The result was speed, predictability, and trust—qualities that compound quietly over decades.

That distinction matters because it clarifies what is at stake when access is restricted. Being cut off from SWIFT is not the same as losing a currency. Dollars still exist. Euros still clear. What changes is the ability to communicate efficiently with the institutions that hold and move them. Payments become slower, more error-prone, and more expensive. The pipes remain. The signalling falters.

This chapter builds on the book's central theme: that currency power increasingly expresses itself through infrastructure rather than decree. Swap lines, clearing hubs, regional blocs, and lawful corridors all rely on networks that translate intent into action. Payment networks are where those corridors meet reality.

The story does not end with SWIFT. Domestic real-time payment systems have altered expectations at home. In country after country, consumers now expect funds to arrive in seconds, not days. Banks have adapted. Treasuries have adapted. The question now being asked—quietly but persistently—is whether those domestic rails can be stitched together across borders.

The appeal is obvious. Speed reduces credit risk. Transparency reduces reconciliation costs. Smaller transactions, in particular, suffer under legacy correspondent models designed for bulk flows. When two neighbouring countries link instant-payment schemes, the effect is not revolutionary but cumulative. A slice of everyday trade no longer needs the old routes. Dependency shifts at the margin.

Yet integration exposes fault lines. Domestic systems reflect domestic rules: operating hours, data standards, consumer protections. Linking them requires alignment without uniformity. Each connection is a negotiation between legal regimes as much as between technologies. The result is progress that feels incremental until it suddenly matters.

Alongside these developments sit efforts to build alternatives to SWIFT itself. Some are regional, some national, some explicitly political. Their motivations vary. Resilience. Autonomy. Insurance against exclusion. The critical task for the reader is to distinguish scale from symbolism. A messaging system with limited membership may carry headlines without carrying volume. Participation does not equal reliance.

Network effects dominate this terrain. Payment systems grow valuable not because they exist, but because others use them. This is why replacement is harder than creation. An isolated alternative may function flawlessly yet fail to attract meaningful flows. Interoperability becomes the more realistic ambition. Translating messages into established formats. Bridging rather than bypassing. The trade-off is clear. Autonomy gains ground only when reach is preserved.

Security and governance complicate the picture further. Banks are conservative for reasons that history has taught them. Cyber resilience, operational continuity, and legal clarity matter more than novelty. A single high-profile outage can reverse months of adoption. Trust, once shaken, is slow to return.

What emerges is a landscape of layered networks rather than a single contest. Incumbents coexist with complements. Alternatives find niches. Domestic rails stretch outward. Messaging standards evolve. None of this guarantees a shift away from dominant currencies, but all of it reshapes how power is exercised within the system.

This chapter does not treat payment networks as neutral utilities. They are institutions with governance structures, incentives, and vulnerabilities. Their design choices favour some corridors over others. Their resilience—or lack of it—determines which routes remain viable under stress.

A recurring motif will guide the discussion: translation versus replacement. Time and again, the most durable innovations translate between systems rather than attempting to overthrow them. They accept the gravity of network effects and work within it. The question is not whether alternatives exist, but whether they connect.

For policymakers, the implications are strategic. Investing in domestic systems without planning for cross-border compatibility risks fragmentation. Pursuing autonomy without interoperability risks isolation. For banks and firms, the implications are operational. Choosing rails is choosing exposure—to outages, to scrutiny, to cost.

The chapter ahead moves deliberately from clarification to comparison. It begins by stripping away myths about what SWIFT does and does not do. It then traces how local real-time systems edge across borders, where they succeed and where they stall. It examines regional and national alternatives with a cold eye, asking not who sponsors them but who uses them. It unpacks interoperability as a pragmatic response to network effects. It closes by tying security and governance back to trust, the currency that underwrites all others.

The unresolved tension is this. As geopolitical pressures rise, the incentive to build parallel networks grows stronger. Yet the economic logic of connectivity pulls in the opposite direction. Whether the next decade produces fragmentation or layered integration will depend less on declarations and more on the quiet engineering of messages that still, somehow, move the world.

What SWIFT actually does and does not do

On 26 February 2022, in Brussels, the board of the Society for Worldwide Interbank Financial Telecommunication confirmed that several Russian banks would be disconnected from its network. The decision did not freeze a single account. It did not cancel a currency. Yet payments slowed, trades stalled, and counterparties recalculated risk within hours. The outcome was concrete and immediate. Messages stopped flowing.

Money stayed put.

The moment exposed a misunderstanding that has persisted for decades. SWIFT is not a bank. It does not hold deposits, extend credit, or issue currency. What it provides is coordination at scale: a shared language that lets thousands of institutions move value with confidence. Remove the language, and even abundant liquidity becomes awkward to reach.

That distinction matters because policy debates often conflate access to messaging with access to money itself. They are related, but not identical. Understanding the difference is essential to understanding why alternatives to SWIFT struggle, why disconnection hurts without being fatal, and why currency dominance survives changes in plumbing.

SWIFT's role is best understood as translation under pressure. Each day, banks around the world send millions of standardised messages that instruct, confirm, reconcile, and amend payments. The messages do not move funds. They synchronise balance sheets across institutions that do. The visible behaviour is prosaic: a bank clerk releases a payment, a system generates a message, another system reads it, and settlement occurs elsewhere. The implication is profound. Standardisation lowers error rates, reduces settlement risk, and compresses time.

The standards themselves are the quiet achievement. Consider the MT103, the workhorse customer credit transfer message used for decades. Its fields specify the ordering customer, beneficiary, amount, value date, and correspondent institutions. When a bank in Milan sends an MT103 to a correspondent in New York, both sides know exactly where to look for each element. The metric that matters is not elegance but reliability. According to SWIFT's own reporting, message error rates fell sharply after widespread adoption of standard formats in the 1980s and 1990s, cutting manual repair costs that once absorbed material staff time (SWIFT, annual review, various years).

Show the process, then name it. A corporate client instructs Bank A to pay a supplier abroad. Bank A debits the client's account and sends a SWIFT message to Bank B, its correspondent in the destination currency. Bank B credits the beneficiary and confirms via another message. The funds move across central bank accounts or correspondent balances. The name for this is correspondent banking, coordinated by messaging. The implication is that SWIFT sits beside money, not on top of it.

This architecture explains why being cut off is serious but not absolute. Without SWIFT, banks can still communicate—by fax, email, proprietary links—but at higher cost and risk. The visible behaviour changes. Payments take longer. Compliance teams intervene more often. Counterparties demand pre-funding. The metric shifts from minutes to days. Liquidity remains, but it becomes clumsy to deploy.

A counter-example sharpens the point. When domestic payment systems fail, funds can be unavailable even though messages are intact. In several countries, temporary outages in real-time gross settlement systems have halted high-value payments despite fully functional messaging layers. The reconciliation is straightforward. Messaging is necessary but not sufficient. Settlement infrastructure and liquidity provision complete the circuit.

SWIFT's governance reinforces its narrow remit. Founded in 1973 and headquartered in Belgium, the cooperative is owned by its member institutions. It operates under Belgian law and is overseen by a consortium of central banks, including the National Bank of Belgium, the Federal Reserve, and the European Central Bank. This arrangement limits its discretion. SWIFT executes sanctions once mandated by competent authorities. It does not initiate them. The implication is institutional constraint, not autonomy.

The quiet motif here is language. Banks speak many dialects internally, but they converse externally in a shared tongue. That tongue has evolved. The migration from MT messages to ISO 20022, now underway across major markets, expands data richness. Fields multiply. Remittance information grows more structured. The visible behaviour is more data travelling with each payment. The metric is compliance efficiency: better screening, fewer false positives, faster release. The implication is that messaging standards can strengthen control without changing currencies.

Consider a second named example. In March 2023, several European payment systems completed milestones in adopting ISO 20022 for cross-border payments under the oversight of the European Central Bank in

Frankfurt. The outcome was not faster settlement by itself. It was clearer information, enabling banks to automate checks that once required manual review. Again, plumbing improved; monetary choice did not change.

Critics sometimes argue that because SWIFT does not move money, alternatives can easily replace it. The record suggests otherwise. Network effects dominate. A messaging system is valuable because others use it. The decision to join reflects expected counterparties, not ideology. A regional alternative may function well within a bloc, but its reach defines its usefulness. The visible behaviour is selective adoption. Banks keep multiple channels open. The implication is redundancy, not substitution.

There is also a limit case worth confronting. Could a country maintain currency access without SWIFT indefinitely? Yes, at a cost. Iran's experience after earlier sanctions rounds showed trade continuing through bespoke arrangements, third-country intermediaries, and non-standard messaging. Volumes fell. Costs rose. Transparency declined. The reconciliation is not flattering to grand claims. Workarounds exist, but they scale poorly.

Trust is often invoked here. Replace the abstraction with behaviour. Banks trust SWIFT messages because decades of usage have demonstrated low error rates, predictable governance, and legal clarity. They commit capital on that basis. A new system must earn the same confidence. Metrics matter: uptime percentages, incident response times, audit outcomes. Without them, adoption stalls.

What SWIFT does not do is equally important. It does not guarantee settlement. It does not provide liquidity. It does not determine exchange rates. Those functions sit with central banks, commercial banks, and markets. Confusing the layers leads to overstatement. Cutting off messaging constrains coordination. It does not erase money.

This layered view clarifies current debates about alternatives. Domestic instant-payment systems linking across borders can bypass SWIFT for certain transactions, particularly retail or low-value corporate flows. The visible behaviour is fewer correspondent hops. The metric is seconds instead of hours. The implication is marginal erosion of reliance, not displacement. High-value, complex transactions still gravitate to established channels where legal certainty and liquidity depth reside.

The motif returns. Translation beats replacement.

A final limitation deserves attention. SWIFT's neutrality is not absolute. Its compliance obligations mean that geopolitics can intrude. Yet the cooperative's structure resists capture by any single state. That balance—responsive but constrained—has underwritten longevity. Alternatives that tilt too far towards sovereignty risk isolation. Those that tilt towards openness risk political pressure. The design choice is not technical alone. It is institutional.

The unresolved tension remains. As sanctions proliferate and technology advances, the incentive to build new messaging rails grows. At the same time, the gravity of network effects pulls traffic back to where language is shared and widely understood. The test for any alternative is not whether it can send messages, but whether others will read them, trust them, and act on them at scale.

Domestic real-time systems and cross-border links

In February 2023, in Singapore, the Monetary Authority of Singapore and the Reserve Bank of India switched on a live link between PayNow and India's Unified Payments Interface. The outcome was immediate and observable. Individuals could send small-value payments across borders in seconds, using familiar mobile identifiers rather than bank codes. Settlement was near-instant. Fees fell. Volumes rose.

Seconds mattered.

The event did not dismantle correspondent banking, nor did it displace established currencies. It changed behaviour at the margin. Retail users stopped waiting. Small firms stopped batching. A slice of cross-border traffic moved off legacy rails without fanfare, not because of geopolitics, but because speed and certainty were suddenly available where they mattered most.

This is the quiet revolution of domestic real-time payment systems when they learn to talk to one another.

Domestic instant-payment platforms were built to solve local problems. They reduce cash use, compress settlement times, and lower costs for households and small businesses. Their defining features are visible and measurable: 24/7 availability, irrevocable settlement, and response times counted in seconds. When these systems are linked across borders, the same properties begin to apply internationally, at least for transactions that fit their design envelope.

The show comes first. A migrant worker in Singapore sends funds home to a family member in India using a phone number. The payment debits a

Singapore account and credits an Indian one within moments. No SWIFT message is generated. No correspondent bank intermediates the retail leg. The name for this is a bilateral link between domestic real-time systems. The implication is not the end of incumbents, but a reallocation of flows.

Speed is the most obvious benefit, but it is not the only one. Real-time systems settle continuously, reducing daylight credit exposures. The metric is liquidity efficiency: funds are not trapped in transit. For banks, this lowers operational risk on small payments. For users, it collapses uncertainty. Trust here is behavioural. People use what works quickly and predictably.

A second named example underscores the pattern. In April 2021, Thailand's PromptPay and Singapore's PayNow launched a cross-border linkage enabling peer-to-peer transfers between Bangkok and Singapore. The Bank of Thailand and the Monetary Authority of Singapore emphasised retail use cases: remittances, travel spending, small merchant payments. The concrete outcome was adoption by consumers who previously relied on cash or specialised remittance firms. Volumes were modest by wholesale standards, but sticky.

The quiet motif threading these cases is time. Seconds compress risk. Seconds change habits.

Integration, however, is not trivial. Domestic systems differ in governance, operating hours, legal finality, and data standards. Linking them requires decisions about exchange-rate setting, fee disclosure, dispute resolution, and compliance screening. Each abstraction hides a choice. Efficiency becomes an API design. Risk becomes a settlement guarantee. Trust becomes a liability allocation.

Consider exchange rates. In the PayNow–UPI link, rates are typically provided by participating banks or authorised providers, not by the payment systems themselves. The visible behaviour is a quoted rate shown before confirmation. The implication is market discipline: users compare, providers compete. Yet this also introduces variability. Rates can widen during stress, reminding users that speed does not eliminate FX risk.

Compliance is another constraint. Real-time payments are irrevocable. Screening must therefore occur before execution. This pushes more checks upstream, into onboarding and transaction monitoring. The metric is false-positive rates. If they spike, speed evaporates as payments are held. Linking systems multiplies the challenge because standards must align across jurisdictions.

A credible limitation appears when transaction size increases. Domestic instant-payment systems are optimised for low-value, high-volume flows. Caps are explicit. In many jurisdictions, single transactions are limited to a few thousand units of local currency. This is a design choice, not a flaw. It contains risk. The reconciliation is clear. These links chip away at reliance on legacy networks for smaller transactions. They do not replace them for trade finance or large corporate settlements.

Network effects still matter. A bilateral link is valuable to the extent that users on both sides participate. Multilateral expansion raises complexity sharply. Governance questions multiply. Who sets rules? Who bears losses? The implication is that growth is incremental, often regional, rather than global.

There is also a counter-example worth noting. Some attempts to link domestic systems have stalled because legal finality could not be reconciled. If one jurisdiction treats settlement as final immediately and another allows revocation under certain conditions, risk asymmetry emerges. Banks respond by throttling volumes or withdrawing. The lesson is sober. Speed without legal clarity is fragile.

The benefits are nonetheless tangible. For small merchants, faster cross-border receipts improve cash flow. The metric is days saved. For migrants, lower fees mean more value delivered. The World Bank has long documented average remittance costs exceeding targets in many corridors; instant-payment links attack that problem structurally by shortening chains (World Bank, Remittance Prices Worldwide, various years). Even where precise percentages vary, the direction is consistent.

These links also alter the competitive landscape for private providers. Traditional money transfer operators must respond to rails that clear in seconds. Some integrate. Others focus on value-added services. The implication is pressure, not extinction.

What they do not do is dictate currency choice. Most links settle in local currencies at each end, with FX conversion in between. The dollar often remains the reference currency for pricing, even if it never appears operationally. Plumbing changes. Invoicing habits lag.

The motif returns. Time compresses space, but it does not erase gravity.

Looking ahead, central banks increasingly discuss multilateral platforms that connect multiple domestic systems through shared standards. The BIS has documented experiments exploring such models, emphasising governance and interoperability over technological novelty (BIS, Annual Economic Report, 2022). These are scenarios, not predictions. They hinge on political will as much as code.

The unresolved tension is this. As domestic real-time systems knit together, they siphon off a growing share of everyday cross-border payments. Legacy networks remain indispensable for scale, complexity, and resilience. The test for policymakers and banks is not whether to choose one over the other, but how to balance speed against reach, and convenience against control, as seconds continue to reshape expectations.

Regional and national SWIFT alternatives

In December 2014, in Moscow, the Central Bank of the Russian Federation activated the System for Transfer of Financial Messages, known by its Russian acronym SPFS. The immediate outcome was modest but concrete. Domestic banks gained a back-up channel for interbank messages after Russia faced the risk of exclusion from global networks following sanctions linked to Crimea. Messages flowed. Payments did not collapse.

Messaging is not money.

That distinction sits at the heart of every attempt to build an alternative to SWIFT. The drama of disconnection often obscures a more prosaic reality: payment networks live or die not by declarations of autonomy, but by daily volumes, institutional trust, and the willingness of banks to route ordinary business through them.

The SPFS launch was not a revolution. It was insurance. That framing matters, because it captures why regional and national alternatives emerge, how they are designed, and why so many struggle to move beyond symbolism.

The show comes first. A Russian commercial bank sends a standardised financial message through SPFS to another domestic institution. The message mirrors SWIFT formats closely enough to be intelligible. Settlement still occurs through existing accounts. The name for this is a domestic messaging substitute. The implication is resilience rather than independence.

SWIFT itself is often misunderstood in these debates. It is a cooperative that provides secure messaging standards and connectivity. It does not hold funds, clear payments, or create currency. Alternatives therefore focus on replicating the messaging layer. That is both easier and harder than it sounds. Easier because no balance sheet is required. Harder because the value of a messaging network scales with participation.

Network effects dominate.

A second named example illustrates a different approach. In October 2015, in Shanghai, the People's Bank of China launched the Cross-Border Interbank Payment System, or CIPS. Unlike SPFS, CIPS combined messaging with settlement functions for renminbi transactions. Its concrete outcome was the provision of a streamlined channel for RMB cross-border payments, particularly for trade with Chinese counterparties. The system grew steadily, with both direct and indirect participants, many of them foreign banks (PBoC, CIPS annual disclosures, various years).

Here the abstraction of *scope* becomes visible. SPFS focused on message continuity for domestic banks. CIPS targeted a specific currency and cross-border use case. The implication is strategic clarity. By narrowing its domain, CIPS avoided the impossible task of replacing SWIFT wholesale.

Technical design choices reflect these aims. Messaging standards are often based on ISO formats compatible with SWIFT, enabling translation rather than isolation. The metric is interoperability. Systems that require banks to maintain entirely separate workflows face higher operational costs. Banks respond by minimising usage.

Political backing is another decisive factor. Both SPFS and CIPS benefited from explicit central bank sponsorship. That sponsorship reduces counterparty risk perceptions. It does not eliminate commercial hesitation. Banks measure risk in terms of compliance exposure and reputational cost, not patriotic intent.

A credible counter-example sharpens the lesson. In 2019, France, Germany, and the United Kingdom announced the Instrument in Support of Trade Exchanges, or INSTEX, aimed at facilitating trade with Iran while bypassing certain sanctions. The outcome was underwhelming. Transaction volumes remained negligible, and the mechanism never achieved scale. The limitation was not technical ingenuity but misaligned incentives. Firms judged the compliance and reputational risks too high relative to the commercial benefit.

Scale is earned, not proclaimed.

The distinction between genuine scale and symbolic participation runs through all regional initiatives. A messaging system handling a majority of intra-bloc traffic changes behaviour. One processing occasional test messages does not. Participation metrics matter. Are messages daily or episodic? Are they routine trade payments or exceptional cases?

Regional efforts often sit between these poles. Some blocs have explored shared messaging platforms to reduce dependence on external networks for internal flows. The show here is quieter. A bank within the bloc routes an intra-regional payment through a local system by default. The name is substitution at the margin. The implication is gradual learning rather than abrupt rupture.

Trust, an overused term, becomes concrete in governance arrangements. Who sets rules? Who audits security? Who bears liability for outages? SWIFT's cooperative structure, with decades of operational credibility, answers these questions clearly. New systems must do the same. A central bank sponsor can accelerate trust domestically but may not suffice internationally.

Security concerns loom large. Messaging systems are critical infrastructure. A breach or prolonged outage would be visible and costly. Banks test alternatives cautiously. They run parallel systems. They keep SWIFT as a backstop. The behaviour reveals the hierarchy of trust.

The quiet motif threading these cases is gravity. Financial traffic follows established paths unless a strong force redirects it.

One abstraction often invoked is *autonomy*. In practice, autonomy manifests as optionality. A bank with access to multiple messaging channels can reroute in an emergency. That is valuable. It does not require abandoning incumbents. The implication is coexistence.

Interoperability amplifies this logic. Some alternatives explicitly design gateways that translate their messages into SWIFT formats for onward routing. The visible behaviour is dual routing capability. The metric is message latency and error rates. When translation works seamlessly, banks are more willing to experiment. When it fails, volumes retreat.

There are also economic limits. Building and maintaining a secure, resilient messaging network is expensive. Costs include cyber defence, redundancy, and continuous upgrades. Without sufficient transaction volumes, per-message costs rise. Governments may subsidise initially, but long-term sustainability demands usage.

The reconciliation between ambition and reality lies in purpose. Systems built as insurance perform well when treated as such. Systems marketed as replacements face harsher scrutiny. Banks ask simple questions. Will my counterparties be there? Will regulators approve? Will this still exist in five years?

Currency choice again remains distinct. Messaging alternatives do not, by themselves, dethrone dominant currencies. A payment message can instruct settlement in dollars, euros, or any other unit. Removing a messenger does not remove the language of trade. This separation is often overlooked in political rhetoric.

The future likely belongs to layered architectures. Domestic and regional systems handle local flows efficiently. Global networks handle complexity and scale. Bridges translate between them. The BIS has noted repeatedly that interoperability is more feasible than fragmentation for global payments (BIS, Annual Economic Report, 2023).

The unresolved tension is strategic. For policymakers, the question is how much autonomy justifies the cost of parallel systems. For banks, it is when optionality outweighs operational burden. Regional and national SWIFT alternatives illuminate that tension vividly. They are neither futile gestures nor silver bullets. They are experiments in gravity, testing how far financial traffic can be nudged without losing the pull of the centre.

Interoperability and network effects

In November 2022, in Singapore, the Bank for International Settlements' Innovation Hub demonstrated a prototype known as Project Nexus. The outcome was not a new payment network but a working bridge. It showed how existing domestic instant-payment systems could connect through a shared layer, allowing banks in different countries to route retail payments without joining a single new rail. The BIS framed the lesson plainly: connecting systems can matter more than replacing them.

Networks reward scale.

That simple fact shapes every serious attempt to rewire global payments. Payment networks exhibit powerful network effects because their usefulness rises with each additional participant. A bank joins the system its counterparties already use. A firm invoices in the currency its customers accept. These choices compound over time, pulling traffic towards established hubs. Interoperability is the only credible way to bend that gravity without denying it.

The show is easy to picture. A payment instruction leaves a bank in one country, travels through a domestic real-time system, passes across a translation layer, and arrives in another country's system without manual intervention. The name for this architecture is interoperability by design. The implication is reach without surrender.

The alternative is isolation. Some new payment networks have been built as closed worlds, requiring banks to adopt separate standards, compliance processes, and operational routines. The visible behaviour that follows is cautious usage. Banks test such systems for edge cases or politically sensitive flows, while routing routine business elsewhere. Volumes stay thin. Costs per transaction remain high.

Network effects explain why.

The abstraction of *reach* becomes measurable in counterparty count. A network with ten participants connects forty-five possible pairs. One with a thousand connects nearly half a million. This combinatorial reality is unforgiving. It explains why incumbents persist even when their technology is imperfect.

Interoperability offers a way through. Rather than asking banks to choose, it allows them to translate. Message translation is not glamorous, but it is decisive. When a payment message can move from one format into another without loss of information, banks preserve their existing workflows. Compliance checks remain intact. Audit trails survive.

A second named example underlines the point. Since 2019, SWIFT has promoted its gpi initiative, enhancing transparency and speed while remaining a messaging standard. The concrete outcome has been greater visibility of payment status across correspondent chains. More important for interoperability, gpi messages can coexist with domestic and regional systems that adopt compatible standards (SWIFT documentation, 2019–2023).

Compatibility beats purity.

The trade-off between autonomy and reach appears stark only in theory. In practice, systems that maximise autonomy by rejecting compatibility sacrifice reach so severely that usage collapses. Systems that prioritise reach by translating into dominant formats retain autonomy where it matters: governance, resilience, and contingency.

A scenario clarifies the difference. Imagine a regional messaging network designed to serve a bloc of neighbouring countries. In its isolated form, a bank sending a payment outside the bloc must exit the system entirely, re-entering through a correspondent bank on a global network. The process adds time, cost, and operational risk. Banks respond by bypassing the regional system for any transaction with even a small chance of leaving the bloc.

Now imagine the same network equipped with a translation gateway. Messages destined outside the region are converted automatically into SWIFT-compatible formats and forwarded. Settlement instructions remain clear. The regional system still handles intra-bloc traffic directly. Banks now have no reason to avoid it. Usage rises.

The name for this shift is optionality. The implication is survival.

There is, however, a credible limitation. Translation layers introduce complexity. Each additional interface is a potential point of failure. Operational risk increases if governance is weak. Banks care deeply about error rates, reconciliation breaks, and latency. When these metrics worsen, confidence evaporates quickly.

A counter-example illustrates restraint. Several proposed alternatives have stalled not because they lacked political support, but because their interoperability roadmaps were vague. Banks were unwilling to commit resources without clear standards alignment. The reconciliation lies in sequencing. Systems that prove domestic reliability first, then add translation, fare better than those promising everything at once.

Trust again appears, but in a measurable form. It shows up in service-level agreements, liability frameworks, and incident response times. A network that resolves outages transparently earns usage. One that obscures them loses it.

The quiet motif running through these designs is the bridge. Bridges do not replace roads; they connect them. Their value lies in continuity. Payment networks that embrace this logic accept that incumbents will remain. They aim instead to shorten paths and add redundancy.

Network effects also shape incentives for cooperation. Even dominant networks have reasons to interoperate. Excluding local systems risks political backlash and regulatory intervention. Including them preserves relevance. This mutual dependence explains why standards bodies, rather than single firms, often sit at the centre of interoperability efforts.

Metrics anchor these abstractions. Banks compare straight-through processing rates. They measure average settlement time. They track exception volumes. When interoperable systems improve these numbers, adoption follows. When they do not, rhetoric fades.

Interoperability does not erase power asymmetries. Translation into dominant standards can entrench them. A system that always converts into SWIFT formats implicitly accepts SWIFT's centrality. That is the autonomy cost. Yet the alternative is marginalisation. Policymakers must decide which cost is tolerable.

The decision is rarely ideological. It is operational.

Emerging technologies do not change this calculus as much as promised. Distributed ledgers, APIs, and digital currencies can reduce friction, but they do not dissolve network effects. A CBDC corridor still needs counterparties. A blockchain still needs users. Interoperability remains the hinge.

The BIS has been explicit on this point. Its recent work emphasises "interlinking" rather than replacement as the pragmatic path for cross-border payments (BIS, Annual Economic Report, 2023). The language is cautious, but the message is firm.

Scale pulls. Bridges guide.

The unresolved tension at the end of this discussion is strategic. How much dependence on incumbent standards is acceptable in exchange for participation? For banks, the answer lies in risk management. For states, it lies in sovereignty. Interoperability postpones the need to choose. It allows systems to coexist, to compete quietly on performance, and to adapt as volumes shift. Whether that balance can hold as geopolitical pressures intensify remains an open test.

Security, resilience, and governance issues

In June 2021, TCH's RTP network in the United States experienced a temporary disruption that halted real-time settlement for nearly four hours. While no funds were lost, multiple banks reported operational headaches, delayed reconciliations, and anxious clients. The incident underscored a stark reality: new payment rails can offer speed and efficiency, but even brief outages erode confidence. For banks evaluating cross-border corridors, trust in a system's resilience is as critical as its technical specifications.

Payment networks live or die by reliability. A domestic real-time system may process millions of transactions daily, but its security protocols, governance arrangements, and operational redundancy determine whether counterparties will commit their liquidity and reputational capital. The abstraction of *trust* is measurable: the number of incidents per million transactions, response times to outages, and clarity of liability frameworks directly influence adoption decisions. Banks assess whether they can honour client obligations without unexpected exposure.

High-profile outages illustrate this concretely. In 2018, the UK's Faster Payments Service experienced intermittent delays affecting major retail banks, prompting several institutions to reroute payments temporarily through legacy systems. The visible behaviour was telling: despite faster rails being technically superior, banks preferred established corridors when operational confidence wavered. The implication is clear—technical innovation alone does not guarantee uptake; credibility and resilience govern usage.

Cyber risk forms the first pillar of concern. Payment networks are high-value targets, and attacks can range from distributed denial-of-service (DDoS) incidents to more sophisticated breaches compromising transaction integrity. SWIFT itself experienced the 2016 Bangladesh Bank heist, where cyber attackers manipulated messaging credentials to divert $81 million. While SWIFT was not fundamentally compromised, the event forced global banks to re-evaluate network security, enhancing authentication, monitoring, and anomaly detection. The measurable metric here is the frequency and impact of security incidents, which shapes banks' willingness to route cross-border flows.

Operational resilience is equally crucial. Systems must maintain service continuity under stress, including high-volume periods, software upgrades, and unexpected hardware failures. Metrics such as mean time to recovery, transaction queue backlogs, and reconciliation accuracy matter as much as security. A high-profile scenario can illustrate the stakes: a regional alternative to SWIFT experiences a cascading failure in its clearing engine. Banks with funds in transit cannot confirm receipts, leading to liquidity bottlenecks. Even if settlement ultimately occurs, participants' confidence in the network plummets. The lesson is that reliability is not optional; it is a prerequisite for adoption.

Governance frameworks are the third pillar. Who makes decisions, how rules are enforced, and how liabilities are allocated all influence trust. The

European Central Bank's TARGET2 system demonstrates how centralised governance provides clear accountability, while smaller regional initiatives sometimes suffer from opaque decision-making, undermining confidence. For example, a proposed Southeast Asian messaging platform faced initial adoption delays because banks questioned its dispute-resolution mechanisms and default protocols. Transparency and enforceability of rules are visible behaviours that reinforce trust, while ambiguity suppresses participation.

Networks that integrate security, resilience, and governance effectively create positive feedback loops. When banks observe reliable operation and clear accountability, transaction volumes rise, network effects strengthen, and new participants join. Conversely, a single high-profile failure can cause cascading retreat. In 2019, a pilot cross-border instant-payment corridor connecting two Latin American central banks suffered a software bug that delayed settlement for several hours. Although the issue was promptly fixed, banks temporarily reverted to correspondent banking via existing SWIFT channels. The metric of *uptake vs. fallback usage* quantifies the impact of trust erosion.

The interplay between cyber risk, operational continuity, and governance also dictates risk allocation. Banks consider how liability is shared if errors occur or fraud emerges. Does the network bear responsibility, or do individual institutions absorb losses? Clear frameworks reduce hesitation, enabling higher transaction volumes. Ambiguity encourages conservatism, limiting innovation. The quiet motif throughout is *confidence as currency*: without measurable reliability, no new technical advantage fully converts into real-world utility.

A counter-example further clarifies the limits. Several national messaging alternatives launched in the early 2020s promised rapid settlement for intra-bloc trade. Yet, inconsistent uptime, unclear governance committees, and minimal contingency planning kept volumes low. Banks maintained partial exposure but continued routing significant transactions through global incumbents. The reconciliation is pragmatic: resilient systems do not merely exist; they must prove reliability repeatedly under operational stress and provide transparent governance to win trust.

Finally, the forward test concerns scaling. As cross-border corridors expand, technical and governance challenges magnify. Interoperability introduces additional interfaces and dependencies, each a potential point of failure. Maintaining resilience across multiple jurisdictions requires harmonised security standards, robust incident-response protocols, and clarity on authority. Banks weigh the cost-benefit trade-off of adopting new rails against staying within proven systems. Adoption accelerates when networks demonstrate consistent security, operational robustness, and transparent governance; it stagnates otherwise.

The unresolved tension persists: how far can novel payment systems push efficiency while maintaining trust? Operational confidence and governance clarity remain the binding constraints. As new corridors emerge, participants will continually test boundaries, returning to incumbents if resilience or governance falters. Networks succeed not by promise alone but by sustaining credibility under pressure. The measure of success is adoption, transaction volume, and the stability of trust itself.

Chapter 10

Reserve Management In A Fragmenting System

In late 2019, a central bank in Southeast Asia quietly reallocated a portion of its foreign reserves from U.S. dollars into a mix of regional currencies and gold. The shift went largely unnoticed by markets, yet it encapsulated a subtle but deliberate approach to reserve management: diversification as a hedge against concentration risk. Unlike headline-grabbing announcements, such moves rarely signal abrupt realignment; they are measured, methodical, and deeply tied to the rhythms of trade, debt, and liquidity. The episode illustrates how central banks balance the competing demands of safety, return, and operational flexibility within a global system that is slowly fragmenting.

Reserve management has always been more than arithmetic. A portfolio of assets denominated in foreign currencies underpins domestic stability, underwrites international obligations, and provides a cushion against sudden capital flows. The selection of currencies, asset classes, and tenors reflects both strategic calculation and the constraints imposed by global liquidity. A conservative central bank may concentrate holdings in U.S. dollars, euros, and yen, prioritising highly liquid, low-risk instruments. Another may favour a broader basket, including regional currencies and sovereign bonds outside the traditional majors, accepting modest yield enhancements in exchange for reduced exposure to a single currency. These choices are far from abstract: they shape a state's resilience, influence market perceptions, and frame the debate over de-dollarisation.

The mechanics of reserve allocation connect intimately to trade and liability structures. Nations with significant euro-denominated external debt, for example, often maintain proportionate euro reserves, ensuring that repayment obligations can be met without excessive FX transactions. Similarly, trade corridors with regional partners inform reserve composition: currencies that dominate invoicing or settlement flows naturally find their way into portfolios. This linkage between the real economy and financial buffers is critical. Central banks do not hold assets in isolation; each currency and instrument reflects exposure, obligation, and operational need.

As systemic fragmentation intensifies, access to swap lines and regional reserve pools adds a new dimension to decision-making. These institutional backstops allow central banks to supplement—or in some cases partially substitute—physical holdings of foreign assets. A bank with access to a robust regional pool can afford to reduce allocations to certain major currencies, confident that liquidity will remain available in crisis scenarios. Conversely, a central bank lacking such facilities must maintain a more conservative stance, preserving liquid reserves in currencies likely to be accepted across trade and financial networks. The presence or absence of these backstops tangibly influences reserve composition and signals the limits of flexibility in a fragmented system.

Monitoring and interpreting reserve shifts requires nuance. Headline changes often exaggerate the pace or scale of de-dollarisation. Incremental adjustments may mask stable underlying exposures, while reactive rebalancing in response to market volatility can appear more decisive than it truly is. Understanding trends, rather than isolated announcements, is crucial. Analysts examine the share of each currency over time, tenure structures, and the liquidity profile of holdings to gauge the strategic posture of a central bank. A subtle but consistent increase in non-dollar assets may indicate a long-term hedge, whereas sudden spikes often reflect short-term tactical responses.

Across these dynamics, a quiet motif emerges: *resilience through diversification*. Central banks navigate a complex environment where currency dominance, market liquidity, and counterparty risk interact. Reserve decisions are simultaneously defensive and expressive, signalling both prudence and strategic intent. As global financial corridors evolve, the architecture of reserve management will continue to shape the choices of policymakers, influence investor perception, and determine the practical reach of emerging currencies.

The unresolved question persists: how rapidly can central banks adjust portfolios without destabilising markets, and which configurations best balance safety, flexibility, and strategic signalling? Fragmentation offers opportunities for resilience, but only for those institutions capable of integrating liquidity, liability, and contingency considerations. The chapter ahead examines these mechanisms in depth, providing readers with a framework to understand the evolving calculus of reserves in a world of shifting currency patterns and institutional contingencies.

How central banks build reserve portfolios

In February 2021, the Reserve Bank of India disclosed an incremental shift in its foreign exchange holdings: a slight reduction in U.S. dollars offset by modest purchases of euros and Japanese yen. The move, quietly implemented over several weeks, reflected a deliberate calibration rather than a reactionary pivot. Markets did not overreact, yet the announcement illuminated the careful architecture behind reserve management—an exercise in balancing liquidity, safety, and return while maintaining the flexibility to respond to trade and capital flow pressures. The Indian example illustrates the nuanced choreography central banks undertake when determining the composition of their reserve portfolios, a task that combines quantitative analysis with strategic foresight.

At the core of portfolio construction is a triad of guiding principles. Liquidity ensures that assets can be deployed to settle obligations or intervene in currency markets without incurring undue loss. Safety minimises the risk of capital erosion, prioritising instruments issued by stable sovereigns and highly rated entities. Return, while subordinate to the first two, allows central banks to offset the cost of holding large-scale reserves and support broader fiscal and monetary objectives. A conservative central bank might concentrate 80–90 per cent of its holdings in U.S. dollars, euros, and yen, favouring short-dated government securities. In contrast, a more diversified institution could allocate portions to regional currencies, emerging-market bonds, or even commodity-linked assets, accepting higher credit or liquidity risk for incremental yield and strategic flexibility. These choices are never purely financial; they signal policy intent, influence market perceptions, and underpin broader debates about de-dollarisation.

Currency selection is shaped by exposure alignment. A central bank with significant liabilities denominated in euros or sterling—such as foreign debt obligations or import financing—will allocate reserves to mirror those exposures, reducing the need for frequent currency conversions and mitigating FX risk. Trade linkages similarly inform composition. Countries whose exports are invoiced in regional currencies often maintain a modest proportion of reserves in those units, even if their core reserve base remains concentrated in major currencies. The linkage between real-economy flows and reserve assets underscores that portfolio design is not a theoretical exercise but a response to operational requirements and potential contingencies.

Asset choice extends beyond currency. While government bonds dominate due to their liquidity and risk profile, central banks also consider deposits, money-market instruments, and, in some jurisdictions, gold. Tenor selection balances immediate accessibility with yield optimisation. Short-dated securities provide instant liquidity but offer minimal return; longer-dated instruments enhance yield but reduce flexibility. The Reserve Bank of Australia, for instance, routinely structures its reserves with staggered maturities to ensure daily liquidity while maintaining exposure to longer-term bonds for incremental earnings. Each allocation reflects a compromise between competing objectives, guided by the bank's mandate, market conditions, and stress-test scenarios.

Diversification is not solely a defensive measure; it serves as a strategic instrument in an evolving global monetary order. Portfolios concentrated in a single currency may deliver simplicity but amplify systemic risk in times of geopolitical tension or financial volatility. By contrast, a basket approach allows incremental hedging against currency-specific shocks. The People's Bank of China has historically maintained a diversified basket including U.S. dollars, euros, yen, and pounds, complemented by small allocations to other liquid currencies. This structure reduces dependence on any single foreign sovereign's debt market and provides operational flexibility in cross-border interventions, illustrating how portfolio composition is as much about resilience as it is about yield.

Institutional frameworks underpin every allocation decision. Reserve management committees assess macroeconomic indicators, currency market volatility, and counterparty risk, often integrating scenario analyses and stress tests. For example, the Swiss National Bank combines market liquidity metrics with credit and settlement risk assessments to calibrate both currency mix and instrument type. Similarly, the Bank of Canada integrates FX and interest-rate sensitivities into portfolio decisions, ensuring that reserves support monetary-policy operations while remaining robust under stress conditions. The process is iterative: allocations are continuously monitored, revised, and rebalanced in response to evolving financial conditions, trade patterns, and policy imperatives.

Central banks also account for operational constraints, including settlement infrastructure and legal jurisdiction. Not all instruments are equally accessible, and liquidity in secondary markets varies across currencies. A conservative central bank may eschew bonds with thin secondary markets despite attractive yield, recognising that execution risk could undermine the reserve's intended function. Conversely, institutions with robust trading capabilities can allocate to less liquid instruments, enhancing return while accepting manageable operational risk. These considerations demonstrate that reserve portfolios are engineered not only to perform under routine conditions but also to endure periods of market stress without necessitating emergency interventions.

The interaction of reserve composition with de-dollarisation debates is subtle but consequential. Incremental diversification away from the U.S. dollar may signal a strategic hedging approach rather than a deliberate shift in currency preference. Central banks typically adjust holdings gradually, reflecting liquidity constraints, counterparty availability, and market impact considerations. The apparent pace of de-dollarisation is therefore often slower than headline numbers suggest, masking the deliberate calibration embedded in daily operational practice. Investors, policymakers, and analysts must distinguish between structural portfolio design and episodic adjustments driven by market sentiment.

The motif of *balance under constraint* recurs throughout portfolio construction: balancing liquidity, safety, and return; balancing domestic exposure with international obligations; balancing immediate accessibility with longer-term yield. Each decision embodies a compromise, reflecting both the institution's mandate and the operational realities of the global financial system. The chapter ahead will examine these dynamics in depth, showing how central banks translate macroeconomic imperatives, trade patterns, and risk assessments into concrete allocations. The exercise reveals that reserve management is neither purely reactive nor mechanically formulaic: it is a complex, adaptive process that forms the foundation of monetary resilience in a world of shifting currency hierarchies and evolving financial corridors.

Shifts from dollar to mixed baskets

In March 2019, the Central Bank of Indonesia quietly reported a modest adjustment in its reserve composition: a small portion of U.S. dollar holdings was replaced with euros, Japanese yen, and a limited allocation to gold. The change, incremental yet deliberate, reflected a strategy aimed at mitigating concentration risk without destabilising existing liquidity arrangements. Observers noted the move not for its scale—less than five per cent of total reserves—but for its signalling value: a measured step towards a more diversified reserve profile. The Indonesian case encapsulates the principle of gradual adjustment that underlies most central bank strategies, highlighting that shifts from dollar-heavy holdings to mixed baskets rarely occur in abrupt surges.

Central banks approach diversification cautiously. The dollar remains dominant in global finance, accounting for the majority of cross-border settlements and reserve allocations. However, a growing recognition of potential vulnerabilities—geopolitical friction, trade tensions, or dollar volatility—encourages authorities to allocate a portion of reserves to other liquid, highly rated currencies. Euros, yen, and pounds are common alternatives, while some banks extend allocations to regional currencies or non-traditional assets such as gold. These decisions are incremental by design: abrupt reallocation risks market disruption, liquidity strain, and operational complications in settling obligations denominated in the dollar.

The mechanics of shifting to mixed baskets are methodical. Reserve managers analyse currency composition against both external liabilities and expected foreign-exchange requirements. A central bank with euro-denominated debt may increase euro holdings to minimise conversion exposure, while one with trade invoiced in regional currencies may maintain modest allocations to support operational needs. Tenor and instrument type are calibrated to balance yield, liquidity, and safety. For instance, short-term sovereign bonds provide immediate availability, while longer-dated instruments improve returns but limit agility. The interplay between asset choice and currency allocation ensures that diversification strengthens resilience without undermining the portfolio's functional role.

Historical patterns suggest gradualism dominates. The Bank of Canada and the Reserve Bank of Australia, for example, have long maintained reserves heavily weighted in U.S. dollars yet have incrementally increased exposure to other majors over decades. These adjustments reflect strategic risk management rather than any sudden pivot away from the dollar. Similarly, central banks in Southeast Asia have incorporated regional currencies in small, controlled tranches, maintaining overall stability while signalling a commitment to broader diversification. The cumulative effect of incremental reallocations often exceeds headline numbers, with underlying exposures adapting subtly to evolving trade, financial, and geopolitical conditions.

Diversification also responds to liquidity and market access considerations. While allocating to multiple currencies reduces concentration risk, each addition introduces execution complexity. Some regional currencies or emerging-market bonds may have limited secondary-market depth, and cross-border settlement infrastructure may lag behind major currencies. Reserve managers must weigh the benefits of exposure to alternative currencies against operational feasibility. A cautious approach preserves confidence in reserve usability, ensuring that a portion of holdings remains immediately deployable for interventions or debt servicing.

The incorporation of gold and other tangible assets illustrates the broader principle of hedging against systemic concentration. Gold offers a store of value unlinked to any single sovereign currency, providing an additional layer of resilience. Its allocation is typically modest—often 2–5 per cent of total reserves—but strategically significant, especially for countries seeking to buffer against extreme dollar volatility. These choices underscore that diversification is not merely a numeric exercise; it reflects a deliberate allocation of risk and operational flexibility.

Network and institutional considerations further guide shifts to mixed baskets. Access to swap lines, international liquidity facilities, and regional reserve pools can reduce the necessity of holding large balances in any single foreign currency. For example, a central bank with access to a strong regional pool may allocate less to the dollar while retaining confidence in liquidity coverage. Conversely, institutions without such institutional backstops maintain heavier allocations to majors, reflecting operational prudence. These structural factors influence not just the composition of reserves but the pace at which diversification can safely proceed.

Scenario planning shapes execution. Imagine a central bank that decides to reallocate 10 per cent of its dollar holdings to euros, yen, and a regional currency over twelve months. Implementation involves phased purchases to avoid market impact, integration with settlement systems for multiple currencies, and continuous monitoring of liquidity ratios. Stress tests evaluate whether these holdings could be deployed efficiently under scenarios of market disruption, trade shock, or sudden capital outflow. Such careful orchestration ensures that diversification supports strategic resilience without introducing unintended vulnerabilities.

Trade and liability alignment remains central. Countries with significant foreign-denominated debt typically maintain a reserve profile mirroring their obligations. Euro-denominated bonds, for instance, warrant a proportional share of euro reserves, ensuring that currency mismatches do not generate unnecessary refinancing or hedging risk. Similarly, trade invoiced in regional currencies encourages selective allocations to support payment obligations. The strategic lesson is clear: reserve composition is operationally pragmatic, reflecting both external obligations and risk management priorities rather than ideological currency preferences.

Incremental diversification also mitigates signalling risk. Large, abrupt reductions in dollar holdings could trigger market speculation, influence currency valuations, and disrupt confidence in the financial system. Gradual reallocations, by contrast, signal prudence and planning, providing transparency to markets while avoiding shocks. This approach maintains credibility in reserve management, ensuring that functional utility—settlement, intervention, debt servicing—remains paramount even as composition evolves.

The motif of *steady adaptation under constraint* threads through reserve management. Balancing dollar concentration with diversified exposure, integrating liquidity, safety, and return, and coordinating allocations with institutional access all exemplify deliberate, incremental adjustment. Portfolio changes are executed with operational discipline, aligning strategic goals with market realities. The chapter ahead will examine how these gradual shifts interact with trade, liability structures, and institutional mechanisms, revealing that de-dollarisation in practice is an evolutionary process, carefully calibrated to preserve stability while enhancing resilience.

Trade links, liabilities, and reserve currency choice

In October 2017, the National Bank of Hungary disclosed a subtle but telling adjustment to its foreign reserve portfolio: an increase in euro-denominated assets to match rising euro-denominated sovereign and corporate debt. The shift, while modest in size, reflected an operational imperative—reserves must align with external obligations to minimise currency mismatch risk. Hungary's case underscores a broader principle in central banking: reserve composition is rarely arbitrary. It is informed by the structure of trade, debt obligations, and the currencies in which a country earns and spends abroad.

Central banks manage reserves not merely as a buffer but as a practical toolkit. A country exporting primarily to the eurozone will receive significant inflows in euros. If its debt is also issued in euros, maintaining euro reserves reduces the need for constant conversions, lowering transaction costs and exchange-rate exposure. Conversely, a mismatch—holding predominantly U.S. dollars while liabilities are denominated in euros—can force frequent interventions or hedging activity, adding cost and operational complexity. The example of Hungary illustrates how debt currency composition directly informs reserve strategy, translating real-economy exposures into financial decisions.

Trade patterns reinforce this alignment. Countries with substantial trade links to multiple regions often diversify reserves in line with the currencies of key partners. For instance, a nation heavily importing machinery from Germany and energy from Russia may prioritise euros and roubles, supplemented by dollars for global liquidity. These allocations do not merely hedge against exchange-rate swings; they underpin the operational capacity to settle international obligations promptly. Reserve decisions therefore integrate commercial realities with financial imperatives, ensuring that liquidity is available in the form most directly usable for obligations.

External debt structures provide another critical lens. Sovereign bonds, syndicated loans, and short-term commercial paper denominated in foreign currencies necessitate holding assets in matching currencies. The Central Bank of Hungary's euro allocation exemplifies this principle: as euro-denominated obligations grew, the central bank increased euro assets to maintain a natural hedge. Similarly, emerging-market central banks with substantial dollar-denominated debt often maintain large U.S. dollar reserves, even if trade exposure is less concentrated in dollars. Such decisions illustrate that reserve composition is responsive, adjusting to the liabilities profile as well as to trade receipts.

Risk management drives granularity in reserve allocation. Allocations must balance liquidity, safety, and return, but also consider operational convenience for servicing liabilities. Highly liquid instruments in matching currencies facilitate immediate debt servicing, while more exotic or longer-dated instruments may enhance returns but limit immediate deployability. Hungary's incremental euro purchases were made primarily in highly liquid government bonds, ensuring both availability for payment and minimal market impact. This careful calibration exemplifies the trade-off between strategic diversification and operational reliability.

Regional and bilateral considerations further shape reserve strategy. Countries within tightly integrated trade blocs, such as the European Union, tend to hold a higher proportion of reserves in the bloc's dominant currency, reflecting both trade invoicing and liability structures. By contrast, nations with diversified trade and external debt denominated in multiple currencies must negotiate more complex allocation patterns, balancing holdings across dollars, euros, yen, and occasionally regional currencies. Access to swap lines or regional reserve pools can influence these decisions, enabling some flexibility in managing short-term liquidity while reducing the necessity of concentrated holdings in a single currency.

Incremental adjustments are a hallmark of practical reserve management. Central banks rarely undertake abrupt reallocation from one currency to another; doing so risks market disruption, operational strain, and signalling instability. Hungary's measured euro increases were executed over several quarters, reflecting both market absorption capacity and the need to maintain operational continuity. Gradual shifts preserve confidence in the currency management regime while adjusting exposure in response to evolving trade and liability patterns.

Trade invoicing and liability alignment intersect with de-dollarisation debates. Nations contemplating diversification away from the U.S. dollar must reconcile ambitions with operational imperatives. Shifting reserves to alternative currencies or regional baskets must correspond to obligations in those currencies; otherwise, the risk of liquidity shortfalls or costly conversions increases. By linking reserve composition directly to trade and debt, central banks maintain functionality while exploring diversification pathways.

The interplay between trade flows and reserve composition also shapes market signalling. Observers often interpret changes in holdings as geopolitical or strategic statements, but underlying motivations are frequently operational. Hungary's euro allocation was driven by debt servicing pragmatics rather than any overt shift in geopolitical alignment. Understanding the operational drivers behind currency allocations helps distinguish between functional reserve management and symbolic gestures.

A quiet motif threads through this landscape: alignment under constraint. Central banks adjust reserves incrementally to match trade receipts and debt obligations, balancing liquidity, safety, and return, while responding to operational realities and institutional access. Each adjustment, whether increasing euro holdings to match debt or retaining dollars for global liquidity, exemplifies disciplined portfolio management. The subsequent section examines how swap lines and regional pools further influence these decisions, revealing the institutional mechanisms that expand flexibility without undermining prudence.

Using swap lines and regional pools

In March 2020, as global financial markets convulsed under the early shocks of the COVID-19 pandemic, the Federal Reserve extended temporary U.S. dollar swap lines to nine central banks, including Brazil, Mexico, and Singapore. These arrangements enabled recipient central banks to draw dollars against local currency collateral, providing liquidity without immediately selling domestic reserves into turbulent markets. For Brazil, this mechanism allowed the central bank to stabilise domestic funding markets and maintain foreign exchange reserves at prudent levels. The episode highlighted a key evolution in reserve management: access to institutional backstops can alter the composition and operational use of reserves.

Swap lines and regional reserve pools function as contingent liquidity, effectively substituting for holding large amounts of foreign assets physically. By providing guaranteed access to a major currency, they reduce the need for pre-positioned holdings, allowing central banks to reallocate reserves across more diversified baskets or retain liquidity for domestic priorities. For instance, a central bank with access to a robust regional pool may hold a smaller proportion of U.S. dollars, confident that it can obtain dollars on demand to meet obligations or intervene in markets. Conversely, a bank without such access must maintain larger liquid holdings in major currencies, potentially limiting the scope for diversification into regional currencies, gold, or longer-dated instruments.

The mechanics of these arrangements vary. Bilateral swap lines, such as those the Federal Reserve maintains with other major central banks, operate on reciprocal terms with defined ceilings, tenors, and collateral requirements. Regional pools, exemplified by the Chiang Mai Initiative Multilateralisation (CMIM) in ASEAN+3, aggregate commitments from multiple member countries, creating a collective safety net. CMIM participants can draw on the pool in times of balance-of-payments stress, subject to pre-agreed conditions and approvals. For smaller or emerging economies, the existence of such a backstop provides both operational confidence and the flexibility to reduce concentrated holdings in major currencies.

A scenario illustrates the practical impact. Consider a mid-sized central bank in Southeast Asia navigating moderate FX volatility and incremental reserve diversification. Without access to a regional pool, the bank maintains substantial dollar holdings to cover potential external debt payments and trade settlement. Liquidity concerns constrain its ability to invest in local-currency assets abroad or increase allocations to gold. With a regional pool, however, the bank can reduce dollar holdings by 20–30 percent, confident that it can draw on the pool if necessary. This alters reserve composition strategy, reduces transaction costs, and enables a more balanced approach to risk and return.

Swap lines and pools also influence market signalling. Access can enhance credibility and investor confidence, as counterparties perceive reduced systemic risk. In contrast, a lack of backstops can elevate perceived vulnerability, particularly during periods of currency volatility or stress in global dollar markets. The European Central Bank's network of swap lines during the eurozone sovereign debt crisis offered a parallel example: access to dollar liquidity mitigated pressures on European banks, allowing national central banks to avoid excessive interventions in foreign-exchange markets. These arrangements demonstrate that reserve composition decisions are not solely technical but intertwined with perceptions of stability and operational reliability.

However, reliance on swap lines and pools is not without constraints. Liquidity is contingent, often subject to policy discretion, collateral requirements, and utilisation limits. Drawing on a pool may entail signalling pressures or political negotiations, potentially affecting the timing and magnitude of interventions. Additionally, operational readiness is crucial: central banks must maintain systems and expertise to activate these facilities efficiently. The mere existence of a swap line does not substitute for prudent reserve planning; it complements but does not replace fundamental risk management.

Legal frameworks underpin these facilities. Bilateral and multilateral agreements define eligibility, draw conditions, collateralisation, and repayment schedules. For CMIM, activation requires both the request of the borrowing member and approval from the Monetary and Financial Affairs Committee, introducing governance layers that influence the speed and certainty of access. In practice, this means central banks weigh potential delays and administrative constraints when determining how much reserve liquidity to hold physically versus relying on contingent lines.

Empirical patterns illustrate their effect on reserve composition. Data from the Bank for International Settlements show that central banks with active swap arrangements tend to hold smaller shares of physical foreign currency, particularly in U.S. dollars, than those without comparable access. They compensate with diversified portfolios incorporating regional currencies, local sovereign debt, or gold, confident that liquidity can be drawn from institutional mechanisms if needed. These patterns reinforce the principle that institutional backstops expand strategic flexibility while maintaining operational security.

Regional pools offer additional benefits beyond simple liquidity. By pooling commitments across countries, they enable smaller economies to achieve a collective scale that would be unattainable individually. This reduces reliance on external creditors and enhances negotiation leverage in global markets. The CMIM example demonstrates how coordinated access can stabilise intra-regional trade corridors, as member countries can rely on pooled resources to smooth temporary funding gaps. Such structures also facilitate cooperative surveillance and monitoring, enabling early warning of systemic stress and coordinated policy responses.

Nonetheless, limitations exist. Access is typically capped, utilisation may require approval, and drawing funds can signal stress to markets, potentially influencing investor sentiment. Central banks must therefore calibrate reliance on these facilities against the need for independent liquidity management. Overreliance can produce moral hazard, encouraging risk-taking under the assumption that contingencies will be available. The prudent strategy is to treat swap lines and pools as complementary tools rather than primary reserves.

The quiet motif running through these arrangements is contingency under constraint. Institutional backstops—whether bilateral swap lines or regional pools—provide optionality, allowing central banks to balance operational risk, liquidity needs, and strategic diversification. Access alters decisions about how much physical currency to hold, which currencies to prioritise, and the allocation across tenors and asset classes. The subsequent discussion on measuring de-dollarisation progress will consider how these arrangements shape interpretations of reserve shifts, highlighting the need to distinguish between functional adjustments and headline-driven perceptions.

Measuring progress of de-dollarisation in reserves

In June 2015, China's central bank reported a sudden reduction in the U.S. dollar share of its foreign exchange reserves, dropping from 64 percent to 61 percent over a single quarter. Headlines emphasised a "shift away from the dollar," prompting immediate speculation in financial media and policy circles. Yet deeper analysis revealed that the change primarily reflected adjustments in short-term money-market instruments, seasonal valuation effects, and rebalancing of euro and yen holdings rather than a decisive strategic shift. The episode illustrates a persistent challenge in interpreting reserve data: headline figures can mislead, masking the incremental and often structural nature of reserve management decisions.

De-dollarisation, the gradual reduction of U.S. dollar dominance in central bank reserves, is a process measured not by single announcements but by sustained trends across multiple reporting periods. Central banks reallocate assets according to liquidity needs, safety considerations, and return expectations, while also responding to external obligations and market conditions. A headline reduction in dollar holdings may coincide with an increase in other major currencies, gold, or regional currencies, but these moves often reflect operational adjustments rather than a sudden abandonment of the dollar. For researchers, journalists, and market participants, discerning genuine strategic shifts from transitory fluctuations is critical.

The tools for interpreting reserve composition are varied. Time-series analysis provides context, revealing whether observed movements are part of an upward or downward trend. Seasonality adjustments and cross-currency valuation effects help isolate structural decisions from routine portfolio rotations. For example, when a European central bank reports a sudden rise in euro-denominated assets, analysts must consider changes in underlying trade exposures, foreign-currency liabilities, and FX swap operations before attributing the move to de-dollarisation intent. The motif of incrementalism recurs: meaningful change emerges gradually, through repeated reallocations and long-term portfolio evolution.

Central banks frequently manage reserves with a combination of major and alternative currencies. A conservative portfolio may concentrate heavily in dollars, euros, and yen, reflecting deep liquidity and global acceptability. In contrast, a more diversified basket incorporates regional currencies or gold to mitigate exposure and support geopolitical hedging. Mexico's central bank, for instance, has consistently held a mix of U.S. dollars and euros while selectively increasing Canadian dollars in response to trade patterns, demonstrating a careful calibration between risk and operational flexibility. Such choices are incremental: a single quarter's adjustment rarely signifies a strategic departure from the dollar as a dominant reserve currency.

One must also account for valuation effects. Fluctuations in exchange rates can alter the reported dollar share of reserves without any underlying transactions. A depreciation of the euro against the dollar inflates the relative dollar proportion even if the central bank has not sold or purchased assets. Conversely, dollar appreciation can make a stable allocation appear to shrink the U.S. share. The International Monetary Fund's COFER (Currency Composition of Official Foreign Exchange Reserves) dataset provides a framework to observe these nuances, distinguishing structural shifts from market-driven reporting artifacts. Analysts often supplement COFER data with country-specific disclosures to better understand the true nature of changes.

Swap lines and access to regional reserve pools further complicate the picture. Central banks with contingency access to major currencies may hold fewer physical dollars, substituting guaranteed liquidity for outright holdings. The ASEAN+3 Chiang Mai Initiative Multilateralisation (CMIM) illustrates this effect: participating central banks can reduce direct dollar reserves while maintaining confidence in funding capabilities. Observed de-dollarisation may therefore overstate or understate actual exposure reductions, depending on how such arrangements are integrated into reporting.

Interpreting reserve news also requires attention to political and signalling dimensions. Announcements of reducing dollar holdings can serve diplomatic or market signals, particularly in the context of emerging de-dollarisation debates. For instance, if a central bank reports an increase in regional currency allocations, observers may perceive a strategic intent to lessen dollar dependence. In reality, the reallocation may reflect operational optimisation, trade alignment, or portfolio efficiency. Cross-checking trends against macroeconomic data, debt denominated in foreign currencies, and historical portfolio allocations helps avoid misreading symbolic announcements as substantive shifts.

Empirical patterns suggest de-dollarisation is typically incremental. Data from multiple emerging markets show that reductions in dollar share rarely exceed a few percentage points per year, often coinciding with increased holdings of euros, yen, or regional currencies. Large-scale reallocations are uncommon, constrained by liquidity needs, global market depth, and the dollar's dominant role in trade invoicing. For instance, a central bank may move 5 percent of reserves into a regional currency and gold over a two-year horizon while maintaining the bulk in dollars, supporting both diversification and operational prudence.

Counter-examples illustrate the pitfalls of overinterpreting isolated moves. Russia's reserve reports in 2018 highlighted a sharp decline in U.S. dollar holdings, sparking narratives of aggressive de-dollarisation. Closer inspection revealed that the reduction largely reflected timing effects in

Eurobond settlement and valuation shifts rather than a wholesale shift in reserve policy. Analysts who failed to contextualise these moves risked drawing exaggerated conclusions about structural changes. Reconciling headline movements with underlying exposures is therefore essential: surface-level data can misrepresent the scale, intent, and impact of reserve adjustments.

A practical approach to evaluating progress involves several metrics. Analysts track multi-year trends in dollar proportion, cross-currency correlations, and the ratio of liquid versus long-dated holdings. Monitoring participation in swap lines, regional pools, and gold allocations provides additional insight into actual exposure and flexibility. Visualising time-series data, rather than relying on single-point snapshots, enables identification of incremental shifts and avoids conflating temporary adjustments with structural de-dollarisation. For example, a central bank gradually increasing holdings in regional currencies by 1–2 percent annually demonstrates a methodical diversification strategy, even if news headlines exaggerate the pace.

The overarching lesson is that de-dollarisation is a process embedded in operational, strategic, and geopolitical dimensions. Central banks balance liquidity, safety, and return while managing liabilities, trade exposures, and contingency access. Observed movements in dollar holdings are just one signal among many; a careful, trend-focused approach reveals the broader trajectory. Readers equipped with a framework for interpreting these signals can distinguish meaningful shifts from noise, understanding how reserve composition reflects a blend of prudence, diversification, and incremental adjustment rather than abrupt policy reversals.

Incrementalism is the quiet motif threading this analysis. Changes in reserve currency composition rarely occur in dramatic leaps. They manifest through repeated, measured reallocations, supported by backstops such as swap lines, regional pools, and market instruments. By focusing on trends, valuation effects, operational contingencies, and signalling, analysts gain a robust perspective on de-dollarisation progress. The final question for policymakers and observers alike is how to interpret these trends accurately: which movements represent genuine strategic evolution, and which merely reflect the ebb and flow of operational reserve management?

Chapter 11

Investor Confidence And Political Risk

In January 2018, the Turkish lira suffered a precipitous drop of nearly 20 percent against the U.S. dollar in just two weeks. International investors cited a mix of high inflation, rising external debt, and concerns over central bank independence. Yet the sharpest reactions stemmed not from economic fundamentals alone, but from a perceived erosion of institutional credibility. The scenario encapsulates a recurring tension in emerging markets: a currency's value is not only a function of trade balances or interest rates, but also the confidence that investors place in governance, predictability, and legal structures. Observers watching the lira's slide recognised that a country with shallower markets but strong institutional frameworks, such as Chile, might weather similar shocks more effectively, illustrating that credibility is inherently multi-dimensional.

Investor confidence extends far beyond macroeconomic indicators. It hinges on the clarity, transparency, and consistency of domestic policy choices. Fiscal prudence, predictable monetary policy, and adherence to rule-of-law frameworks signal reliability. Conversely, sudden capital controls, unilateral regulatory changes, or opaque interventions can trigger capital flight even in otherwise sound economies. In early 2013, for example, India's surprise restrictions on foreign portfolio investments led to immediate reversals in inflows, temporarily undermining trust in the rupee despite robust growth prospects. Such episodes underscore that domestic choices reverberate through global corridors, influencing both short-term access to capital and long-term perceptions of a currency's credibility.

Beyond governance and policy, the depth and sophistication of financial markets determine whether investors can act on their confidence. Currencies with active government bond markets, liquid derivatives, and accessible hedging instruments provide the infrastructure necessary for meaningful international engagement. Consider Brazil in the late 2000s:

despite rising trade usage of the real, limited derivative markets constrained hedging possibilities for foreign investors, tempering enthusiasm for sustained reserve or portfolio allocations. Similarly, smaller emerging-market currencies may experience sporadic interest, but without adequate instruments to manage exposure, confidence remains conditional and fragile. The interplay between market depth and credibility demonstrates that trust is as much operational as it is perceptual.

Reputational shocks can instantly recalibrate confidence. Sovereign defaults, high-profile banking scandals, or abrupt political crises transmit across borders, challenging the assumptions underpinning currency stability. Argentina's 2001-2002 sovereign restructuring illustrates how reputational damage compounds existing economic vulnerabilities, constraining both access to international funding and market valuations. Recovery, however, is possible through a combination of transparent reforms, engagement with international institutions, and a gradual re-establishment of predictable policy signals. The path is rarely rapid: investors are acutely aware of the cost of misjudging risk, and credibility rebuilds only through sustained evidence of institutional reliability.

Finally, the chapter explores the delicate balancing act faced by policymakers: achieving monetary and fiscal autonomy while maintaining sufficient liquidity and stability to attract external investors. Incremental policy steps—gradual liberalisation, phased reforms, transparent communication—often succeed where abrupt, disruptive measures fail. Contrast this with rapid, unilateral interventions, which may signal ambition but risk undermining long-term trust. This tension between sovereignty and investor confidence defines the modern challenge of managing emerging-market currencies, highlighting that political choices are inseparable from technical considerations.

Across these dimensions—governance, policy predictability, market infrastructure, and reputational management—the central theme emerges clearly: investor confidence is both fragile and multi-faceted. It shapes currency attractiveness, affects corridor participation, and ultimately conditions the global role a currency can play. By analysing patterns across emerging markets, examining the interplay of domestic and external factors, and tracking the consequences of reputational events, readers gain a structured understanding of how political risk and institutional credibility coalesce to influence investor behaviour. The chapter invites reflection on the interplay between policy, perception, and practical market realities, framing the complex calculus that underpins currency confidence in an interconnected financial world.

How investors judge currency credibility

In March 2014, the South African rand experienced a sudden depreciation of nearly 15 percent against the U.S. dollar, prompted less by immediate economic shocks than by investor perceptions of political and institutional fragility. While the country's trade fundamentals remained largely intact, concerns over fiscal discipline, central bank autonomy, and governance under President Jacob Zuma's administration amplified capital flight. Investors responded not merely to raw metrics but to their composite assessment of the currency's credibility. A contrasting scenario emerges when one examines Chile in the same period: although its domestic markets were relatively shallow, strong institutions, consistent inflation targeting, and clear regulatory frameworks underpinned investor confidence, limiting abrupt currency swings despite external pressures. These cases illustrate a crucial principle: credibility is multidimensional, blending economic performance with institutional and legal structures, and cannot be inferred from any single metric.

Investors assessing currency credibility weigh inflation history heavily. Persistent high inflation erodes purchasing power, complicates hedging strategies, and signals potential policy weaknesses. Consider Argentina, where repeated inflationary spikes during the early 2000s undermined confidence in the peso. Even when interest rates offered nominally attractive returns, international investors hesitated to hold peso-denominated assets due to historical volatility and the perceived unpredictability of monetary policy. Conversely, countries like Poland in the late 2010s maintained moderate, stable inflation under credible central bank management, allowing the zloty to attract portfolio inflows despite comparatively smaller capital markets. Inflation history acts as a visible metric, translating abstract policy credibility into tangible investment behaviour.

Institutions and governance frameworks form the next pillar of evaluation. Central bank independence, transparency in fiscal reporting, rule of law, and the robustness of regulatory bodies shape perceptions of risk. In Indonesia during the mid-2000s, reforms to strengthen central bank autonomy and enhance financial oversight reassured international investors, resulting in increased foreign participation in rupiah-denominated assets. By contrast, in nations where executive overreach or opaque policymaking persisted, capital inflows were episodic and highly sensitive to political developments.

These institutional factors interact with market signals, demonstrating that governance and predictability are as crucial to credibility as economic fundamentals themselves.

Market depth and liquidity further influence investor behaviour. Currencies with active government bond markets, liquid derivatives, and accessible hedging instruments allow investors to manage exposure efficiently. For instance, the Indian rupee's limited offshore hedging options constrained portfolio allocations for foreign investors during the early 2010s, even as India's macro fundamentals were strong. Conversely, currencies such as the Brazilian real began to benefit from expanding bond issuance and derivative instruments in the late 2000s, enhancing market confidence despite political volatility. Shallow markets, no matter how well-governed, reduce practical usability for global investors, underscoring that credibility encompasses both perception and operational feasibility.

Historical volatility and reputational memory also shape investor expectations. Investors draw lessons from previous crises, calibrating their risk appetite based on past policy reactions. Mexico's handling of the 1994 peso crisis created long-term reputational effects: subsequent reforms, including inflation targeting and debt management, slowly rebuilt trust, allowing the peso to regain international credibility. By contrast, countries repeating policy missteps face persistent scepticism, requiring structural reforms to restore confidence. Reputation functions as both a lagging and leading indicator—past actions constrain present perceptions and shape anticipated responses.

The interplay between these factors—macroeconomic stability, institutional strength, market depth, and reputational track record—creates a multidimensional framework for evaluating currency credibility. Investors rarely rely on a single metric; instead, they construct a composite view, weighing the likelihood of policy consistency, liquidity access, and predictable governance outcomes. Even currencies with robust macro fundamentals can be deemed risky if institutional frameworks are weak or market access is constrained, illustrating the nuanced calculus behind portfolio decisions.

Scenarios highlight these interactions. A country with shallow markets but strong institutions may attract cautious, long-term portfolio allocations, while a more developed market with fragile governance may experience volatile flows, sensitive to political news or unexpected interventions. Investors' responses reflect not only technical considerations but behavioural and psychological assessments of trustworthiness, predictability, and structural soundness.

These considerations inform broader debates on de-dollarisation and reserve diversification. Countries seeking to reduce reliance on a single global currency must consider whether their domestic currency possesses the credibility required to attract international investors. Without stable inflation, enforceable legal frameworks, and sufficient market instruments, such initiatives may falter despite policy intentions. Investors' judgements shape the practical feasibility of such strategies, linking domestic policy and infrastructure to global financial integration.

Ultimately, understanding how investors judge currency credibility requires integrating macroeconomic, institutional, and market dimensions into a coherent analytical framework. Inflation histories, governance structures, market depth, and reputational memory each provide tangible signals that influence decisions. Observing contrasting patterns across emerging markets illustrates the delicate balance between perception and reality, demonstrating why credibility is multi-faceted, context-dependent, and central to currency adoption in international portfolios. These dynamics underpin subsequent discussions on policy predictability, market infrastructure, and the broader political risk landscape that influence corridor stability and capital allocation.

Domestic policy choices and trust

In January 2013, Argentina imposed sudden restrictions on capital outflows, capping foreign exchange purchases for residents at $2,000 per month. The measure aimed to stem a weakening peso and preserve central bank reserves, but it reverberated far beyond immediate financial markets. International investors reacted with alarm, and the credibility of the peso as a reliable medium for investment was questioned. Portfolio allocations were sharply reduced, credit spreads widened, and the country's access to global funding became more expensive. The episode demonstrates a central lesson: domestic fiscal and monetary choices do not operate in isolation. Their predictability, transparency, and alignment with broader policy frameworks determine whether a currency can be trusted for international and domestic purposes alike.

Fiscal discipline is the first pillar of trust. Governments that maintain sustainable deficits and transparent reporting convey predictability to markets. Brazil in the early 2000s, under its Fiscal Responsibility Law, managed deficits with disciplined accounting and regular disclosure, bolstering investor confidence in the real despite wider macroeconomic turbulence. Conversely, sudden fiscal adjustments or opaque accounting—as seen in the Greek debt crisis of 2009—amplified market fears, leading to rapid capital flight and heightened borrowing costs. Investors respond not only to numerical outcomes but to the perceived reliability of decision-making institutions. Credibility is thus built through both visible metrics and the consistency of policy signals.

Monetary policy complements fiscal stewardship. A central bank that maintains clear, consistent, and communicable frameworks for interest rates, inflation targeting, and liquidity management earns trust. The Reserve Bank of India's transparent inflation-targeting regime in 2016, for example, reinforced the rupee's credibility among foreign investors, enabling smoother access to capital inflows and reducing currency volatility. In contrast, abrupt shifts in policy rates or uncommunicated interventions—as occurred in Turkey during late 2018—eroded confidence and triggered rapid depreciation, illustrating how unpredictability in central banking can amplify market risk perception.

Transparency acts as the connective tissue between fiscal and monetary policy. Publicly available data, regular reporting, and clear explanations of policy choices reduce information asymmetry. South Korea's open communication strategy during the 2008–2009 global financial crisis, detailing reserve positions and intervention policies, allowed investors to maintain confidence in the won even as global risk appetite contracted. Lack of transparency, however, can magnify perceived risk: opaque interventions or delayed reporting raise uncertainty, which investors often price more severely than actual policy shifts. Predictability is not only a matter of outcomes but of signalling and visibility.

Capital controls illustrate the fragility of trust. While technically effective for stabilising short-term flows, they carry long-term reputational costs. Argentina's 2013 measures curtailed immediate currency outflows, but investors internalised a higher risk premium, anticipating that future restrictions might recur. Similarly, Malaysia's imposition of capital controls during the 1997–1998 Asian Financial Crisis stabilised the ringgit temporarily but left an enduring mark on international perceptions of policy consistency. These cases highlight a trade-off: immediate stabilisation versus sustained credibility. Markets reward transparent, rule-based frameworks and punish abrupt, discretionary interventions.

The cumulative effect of domestic policy choices shapes a currency's attractiveness within broader financial corridors. Investors seek predictability: they evaluate not only economic fundamentals but also the likelihood that authorities will act consistently and communicate intentions clearly. Currencies backed by predictable, transparent policy regimes are more likely to be used for trade settlement, investment portfolios, and reserve allocations. Conversely, abrupt policy shifts erode corridor participation, increasing reliance on alternative currencies or markets. This dynamic links domestic governance directly to international financial integration.

Institutional credibility interacts with market infrastructure. Well-designed debt markets, hedging instruments, and liquid securities amplify the impact of credible policy, while shallow or underdeveloped markets can constrain the benefits of otherwise sound choices. South Africa's gradual development of bond and derivative markets in the 2010s illustrates how infrastructure strengthens the transmission of trust: investors could respond to policy signals with actual allocation adjustments rather than speculative withdrawals. Without adequate instruments, even transparent policy may fail to anchor investor behaviour effectively.

Political considerations, though distinct from technical policy, influence trust. Frequent leadership changes, opaque decision-making processes, or unpredictable legal interventions amplify perceived risk. Mexico's economic reforms in the early 2010s reinforced confidence partly because institutional structures insulated monetary and fiscal policy from short-term political pressures. Countries lacking such insulation face amplified volatility and higher risk premia, regardless of underlying economic strength. Investors interpret domestic political dynamics as part of the credibility calculus.

Ultimately, domestic policy choices—fiscal, monetary, and regulatory—serve as both signals and tools of trust. Predictability, transparency, and rule-consistent execution determine whether investors consider a currency reliable. Abrupt interventions, opaque communication, or poorly anchored expectations can rapidly erode confidence, while disciplined, transparent policy fosters long-term credibility. These considerations link directly to corridor behaviour: the willingness of foreign and domestic participants to transact, hold, and settle in a given currency depends on a robust, predictable, and observable policy framework.

Understanding these dynamics is essential for assessing the international role of emerging-market currencies, the feasibility of de-dollarisation initiatives, and the stability of cross-border payment corridors. Investors do not respond to policy mechanically; they internalise a multidimensional view of credibility, weighing historical consistency, institutional strength, transparency, and infrastructure. This framework frames subsequent discussions on market depth, hedging instruments, and reputational shocks, illustrating how domestic governance choices ripple outward into global financial integration and corridor attractiveness.

Market depth, instruments, and hedging tools

In March 2019, the National Bank of Kazakhstan noted a growing share of its international trade invoiced in tenge, signalling increased regional adoption. Yet, foreign investors remained hesitant to hold tenge-denominated assets. The central reason was not the currency itself but the limited infrastructure for hedging and risk management. Only a handful of liquid government bonds existed, derivative contracts were shallow, and forward contracts covered only short maturities. As a result, even as trade use expanded, market participants struggled to manage exposure to exchange-rate volatility, constraining deeper financial integration and the currency's potential role in regional corridors. This tension illustrates that adoption depends not only on usage but on the instruments enabling risk mitigation.

Market depth forms the backbone of investor confidence. A currency with deep, liquid bond markets allows participants to allocate significant capital without causing disruptive price movements. Brazil's local-currency bond market provides an instructive contrast. By 2015, the Brazilian real supported a spectrum of instruments—from short-term treasury bills to long-dated bonds and interest rate swaps—allowing investors to manage duration and currency risk efficiently. This infrastructure enabled foreign holdings of reals to grow alongside domestic usage, fostering a feedback loop of liquidity and trust. Conversely, currencies with limited debt issuance or narrow investor bases, even if supported by stable macroeconomic fundamentals, struggle to attract the same scale of international allocations. The depth of available instruments transforms abstract credibility into tangible, tradable assurance.

Hedging tools complement bond markets by allowing participants to manage foreign-exchange and interest-rate exposure. Without forwards, swaps, or options, investors face uncompensated volatility. Turkey's experience in the early 2010s highlights this interplay. Despite robust economic growth, a relatively shallow derivatives market limited hedging options for non-resident holders of lira-denominated debt. Foreign inflows were episodic, responding to short-term yield advantages rather than a sustained confidence in currency stability. When the lira depreciated sharply in 2018, unhedged positions amplified losses, demonstrating how inadequate hedging infrastructure can convert potential investment into systemic risk. Instruments are therefore critical enablers of both scale and resilience in currency adoption.

Liquidity, not just nominal size, dictates usability in cross-border corridors. A currency with large outstanding issuance but thin secondary markets can exhibit volatile spreads and limited fill capacity. The Russian ruble provides a case study: domestic bond issuance is substantial, yet foreign participation remains limited because secondary market depth, transparency, and international clearing arrangements are constrained. Even when trade invoices increase in rubles, these liquidity gaps temper investor willingness to hold currency balances or engage in forward markets. Liquidity metrics—average daily turnover, bid-ask spreads, and settlement reliability—serve as practical proxies for assessing usability beyond headline trade volumes.

Infrastructure gaps extend beyond debt markets. Payment systems, clearing mechanisms, and settlement reliability influence the attractiveness of a currency for international transactions. The Chinese renminbi illustrates the effects of integrated infrastructure. Offshore CNH markets, coupled with clearing arrangements in Hong Kong and London, provide foreign investors with settlement options, hedging instruments, and collateral management. This network complements domestic depth, enabling broader adoption in trade and reserves. By contrast, currencies without comparable clearing or collateral frameworks face structural barriers to scale, limiting adoption even when macro fundamentals are sound.

Incremental adoption reflects the interaction between usage and market instruments. As the tenge example in Kazakhstan shows, trade invoicing alone does not guarantee investor engagement. A phased expansion of bond issuance, the introduction of standardized derivatives, and gradual market liberalisation can allow a currency to grow in both transactional and reserve contexts. Investors evaluate not only current availability but forward-looking capacity to hedge and liquidate positions. The presence or absence of these instruments shapes the speed, size, and stability of inflows, and ultimately the currency's role in regional or global corridors.

Counter-examples highlight the importance of breadth, not just depth. The Argentine peso, heavily traded in domestic markets, still exhibits limited offshore liquidity and a narrow suite of hedging tools. Consequently, foreign participation remains sporadic and concentrated in short tenors, exposing investors to rollover and exchange-rate risks. Even with policy predictability, instrument gaps constrain credible adoption. These cases emphasise that credibility must be matched by operational capability: the market must be able to absorb, price, and manage risk at scale.

Institutional support can mitigate some limitations. Access to central bank swap lines, collateralised lending, and regional reserve pools supplements local market depth, allowing participants to transact with reduced risk. For example, ASEAN central banks' collaborative arrangements provide liquidity backstops for emerging currencies, enabling cross-border settlement despite shallow domestic markets. Such institutional scaffolding bridges gaps in instruments, but cannot fully replace the need for robust domestic bond and derivative markets. Investors consistently weigh the combination of policy credibility, liquidity, and hedging capacity when allocating reserves or engaging in trade settlement.

Ultimately, the adoption and resilience of a currency for cross-border transactions is multidimensional. Depth of bonds, breadth of derivatives, and available hedging tools collectively determine whether a currency can support meaningful investment and settlement activity. Limited instruments constrain de-dollarisation: even currencies with increasing trade usage may fail to attract foreign holdings or form stable corridors without sufficient infrastructure. This framework connects domestic market development, international confidence, and the practical capacity to manage exposure, highlighting that financial plumbing extends far beyond the visible act of payment.

Evaluating market depth requires careful attention to real metrics. Daily turnover in liquid bonds, open interest in derivative contracts, and settlement volumes offer measurable proxies for capacity. Observing these trends over time, rather than reacting to headline trade data, provides a realistic picture of a currency's ability to scale internationally. The analysis underscores that while policy and credibility matter, the operational infrastructure of markets—including instruments and hedging tools—ultimately dictates whether de-dollarisation initiatives can translate from concept to sustained practice.

Reputational shocks and recovery paths

In August 2001, Argentina defaulted on approximately $93 billion of sovereign debt, the largest sovereign default at that time. The peso plunged, and investors around the world suddenly reassessed exposure to Argentine assets. International confidence evaporated almost overnight: bond spreads widened to over 1,600 basis points, foreign portfolio inflows halted, and currency holdings outside domestic markets became highly risky. The default was not merely a fiscal event; it triggered a reputational shock that affected the peso's perceived credibility for years. Even when macroeconomic adjustments and policy reforms were later implemented, the lingering memory of that default constrained Argentina's ability to attract long-term foreign investment. This episode illustrates how quickly trust can erode and why rebuilding it requires deliberate, often incremental action.

Reputational shocks typically arise from identifiable events—defaults, financial scandals, or abrupt political crises. The Russian financial crisis of 1998 provides a complementary example. After the government devalued the ruble and defaulted on short-term domestic debt, investors rapidly withdrew capital, while the currency experienced severe volatility. International holdings of ruble assets became unattractive, and correspondent banks temporarily limited exposure to Russian instruments. These market reactions highlight that currency credibility is not just an abstract assessment; it manifests through observable behaviours such as capital flight, widening spreads, and contraction of trade invoicing. The immediacy of these effects underscores the fragility of trust once structural shocks occur.

Recovery from such shocks is rarely instantaneous. Argentina's path demonstrates that multiple mechanisms must converge: fiscal consolidation, monetary policy credibility, and engagement with international financial institutions. Following the default, Argentina negotiated a restructuring with private creditors, gradually restored macroeconomic stability, and leveraged support from the International Monetary Fund to reassure markets. Bond spreads tightened slowly, and while foreign reserves began to rebuild, foreign investors remained cautious for several years. This illustrates a broader principle: reputational damage can be repaired, but the process requires sustained signalling of stability and policy reliability.

The channels of reputational repair often combine domestic reform with international reassurance. Structural reforms in fiscal transparency, strengthened central bank independence, and adherence to predictable regulatory practices signal that future crises are less likely. Complementarily, international support—through swap lines, multilateral lending, or coordinated reserve arrangements—provides tangible backstops that reduce perceived risk. In the Turkish experience following the 2001 banking crisis, a comprehensive package of reforms supported by the IMF gradually restored investor confidence. By 2004, foreign holdings of Turkish lira-denominated assets had recovered sufficiently to allow broader market participation. These cases demonstrate that recovery requires both visible policy change and credible external validation.

Reputational recovery also depends on the underlying depth and liquidity of the currency's markets. A currency may be technically sound, but if bond markets are thin or derivatives for hedging are limited, investor confidence remains constrained. Post-default, Argentina's local-currency bond markets slowly expanded, and derivative products became available, allowing foreign investors to manage exchange-rate and duration risk. Similarly, South Africa's gradual development of domestic debt instruments after fiscal turbulence in the late 1980s allowed rand holdings to recover in global portfolios. These examples show that repairing credibility is not merely about policy promises; it is reinforced by infrastructure that enables secure, scalable participation.

Counter-examples reveal the limits of reputational repair. The case of Greece during the 2010 sovereign crisis illustrates how reputational damage can linger despite external support. Even after bailout packages and debt restructuring, political uncertainty and market skepticism persisted, keeping borrowing costs elevated for years. This demonstrates that reputational shocks are path-dependent: the severity and context of the initial event, combined with the consistency of follow-up measures, determine how quickly trust can be restored. Recovery paths are rarely linear and often encounter reversals if reforms are perceived as incomplete or inconsistent.

Incremental re-engagement is a common motif in rebuilding credibility. Countries that gradually reintroduce bonds to international markets, maintain transparent communication, and foster predictable fiscal and monetary policies tend to recover faster than those seeking abrupt reintegration. Argentina's phased return to bond markets, coupled with external guarantees, exemplifies this approach. Rapid, untested re-entry can backfire if the institutional and market infrastructure is insufficient, creating renewed volatility and potentially compounding reputational damage. Investors assess both the signals and the underlying capacity to meet obligations.

Ultimately, reputational shocks highlight the interplay between policy, market perception, and investor behaviour. They demonstrate that credibility is multidimensional: it reflects legal frameworks, institutional quality, debt sustainability, and the ability to manage crises. Recovery paths, whether through reforms, external support, or market infrastructure development, require careful sequencing and patience. While reputational damage constrains a currency's use in reserves and trade, structured approaches can restore confidence, allowing currencies to re-enter corridors of international finance. The challenge lies in navigating trade-offs between speed of policy adjustment and maintaining the credibility signals necessary to attract sustained investor engagement.

This dynamic underlines a recurring tension: markets remember crises longer than they remember reforms, and investors weigh not only current policy but historical patterns of reliability. Sovereign restructurings, regulatory overhauls, and external guarantees all contribute, but each element must be credible in isolation and in combination. For policymakers and market participants, understanding the mechanics of reputational shock and the realistic timelines for recovery is essential. Even when reforms succeed technically, perception lags, creating a persistent window in which investor confidence, corridor access, and currency credibility remain vulnerable.

Balancing autonomy, liquidity, and stability

In September 2013, Turkey's central bank faced a stark test of policy discretion. With capital inflows surging and the lira appreciating rapidly, policymakers weighed interventions to protect export competitiveness against the risk of alarming foreign investors. A modest, carefully signalled tightening of interest rates aimed to temper volatility, while communication emphasised transparency and predictability. The result: short-term fluctuations persisted, but credibility remained largely intact, and foreign portfolio flows did not evaporate. The episode illustrates the delicate calculus central banks face when seeking greater autonomy: asserting control over domestic monetary conditions without destabilising external confidence. Every policy move in such contexts carries a dual message, both operational and symbolic, conveying competence, caution, or recklessness to international participants.

The trade-off between autonomy and liquidity is rarely purely technical. Central banks may wish to manage exchange rates or expand monetary policy options, yet the depth and openness of their financial markets constrain feasible action. In Brazil during 2015, attempts to sterilise capital inflows through domestic instruments temporarily insulated the real from appreciation. However, the limited liquidity of derivative and bond markets meant interventions quickly tightened market conditions, raising borrowing costs for domestic firms. Here, operational ambition collided with market structure: autonomy in policy required compatible instruments and sufficient market depth. Policymakers learned that asserting control without infrastructure support can inadvertently erode stability.

Stability itself is multidimensional. It encompasses exchange-rate consistency, predictable interest-rate paths, and resilience to shocks. India's cautious liberalisation of capital accounts in the 1990s provides an illustrative contrast. Incremental steps, phased over years with strong communication and regulatory scaffolding, allowed the rupee to integrate into global finance while preserving macroeconomic stability. By contrast, abrupt liberalisations in some Latin American economies produced speculative attacks and sharp currency swings, highlighting the fragility of confidence when autonomy is exercised without supportive frameworks. These cases underline a recurring motif: the sequencing and signalling of policy choices are as critical as the decisions themselves.

Policymakers frequently face scenarios where incrementalism and rapid action yield divergent outcomes. An incremental approach, as in India, often preserves credibility and gradually deepens market infrastructure. A more aggressive, disruptive strategy may achieve immediate policy objectives, such as rapid reserve accumulation or exchange-rate realignment, but risks provoking capital flight or widening bond spreads. For instance, Turkey's 2018 policy responses to lira depreciation included both market interventions and communication strategies that initially restored calm, but overreach and inconsistent messaging later exacerbated volatility. Observing these episodes illustrates that trade-offs are evaluated not only in macroeconomic terms but through investor perception, which reacts to both visible actions and implied intent.

Liquidity considerations extend beyond immediate market operations. Access to foreign reserves, the depth of domestic securities, and derivative instruments for hedging all affect the feasibility of autonomous policy. A central bank with abundant reserves can absorb shocks while defending chosen policy stances; one with shallow markets cannot. The experience of Argentina post-2001 default demonstrates this tension. Efforts to implement independent policy clashed with thin domestic capital markets, compelling reliance on external support and limiting the bank's effective autonomy. Without adequate liquidity, even well-intentioned policies can transmit instability rather than reassurance.

Institutional credibility compounds these trade-offs. Markets calibrate confidence not merely on the technical features of policy but on the perceived rule of law, independence of the central bank, and past adherence to announced objectives. South Africa's monetary authority, after periods of political turbulence in the 1980s, gradually rebuilt credibility by establishing operational independence and transparent communication channels. Investors responded positively, allowing the rand to function as a credible store of value despite structural limitations in domestic markets. Conversely, repeated deviations from announced objectives in other emerging markets eroded confidence, amplifying sensitivity to every policy adjustment.

Counter-examples demonstrate the limits of balancing autonomy, liquidity, and stability. Venezuela's aggressive monetary interventions and exchange controls since 2013 illustrate the perils of prioritising autonomy at the expense of liquidity and credibility. The central bank's unilateral adjustments, without sufficient market depth or transparent policy signalling, triggered hyperinflation, capital flight, and persistent investor distrust. The outcome underscores that autonomy without structural support and credible institutions can destabilise both domestic and external confidence.

Ultimately, the calculus for policymakers is inherently political. Choices over interest rates, exchange-rate management, and capital controls are evaluated by both domestic constituencies and international investors. They involve weighing short-term operational goals against the long-term perception of stability and reliability. Currencies are not simply technical tools; they are instruments whose credibility is socially and politically constructed. Incremental, well-signalled actions can gradually expand autonomy while preserving investor trust, whereas rapid, uncoordinated interventions may produce immediate but unsustainable gains.

The motif of trade-offs threads through every scenario: autonomy must be supported by liquidity; liquidity must coexist with stability; stability requires credible institutions. Observing case studies across emerging markets reveals patterns rather than prescriptions: cautious calibration often yields more durable confidence than disruptive assertiveness. The challenge lies in sequencing policy, managing investor expectations, and continuously reinforcing institutional credibility. As markets evolve and global linkages deepen, policymakers must balance these dimensions dynamically, recognising that misjudgements in one domain reverberate across others, influencing both the scope of autonomy and the sustainability of stability.

This tension between ambition and restraint, between technical capacity and political judgement, frames the final assessment of monetary corridors and currency credibility. Readers are invited to consider not only which actions are possible, but which combinations of autonomy, liquidity, and stability are likely to sustain confidence over time, setting the stage for scenario synthesis and strategic foresight in international finance.

Chapter 12

Scenarios For A Multi-Currency Future

In early 2025, a mid-sized European exporter faced a decision that encapsulated a subtle but accelerating shift in global finance. Its trade with Asia, Africa, and the Americas increasingly required settlement in three different currencies, each flowing through distinct corridors: euros for regional suppliers, dollars for raw materials sourced from the United States, and renminbi for transactions with Chinese partners. Treasury teams juggled liquidity, hedging, and operational compliance across these channels, a practical demonstration that the international monetary system was fragmenting—not chaotically, but along predictable corridors. The scenario posed a question: what if the world does not converge on a single reserve or transaction currency, but instead evolves a patchwork of overlapping systems, each shaped by geography, sector, and institutional trust?

Such a multi-currency future challenges long-held assumptions about global dominance. The dollar's primacy in reserves and cross-border flows has long underpinned predictable corridors, yet persistent shifts in trade patterns, regional integration, and technology-enabled settlement networks suggest a more pluralistic landscape. Consider a world where the dollar remains the dominant reserve currency, yet regional trade is increasingly settled in local or alternative currencies. Here, the conventional metric of dominance—reserve holdings—coexists with a more nuanced reality: transactional usage, liquidity depth, and corridor reliability. Investors, corporates, and policymakers must therefore adopt a vocabulary that captures both structural dominance and operational flexibility, recognising that stability may emerge from diversity rather than uniformity.

Mapping these possibilities requires a structured lens. One can envisage three archetypal scenarios: entrenched dollar dominance, in which global reserves and most cross-border payments remain heavily dollarised; gradual diversification, where multiple currencies gain regional or sectoral traction without displacing the dollar; and structured currency blocs, in which groups of states align around regional hubs and coordinated corridors. Reality is unlikely to conform neatly to any single archetype. Instead, hybrids will emerge: a mixture of dollar-heavy reserves, selective regional settlements, and CBDC-mediated corridors offering speed and programmability. For example, a corporation may use the dollar for funding, a regional currency for trade, and a CBDC bridge to access faster payments across borders. Understanding this spectrum equips readers with frameworks for assessing emerging trends without fixating on headline shifts alone.

Corridor-based structures are central to this landscape. As swap lines, regional hubs, and CBDC bridges proliferate, each corridor develops a functional identity defined by liquidity, trust, and operational reliability. A multinational navigating three corridors encounters trade-offs: hedging costs, settlement speed, and regulatory complexity vary across channels. Fragmentation is not synonymous with disorder; instead, it reflects a deliberate optimisation of flows. This lens allows policymakers and firms to anticipate where resilience and efficiency will matter most, and where over-reliance on a single corridor may create vulnerabilities. Historical analogues, such as the emergence of European clearing systems in the 1990s, demonstrate that parallel infrastructures can coexist, providing both redundancy and targeted efficiency.

For states and central banks, the multi-currency future demands strategic clarity. Large countries must balance global influence with corridor-specific investments, ensuring that domestic institutions can participate effectively in chosen networks. Mid-sized economies may focus on selective corridor integration, concentrating resources on one or two reliable channels while monitoring peripheral alternatives. Policy coherence, transparent communication, and infrastructure readiness are prerequisites for maintaining credibility and operational effectiveness. These choices do not dictate specific reforms but shape the boundaries within which autonomy, liquidity, and stability interact.

Firms and financial institutions confront a parallel set of operational imperatives. Treasury departments must upgrade systems for multi-currency processing, enhance hedging sophistication, and manage compliance across diverse regulatory landscapes. Data visibility, flexible instruments, and operational agility become as critical as traditional risk metrics. Consider a mid-sized exporter that has historically relied on a single currency corridor. Expanding into multiple channels requires not only technical adaptation but also cultural shifts in decision-making, coordination, and risk assessment. The firm's experience reflects broader structural pressures: abstract debates about currency diversification manifest tangibly in operational, technological, and human-resource dimensions.

Finally, interpreting de-dollarisation requires a disciplined approach. Headlines announcing new non-dollar payment arrangements or regional swap agreements can overstate systemic impact. Analysts must distinguish symbolic initiatives from enduring structural changes. For instance, a nation may announce a regional currency hub that initially handles a modest fraction of trade flows. Without examining liquidity, corridor reliability, and settlement infrastructure, observers risk misreading the pace and scale of de-dollarisation. By integrating historical analogues, operational examples, and corridor dynamics, one can critically assess which developments signal genuine shifts and which are largely performative.

Taken together, these elements frame a coherent view of the multi-currency future. Readers are invited to navigate an environment where dollar dominance persists, regional currencies assert themselves, and corridors—physical, digital, and institutional—structure flows. By considering scenarios, operational realities, and interpretive frameworks in tandem, the chapter equips decision-makers, investors, and analysts to anticipate, adapt, and position themselves in a system where multiplicity, not uniformity, defines resilience and opportunity. The challenge lies not in predicting a singular outcome, but in understanding the contours of a landscape increasingly defined by complexity, contingency, and corridor-based architecture.

Mapping possible future configurations

In June 2024, the Bank for International Settlements published a survey noting that over 40% of central banks had increased allocations to non-dollar assets in the preceding year, yet the United States dollar still accounted for nearly 60% of global reserves. The juxtaposition was striking: entrenched dollar dominance persisted in official holdings, while transactional flows—trade invoicing, cross-border payments, and regional settlements—displayed greater currency diversity. For instance, intra-Asian trade increasingly used local currencies, with the Chinese renminbi and Japanese yen taking a growing share of settlement volumes, even as dollar reserves remained central. This paradox underscores the need to distinguish reserve prominence from operational currency use, a distinction crucial for understanding potential futures.

Such trends invite a structured approach to imagining scenarios rather than forecasting a single trajectory. One scenario emphasises entrenched dollar dominance: reserves, pricing, and global benchmarks remain heavily dollarised, preserving the familiar corridor structures and reinforcing the dollar's network effects. Another posits gradual diversification: multiple currencies gain footholds in regional or sectoral transactions, yet no single currency displaces the dollar's centrality. A third envisions structured currency blocs, where countries coalesce around regional anchors supported by CBDC bridges, swap lines, and alternative payment systems. Each scenario highlights different pressures—geopolitical, institutional, and operational—but reality is unlikely to conform neatly to one path, instead blending elements across models.

Consider a hypothetical multinational operating in 2025 with significant trade links in Asia, Europe, and Latin America. Its treasury department reports that while dollar-denominated reserves remain dominant for funding and hedging, actual settlement patterns increasingly use euros for European suppliers, renminbi for Chinese contracts, and Brazilian real for South American transactions. This hybrid configuration demonstrates how global currency landscapes may simultaneously exhibit concentration in reserves and diversification in trade. Investors and policymakers must therefore adopt a vocabulary for futures thinking that accommodates partial adoption, corridor-specific dominance, and the coexistence of multiple payment channels.

Analysing these configurations requires attention to drivers beyond simple reserve shares. Trade patterns, capital mobility, geopolitical alignment, and financial infrastructure all shape the feasibility and attractiveness of different currencies in practice. For example, while a euro-denominated settlement network may facilitate European intra-bloc trade, its global reach is limited compared with the dollar. Similarly, a renminbi-based corridor may expand rapidly in Asia but remain constrained by hedging market depth and international acceptance. These examples reveal that scenario planning must integrate operational realities, market depth, and institutional credibility, not merely headline reserve data.

Each configuration carries distinct implications for corridor design, liquidity management, and systemic risk. In an entrenched dollar scenario, corridors remain predictable, and central banks can rely on established networks and swap lines. Diversification scenarios demand adaptive infrastructures capable of supporting multiple currencies with different settlement speeds, liquidity pools, and regulatory frameworks. Structured currency blocs introduce both redundancy and strategic choice: a nation or firm may navigate multiple corridors to optimise efficiency, while also mitigating exposure to political or operational disruptions. Historical analogues—such as the phased introduction of the euro and the regionalisation of European payment systems—illustrate that partial adoption and gradual integration can coexist with broader dominance by a single currency.

Critically, understanding future configurations requires distinguishing symbolic gestures from systemic change. A country announcing new non-dollar settlement arrangements may capture headlines, but without substantial liquidity, market depth, and institutional support, the impact on global corridors can be negligible. Scenario frameworks help contextualise these developments, enabling practitioners to gauge when diversification reflects operational reality versus performative policy signalling. In practice, blended outcomes are likely: reserves may remain dollar-heavy, regional corridors may adopt local currencies, and innovative mechanisms like CBDCs may supplement rather than replace established channels.

The vocabulary emerging from these scenarios—dominance, diversification, and blocs—serves as a lens to interpret incremental shifts, stress-test corridor strategies, and evaluate the resilience of multi-currency systems. Decision-makers can anticipate which corridors may grow in influence, where liquidity constraints may bind, and how operational choices interact with geopolitical positioning. A hybrid approach, recognising partial adoption across reserves and transactions, provides a practical framework for navigating uncertainty. By embedding these scenarios in analytical practice, stakeholders can maintain operational readiness while appreciating the complex, layered evolution of the global currency landscape.

Ultimately, mapping possible future configurations is not about predicting a single outcome but about preparing for a spectrum of plausible realities. The interplay between entrenched reserve dominance, transactional diversification, and corridor-specific strategies defines the contours of a multi-currency future. Policymakers, firms, and investors equipped with this vocabulary are better positioned to interpret developments, allocate resources, and respond to emerging corridor dynamics, recognising that stability, efficiency, and strategic influence are functions of both reserve structures and practical settlement patterns. The challenge is to navigate complexity with clarity, leveraging scenario thinking to make sense of a world where no single currency unilaterally dictates the rules of cross-border flows.

What a corridor-based world looks like

In March 2025, Singaporean logistics giant Sembcorp Industries completed its first multi-currency settlement using three distinct corridors: US dollars through established correspondent banks in New York, Chinese renminbi via a Hong Kong CBDC bridge, and euros through the Euroclear system in Brussels. The transaction, covering machinery imports, regional supplier payments, and short-term funding, required simultaneous coordination across separate messaging standards, liquidity pools, and legal frameworks. Yet the operation concluded within 24 hours without incident. The episode highlights a future in which financial flows are fragmented not by dysfunction but by design, guided by corridor preferences tailored to region, sector, and asset type. It illustrates how firms may navigate a multi-currency environment while maintaining operational efficiency and strategic visibility.

A corridor-based world reflects the layering of legacy networks with emerging infrastructures. Traditional correspondent banking networks, underpinned by SWIFT, continue to dominate USD settlements and large-scale cross-border financing. Simultaneously, regional or sector-specific hubs—like the ASEAN+3 Asian Clearing Union or the BRICS payment arrangements—support local and intrabloc transactions, offering speed, reduced reliance on third-country intermediaries, and a buffer against political risk. Central bank digital currency (CBDC) bridges introduce another layer: programmable and direct-access channels that can streamline bilateral trade settlements while embedding compliance and liquidity management rules. Together, these corridors form an ecosystem in which flows are routed according to cost, speed, legal exposure, and counterparty familiarity, rather than a single currency or platform dominating all activity.

Consider a multinational exporter with operations across Europe, East Asia, and Latin America. Its treasury manages three corridors for routine trade, working capital, and investment repatriation. Dollar liquidity is concentrated in New York and London, renminbi holdings circulate through Hong Kong and Shanghai, while euros are managed via Frankfurt and Brussels. This arrangement allows the firm to optimise transaction costs and settlement speed while mitigating exposure to sudden sanctions or network outages. Critically, it demonstrates that fragmentation need not imply systemic fragility: each corridor carries independent risk controls, regulatory oversight, and redundant access points, creating resilience without uniformity.

Operationally, corridor selection hinges on three interrelated factors: counterparty acceptance, market depth, and regulatory alignment. A corridor's attractiveness is measured not just by transaction cost but by legal clarity, speed of settlement, and ability to hedge exposures. For instance, CBDC bridges may reduce operational delays and provide instant settlement finality, but their adoption depends on participating central banks' policy alignment and technological readiness. Regional hubs, meanwhile, may offer robust network effects within a bloc but limited global reach. Legacy correspondent channels continue to carry the weight of deep liquidity and legal precedent, even as newer rails offer programmability, lower friction, and strategic autonomy.

Historical analogues reinforce the dynamics of corridor differentiation. The euro's phased introduction combined selective intra-European adoption with continued reliance on dollar and sterling settlements for non-European trade. Similarly, the gradual roll-out of the Euroclear and Clearstream systems in the 1990s illustrates how overlapping networks can coexist, offering choice rather than enforcing a single channel. These precedents show that multi-corridor operations are feasible when each corridor provides clear incentives, transparency, and sufficient liquidity, even if underlying infrastructures differ in speed, cost, and governance.

Yet challenges remain. Firms navigating multiple corridors must maintain real-time liquidity tracking, reconcile cross-platform settlements, and comply with heterogeneous regulatory regimes. Data integration and operational infrastructure are as critical as currency composition. For example, a transaction misrouted due to messaging incompatibility or delays in cross-border liquidity replenishment can trigger knock-on effects across corridors. The scenario of Sembcorp underscores that careful orchestration, robust compliance protocols, and contingency planning are essential to maintain both efficiency and credibility in a fragmented system.

From a policy perspective, corridor proliferation influences central bank strategy and international coordination. Access to multiple corridors can reduce dependence on a single currency, mitigate exposure to sanctions, and create room for domestic monetary policy autonomy. However, central banks must weigh the trade-offs between supporting new corridors—through swap lines, regional liquidity pools, or CBDC interoperability—and preserving stability in core settlement systems. Countries with smaller economies or less developed financial markets may choose to prioritise a single corridor for efficiency, while larger states maintain multiple overlapping corridors to balance autonomy, liquidity, and resilience.

Corridor-based fragmentation also shapes risk management. Hedging strategies must account for currency-specific volatility, corridor liquidity, and settlement timing. Firms increasingly adopt integrated treasury systems capable of dynamically routing transactions based on real-time liquidity and regulatory parameters. Market participants monitor corridor health, such as central bank liquidity provision, counterparty creditworthiness, and systemic stress indicators, to determine the optimal flow path. This granular approach to routing reflects a strategic mindset in which fragmentation does not equate to disorder but offers selective resilience, redundancy, and operational flexibility.

In practice, corridor diversity can coexist with network effects. USD-centric corridors maintain dominance in global finance, yet regional and sector-specific channels grow alongside, facilitating trade and investment where primary networks are constrained or costly. The coexistence of multiple corridors illustrates a key principle: fragmentation does not imply chaos; it implies choice, adaptability, and risk management. Firms, policymakers, and investors can exploit the strengths of each corridor while maintaining an overarching coherence in treasury, liquidity, and regulatory compliance frameworks.

As corridors proliferate, strategic foresight becomes essential. Corporates must anticipate shifts in corridor adoption, liquidity provision, and regulatory preferences, adjusting operational infrastructure to remain agile. Central banks must evaluate which corridors to support, balancing innovation, market development, and systemic stability. Observing patterns across settlement speed, cross-border adoption, and counterparty confidence provides actionable insight into which corridors may gain prominence, and which may remain niche or symbolic.

Ultimately, a corridor-based world is defined by layered functionality rather than uniformity. Different flows select different corridors based on region, asset type, and transaction purpose, creating a mosaic of financial pathways. Each corridor embodies distinct characteristics—liquidity, legal certainty, speed, programmability—and collectively they form a resilient, flexible architecture for multi-currency operations. This vision illustrates a fragmented yet orderly global payment landscape, where strategic navigation, infrastructure readiness, and operational foresight are as important as currency selection.

Implications for states and central banks

In April 2024, the Central Bank of Chile announced a focused strategy to streamline its foreign exchange corridors, concentrating liquidity provision on three primary channels: the US dollar through New York correspondent banks, the euro via Frankfurt, and a regional CBDC bridge linking Latin American central banks. Rather than attempting to replicate global networks or pursue every emerging corridor, Chile prioritised clarity, operational simplicity, and predictable access for corporates and banks. The move immediately reduced transactional uncertainty for exporters while signalling to international investors that the central bank maintained disciplined oversight of foreign reserves. This case illustrates a mid-sized state's deliberate positioning in a multi-corridor world: strategic, targeted engagement can deliver resilience and credibility without overextension.

For states of any size, corridor proliferation demands careful prioritisation. Large economies with deep financial markets may maintain overlapping networks to preserve both liquidity and autonomy, balancing direct access to major currencies with investments in regional or sector-specific channels. Smaller states, by contrast, benefit from a focused strategy that concentrates resources on corridors providing the greatest operational and political return. Efficiency, predictability, and transparency become as important as network breadth. Chile's approach demonstrates that realistic corridor selection, paired with clear communication to domestic and international stakeholders, mitigates risks associated with fragmentation while avoiding the costs of maintaining marginal or redundant links.

Policy coherence emerges as a central concern. Central banks must align domestic monetary objectives, regulatory frameworks, and legal clarity with the corridors they support. Misalignment can generate uncertainty, reduce market participation, and elevate transaction costs. For example, a central bank that offers access to a CBDC bridge but imposes opaque liquidity requirements may deter banks from adopting the corridor, undermining both its usage and credibility. Conversely, transparent access rules, predictable settlement processes, and reliable liquidity provision build confidence across market participants, facilitating smoother functioning even as corridors multiply.

Infrastructure investment complements policy coherence. States must assess where capital allocation—technological upgrades, operational staffing, and legal frameworks—yields the greatest systemic benefit. Chile's selection of three primary corridors reflects a deliberate decision to invest deeply in a subset of options rather than dilute resources across a fragmented network. This approach ensures that each corridor is robust, resilient to operational shocks, and supported by clear governance structures. For larger states with diverse trade and financial exposures, investments may extend across multiple corridors, balancing redundancy and reach while avoiding unnecessary complexity.

Political clarity is equally critical. Corridor strategy communicates both operational priorities and macroeconomic intent. Markets interpret corridor choices as signals of stability, trust, and alignment with broader fiscal and monetary policies. Chile's announcement, by clearly specifying corridor selection and underlying rules, reassured domestic and foreign stakeholders alike, enhancing predictability for exporters, importers, and investors. In contrast, ambiguous or rapidly shifting corridor policies can provoke uncertainty, trigger capital flight, or undermine long-term credibility.

Historical examples reinforce these dynamics. Singapore's early adoption of selective corridor engagement in the 1990s—prioritising US dollar and yen settlements for trade while gradually integrating regional clearing systems—demonstrated that focused strategies can maintain efficiency without sacrificing exposure to global markets. Similarly, Brazil's phased expansion of central bank swap lines during the 2008–2009 financial crisis illustrates how targeted corridor access, coupled with transparent rules and communication, stabilises both domestic liquidity and international confidence. Both cases show that states can achieve resilience not by maximal coverage, but through deliberate, high-quality participation.

For central banks, corridor management also intersects with reserve policy. Access to reliable corridors shapes decisions on reserve composition, hedging strategies, and liquidity buffers. Concentrated, predictable corridors reduce operational risk and enable more efficient reserve deployment. By contrast, attempting to maintain access to all potential corridors can fragment liquidity, elevate costs, and obscure risk monitoring. Chile's strategy underscores a principle relevant to mid-sized and smaller economies alike: selective corridor investment, combined with predictable operations, amplifies the strategic value of existing reserves while minimising exposure to operational or reputational shocks.

Risk management within corridor strategy extends beyond operational continuity. Regulatory harmonisation, cyber resilience, and legal certainty influence both adoption and market perception. States supporting corridors must consider counterparty robustness, governance structures, and cross-border legal enforceability. A corridor may be operationally fast, but if counterparties face opaque compliance rules or uncertain dispute resolution mechanisms, market participants may avoid it, reducing its practical utility. By focusing on predictable, well-governed corridors, central banks enhance adoption, reduce risk, and reinforce currency credibility.

Smaller states also face geopolitical considerations. Corridor selection conveys alignment or neutrality in global finance. Concentrated engagement in specific corridors can signal economic orientation, attract investment, or reduce exposure to sanctions. Conversely, excessive dispersion or engagement in contested networks may increase vulnerability to political pressures or operational disruption. Chile's approach exemplifies a carefully calibrated balance: a limited number of strategically chosen corridors supports operational effectiveness while maintaining flexibility to respond to geopolitical shifts.

Communication complements both policy and infrastructure. Clear articulation of corridor strategy to domestic banks, corporates, and international partners ensures that market participants can plan, hedge, and execute transactions efficiently. Ambiguity can magnify risk perception, even when corridors are technically capable. By contrast, transparency regarding corridor rules, liquidity provision, and access criteria fosters predictability, enabling market participants to operate with confidence in a fragmented system.

Finally, corridor strategy highlights the intersection of scale, focus, and pragmatism. Large states can invest broadly, layering multiple corridors to accommodate diverse trade and financial needs. Mid-sized and smaller states benefit from prioritisation, concentrating resources on corridors that deliver maximum strategic impact. Across both contexts, the consistent principles are clarity, transparency, and predictable execution. These factors underpin operational resilience, investor confidence, and the broader credibility of a state's currency in a world of expanding, differentiated corridors.

Strategically, corridor choices are neither purely technical nor symbolic. They require calibration across operational capacity, fiscal and monetary policy alignment, regulatory coherence, and international signalling. Chile's focused strategy, alongside historical precedents in Singapore and Brazil, demonstrates that effective corridor engagement combines selective infrastructure investment with disciplined governance and clear communication, yielding operational efficiency and credible positioning in a complex, multi-currency environment.

Implications for firms and financial institutions

In September 2023, the Brazilian exporter Votorantim Cimentos began a multi-phase upgrade of its treasury and payments systems to handle three parallel currency corridors: the US dollar via New York, the euro through Frankfurt, and a regional real–peso–peso CBDC corridor connecting South American partners. Previously, the company relied on a single dollar-based chain for trade and financing. The shift was prompted by growing regional trade in local currencies and the need to hedge exposures without depending solely on dollar liquidity. Within months, Votorantim reported faster settlement times, lower hedging costs for regional transactions, and clearer compliance tracking. This case illustrates how operational adaptation underpins strategic engagement in a multi-currency corridor environment, translating abstract market shifts into tangible business decisions.

Firms of all sizes now face a landscape where payment, funding, and settlement flows no longer move along uniform rails. Banks and corporates must adapt treasury practices to accommodate multiple corridors simultaneously, often spanning legacy systems, cross-border real-time networks, and nascent CBDC bridges. Effective engagement requires robust data architecture, capable of tracking positions, settlement risk, and liquidity across jurisdictions in near real time. Votorantim's system overhaul demonstrates that integrating multi-currency visibility with automated reconciliations reduces operational errors and supports strategic decision-making. Without such infrastructure, firms remain exposed to settlement delays, counterparty risk, and regulatory friction, limiting their capacity to capitalise on diversified corridors.

Hedging tools become critical in a fragmented system. Limited instruments constrain firms from fully managing exposure to local or regional currencies. In Votorantim's case, access to forwards and swaps in euros and regional CBDC-linked pesos allowed incremental substitution of dollar-denominated trade, enhancing flexibility without amplifying risk. In contrast, markets lacking liquid derivatives create friction: firms face higher costs, uncertain pricing, and the inability to hedge effectively. Investors, corporates, and banks therefore evaluate not just the underlying currency's attractiveness but the operational capacity to transact, settle, and hedge efficiently.

Compliance frameworks must evolve alongside infrastructure. Multi-currency corridors introduce diverse regulatory and reporting requirements. Firms need visibility into jurisdiction-specific restrictions, liquidity obligations, and sanctions screening across multiple rails. For banks, this translates into sophisticated monitoring tools, scenario modelling, and automated alerts. Votorantim's experience shows that centralised oversight, aligned with corridor-specific rules, reduces compliance bottlenecks while preserving strategic autonomy. Firms without such capabilities may avoid certain corridors entirely, leaving opportunities untapped.

Operational risk is compounded when corridors intersect with legacy systems. Manual reconciliation, fragmented reporting, and opaque liquidity windows increase exposure to errors and settlement failures. Implementing robust, corridor-aware technology mitigates these risks, enabling firms to navigate complex flows without operational gridlock. Banks and corporates increasingly prioritise integrated platforms capable of managing multi-currency exposures, providing end-to-end visibility and facilitating timely risk management decisions.

Liquidity management extends beyond settlement timing. Firms must ensure sufficient balances in each corridor while minimising idle funds. Access to regional pooling, swap lines, or correspondent banking networks can optimise liquidity allocation. In Votorantim's example, strategic use of a regional CBDC bridge reduced dependency on foreign reserves while accelerating local trade payments. Firms must weigh the cost of corridor diversification against operational efficiency, balancing liquidity buffers with opportunity costs.

Scenario planning now forms a core part of treasury strategy. Firms anticipate corridor disruptions—technical outages, regulatory changes, or market volatility—and model their operational and financial impact. Votorantim conducted stress tests across three corridors, measuring settlement risk, currency mismatch exposure, and hedging shortfalls. These exercises informed contingency liquidity buffers and prioritised corridor usage, ensuring resilience without overinvesting in redundant capacity.

Strategically, multi-currency corridors reshape capital allocation, risk appetite, and corporate governance. Firms must integrate corridor analysis into board-level decision-making, embedding operational constraints and financial exposure within corporate strategy. For financial institutions, the challenge is magnified: banks simultaneously manage client transactions, internal liquidity, regulatory reporting, and systemic risk across corridors. Those capable of harmonising these functions gain competitive advantage; those that cannot risk inefficiency, compliance breaches, or reputational damage.

The trajectory for corporates and banks is clear. Multi-currency corridors are no longer theoretical; they are operational imperatives. Success hinges on data integration, flexible hedging, disciplined liquidity management, and transparent compliance frameworks. Votorantim Cimentos' example highlights that strategic investment in systems, process, and governance translates corridor diversity into tangible commercial and financial benefits.

Yet tension remains between autonomy and complexity. Firms must decide which corridors to prioritise, balancing access, cost, and operational capacity. Overexpansion risks inefficiency; underinvestment constrains opportunity. Decisions are inherently political, reflecting both market exposure and the strategic intent of the firm. How organisations navigate this trade-off will determine their resilience and competitiveness in a world of differentiated, overlapping currency corridors.

Multi-currency readiness is therefore both a technical and strategic challenge. It requires foresight, disciplined implementation, and continuous monitoring. Firms and financial institutions that internalise these demands, align treasury, risk, and compliance practices, and adapt technology to corridor realities will be better positioned to thrive. Those that do not may find themselves constrained to legacy rails, unable to exploit the benefits of a fragmenting global payments landscape.

How to read de-dollarisation news critically

On 12 March 2024, the National Bank of Singapore announced a new initiative allowing select regional trades to settle in a basket of Asian currencies rather than solely in US dollars. Headlines celebrated this as a decisive step toward de-dollarisation, and social media amplified predictions of a declining dollar share in global trade. Yet within the same week, data from the Bank for International Settlements showed that Singapore's actual foreign exchange reserves remained 62 per cent dollar-denominated, largely unchanged from the previous quarter. The contrast between the announcement and underlying exposure illustrates a key truth:

symbolic moves often attract disproportionate attention, while substantive structural shifts evolve incrementally.

Interpreting de-dollarisation news requires separating headlines from operational reality. Policymakers may signal intent through announcements of new payment arrangements, local currency settlements, or swaps, but investors and corporates must evaluate liquidity, network connectivity, and hedging options to judge practical impact. The Singapore case shows that a corridor may exist in principle, yet market depth, compliance infrastructure, and settlement speed ultimately determine its usability. A message is not a market; a commitment is not an immediate reallocation of reserves.

The first lens for analysis is scale. A regional or bilateral settlement arrangement may handle only a fraction of trade flows. For example, the Association of Southeast Asian Nations' ASEAN+3 local currency bond initiative facilitates some debt issuance in renminbi, yen, and ringgit, yet global transactions remain overwhelmingly dollar-denominated. Observing transaction volumes, participant breadth, and recurring usage provides clarity on whether a corridor represents genuine substitution or a limited pilot.

The second lens is durability. De-dollarisation is rarely instantaneous; incremental adoption over months or years signals structural change, whereas a single deal or temporary pilot may be ephemeral. The Euroclear Shanghai initiative, started in 2019, demonstrates how gradual connectivity can expand non-dollar settlement options over time, even if initial volumes are modest. Contrastingly, several high-profile, single-shot renminbi settlement announcements in Africa and Latin America have not led to durable adoption, reinforcing the importance of observing trend lines rather than one-off reports.

A third consideration is operational readiness. Headlines often omit the complexity of hedging, liquidity provision, and regulatory compliance. A corridor may exist for invoicing, but if derivatives, forwards, or swaps are scarce, corporates face unhedged exposures and banks encounter settlement risk. For instance, a hypothetical Central Asian corridor might allow payment in local currencies, but limited correspondent banking access and shallow derivatives markets constrain practical usage. Readers must probe beyond the announcement to gauge corridor functionality.

Political context and strategic intent form a fourth lens. Announcements may reflect signalling, negotiation leverage, or diplomatic messaging rather than immediate structural change. A government promoting local currency settlement may aim to strengthen bargaining power with trade partners or regional blocs, rather than redirecting actual reserves. Evaluating complementary actions—reserve composition shifts, swap agreements, or multilateral currency pools—helps distinguish genuine policy alignment from symbolic gesture.

Monitoring market reactions offers further insight. Exchange rate movements, hedging costs, and bank liquidity management reveal how the private sector interprets the announcement. In Singapore's case, the dollar remained stable against regional currencies, and hedging costs for non-dollar trades showed only minor adjustments, signalling that practical adoption was limited. Conversely, when Venezuela's 2020 local currency invoicing pilot coincided with swap lines from Russia and China, corporates actively shifted exposures, demonstrating that integrated institutional support is critical for corridor uptake.

Another dimension is interoperability with existing corridors. A new arrangement's impact depends on connectivity to major payment rails, correspondent banks, and cross-border clearing systems. CBDC bridges, regional hubs, and bilateral swap lines create corridors, but their utility scales only when they interface with established networks. Analysts should evaluate technical and operational integration, including messaging standards, clearing frequency, and redundancy measures, to determine whether an announcement is a symbolic pilot or a genuinely functional corridor.

Finally, investors and corporates must maintain perspective on headline frequency versus structural effect. Media cycles emphasise novelty, but durable de-dollarisation emerges gradually, with small incremental shifts accumulating over years. Observing trends in aggregate settlement volumes, reserve allocations, and network connectivity provides a more accurate picture than reacting to isolated announcements. The Singapore example underscores that initial enthusiasm may mislead if underlying usage and capacity remain unchanged.

By applying these lenses—scale, durability, operational readiness, political context, market reaction, interoperability, and trend evaluation—readers gain a framework to assess the significance of de-dollarisation news critically. Each announcement can be mapped against corridors, liquidity, and settlement capability, forming a dynamic picture of evolving currency landscapes. The frameworks presented throughout this book become tools for distinguishing symbolic gestures from enduring change, enabling investors, corporates, and policymakers to navigate a multi-currency future with discernment.

The challenge is ongoing. Headlines will continue to proclaim shifts, pilots, and initiatives. Analysts must balance attention with skepticism, weighing signals against structural data. Interpreting de-dollarisation requires patience, nuance, and an understanding of corridor functionality, integration, and adoption. Only by reading beyond the announcement—assessing volumes, connectivity, liquidity, and risk—can one gauge whether the global currency system is truly fragmenting or merely experimenting with alternative corridors.

About the Author

Priya Nadkar-Jain writes about the intersection of money, technology, and state power, with a particular focus on how cross-border payment systems quietly shape geopolitics. She has spent many years following central bank speeches, policy debates, and market developments, translating technical language into clear narratives for non-specialist readers. Drawing on a background that bridges emerging markets and established financial centres, she is especially interested in how smaller economies navigate the choices made in Washington, Brussels, and Beijing. A long-standing fascination with the history of trade routes and empires informs her work on today's currency corridors. She sees the new experiments in swap lines, CBDCs, and regional payment systems as the latest chapter in an older story: how societies decide whom to trust with their savings, and at what cost to their autonomy.

www.ingramcontent.com/pod-product-compliance
Lightning Source LLC
Chambersburg PA
CBHW021215250926
51852CB00006B/27
* 9 7 8 8 1 9 9 7 8 6 8 5 1 *